SELECTED WRITINGS
ON FEMINISM
AND SOCIALISM

SELECTED WRITINGS ON FEMINISM AND SOCIALISM

BY

LILY BRAUN

TRANSLATED AND EDITED BY

ALFRED G. MEYER

INDIANA UNIVERSITY PRESS
Bloomington and Indianapolis

Manufactured in the United States of America

Library of Congress Cataloging-in-Publication Data

Braun, Lily.
Selected writings on feminism and socialism.

Includes index.
1. Women and socialism.   2. Feminism.   I. Meyer,
Alfred G.   II. Title.
HX546.B72   1987   335'.0088042   86-45942
ISBN 0-253-35101-4

1 2 3 4 5 91 90 89 88 87

For Eva

CONTENTS

IV. Heroism, Individualism, and Joy

V. Children's Liberation

INTRODUCTION

Alfred G. Meyer

Lily Braun was born in 1865 into the German nobility. She received the conventional upbringing of aristocratic girls, designed to prepare her for life as an aristocrat's wife, a lady-in-waiting, or a governess. To such prospects this young woman reacted with growing distaste, since the choices open to her left no room for her strong urge to be active, creative, a participant, and an achiever. More and more openly she rebelled against her assigned roles.

Like so many other late-Victorian radical women, she began her rebellion by doubting Christian dogma because she perceived the glaring discrepancy between confessed beliefs and actual practice. The arrogance of the rich and the squalor of the poor, which she saw before her eyes, induced a revulsion that was both moral and aesthetic. Again, she seems similar to other late-Victorian rebels who in the depth of their souls felt a discrepancy between, on the one hand, being beneficiaries of aristocratic privilege and, on the other, having as women the same low status as children, criminals, or the mentally incompetent. In her case, these sensibilities were fostered or intensified by early and thorough exposure to classical and contemporary literature, a realm into which she learned to escape in hours of misery. Goethe and Nietzsche probably provided the most profound inspiration for the ideas of her adulthood, but the list of important influences was in fact much longer. In 1890, the young Emperor, William II, summarily dismissed her father from his service in an arbitrary exercise of whim; the family then moved to Berlin, where Lily became acquainted with the literary and political avant-garde and took the decisive steps of breaking with her class and her family. She became a militant feminist and quickly moved to the far left of the feminist movement and closer and closer to Marxism, which she openly embraced in December 1895.

The German Social Democratic party (SPD) was a mass party with a strong organization and numerous auxiliaries, run in near-dictatorial fashion by August Bebel and his board of directors. The party's official ideology was what is today dismissed as "vulgar Marxism"—that mix of simplified and misunderstood statements by Engels and Marx together with Darwinist notions codified into an esoteric dogma understood by few though mouthed by all. I would like to summarize it by suggesting that in the SPD Marxism had become Prussianized, to which one might add that the European culture that served as background and determining framework for this process was late Victorianism. But it was primarily the political culture of the post-Bismarckian Reich that shaped the party's political activities: burgeoning capitalism within a society based on aristocratic prerogative and bureaucratic rank-consciousness; authoritarian rule with pseudoparliamentarism; and cultural, regional, denominational, and social cleavages that were so sharp as to inhibit fruitful discourse among groups. This environment helps explain the curious contradictions of German Marxism in the period of the Second International—its revolutionary rhetoric accompanying *attentisme* and reformist practices; much emphasis on electoral victories but strict refusal to have its parliamentary representatives join in any constructive action.

In reaction to these political tendencies Lily Braun became a critic within the movement and therefore was dubbed a Revisionist. She insisted, for instance, that the party must break out of its isolation and work with like-minded radicals outside the movement, communicate with them, and reward them as potential recruits instead of needlessly antagonizing them. The improvements in the political and economic conditions of the working class that might be achieved through such collaboration she regarded not as a substitute for revolution but as a preparation for it: Even major improvements within the framework of capitalism could only raise the workers' consciousness of what might be possible under socialism.

Similarly, although she abhorred violence and vindictiveness and was convinced that within the party and even between classes it should be possible to conduct far more political discourse in gentlemanly, nonviolent fashion, she often conceded that, ultimately, violence would have to be applied to remove the old ruling class and the old system. Braun stressed the moral commitment of the Marxist movement and rejected

Kautsky's amoral philosophy. Her affirmation of moral commitment derived from Prussian-aristocratic character training, its slogan of "noblesse oblige," and from practical, anticlerical Christianity, reinforced by the writings of Rousseau, Goethe, Nietzsche and Plato and by the heroic example of American abolitionists and feminists.

Further, Braun greatly admired British and French socialists and numbered many of them among her friends. To be sure, her admiration was always mixed with criticism of their limitations; yet she often stressed their achievements and was a far more outspoken critic of the SPD than was Eduard Bernstein. She attacked the dogmatism of its ideologists, the authoritarian and bureaucratic pattern of its management, the elitism and vanguardism of its leaders, the patriarchalism and sexism prevalent among its members, and the spirit of Prussianism that tied all these features together into a political culture she thought must be overcome.

Braun distinguished between different modes of oppression, or different alienations, that sometimes reinforced but at other times were unrelated to each other. As a socialist, she dealt, of course, with the alienation of labor under capitalism, and in her major book on the subject she provided a great wealth of statistical material on the political economy of women's work. But whereas most Marxists of her generation treated the alienation of labor exclusively as an economic and political problem, Braun was equally interested in discussing the effects of capitalism in areas that the movement as a whole neglected. To put it most succinctly, she was interested in the human side of capitalist exploitation, in its effect on human beings, their daily lives, and their relations with each other. Her writings show her to have been sensitive to the psychological effect of the competitive rat race: the impact this had on child rearing and education, on career choices and on mate selection, were of particular concern to her. Further, she discussed the prostitution of art under capitalism and the many ways in which the market society perverts creativity and individuality. Finally, she regretted the gray sobriety of modern society, the alienation of joy, and the disappearance of all genuine feeling for rites, celebration, for the enjoyment of nature, for mystery and myth. Most important, she accused capitalism of destroying femininity and of imperiling the most fundamental human relationship, that between mother and child.

Braun's feminism, which predated her commitment to Marxism, was too complex to fit in with the orthodoxies of the socialist movement. Women, she argued, had been oppressed long before capitalism appeared, and they were likely still to be oppressed after it was overthrown. In ancient Greece and Rome they had in effect been slaves. To this oppression Christianity had added the terrible stigma of declaring women to be vessels of sin: by declaring the natural, healthy, and beautiful sexual functions to be filth and abomination, Christianity had struck the cruelest blow at the female sex, had introduced the hypocrisies of the double standard, and had made prostitution a ubiquitous phenomenon. Through Christianity, Braun argued, we had been alienated from our sexuality.

Capitalism had intensified the oppression of women in complex fashion. First, the rise of capitalism coincided with a cultural change that made productive or creative labor the chief standard for measuring a human being's worth. But, as this cultural change took place, women were increasingly forced out of the more meaningful and satisfying lines of work. With the coming of the machine age, moreover, the many productive functions that women had carried out in the home were taken over by factories, so that household management, once a responsible and challenging line of work, had turned into boring drudgery. The middle-class wife had been degraded to a decorative play thing; and indeed bourgeois feminism, according to Braun, could be defined as the self-consciousness of the woman as a doll. Meanwhile, lower-class women had been mobilized in large numbers for wage work in industry. They did the most menial tasks under degrading and health-destroying conditions for wages far below those paid to men. Or else, on the margins of the capitalist system they faced comparable or even worse exploitation and degradation as domestic servants, secretaries, waitresses, dancers, actresses, or prostitutes, while in the countryside they toiled in their own hovels which functioned as the sweatshops of cottage industry.

For Braun the socialist, these were all aspects of the alienation of labor, but for Braun the feminist they were elements of an evil that she deplored at least as much—the alienation and possible destruction of femininity. Like Plato, like Rousseau, Braun believed that women are different from men, that they have different needs, different aptitudes, different sensibilities, different potentials. As a woman, she took pride in those traits that, by and large, she believed to be more humane, more cooperative, and more suitable for the management or the creation of a truly decent society. The liberation of women, therefore, would lift all of human society to a higher level, and women's emancipation was a precondition for general human emancipation. Reading her writings, I sometimes felt she might assert that "feminine is beautiful."

Capitalist society, however, was destroying femininity. The bored fashion doll in the bourgeois drawing room was a travesty of femity, and hard toil under degrading and health-endangering conditions quickly destroyed all traces of it in the working woman.

One of the needs of women that Braun recognized was the exercise of the sexual urge, just as she regarded their ability to love as one of their potentials. But the repressive code of Christian bourgeois morality had destroyed healthy sexuality and had inhibited love; moreover, since it was enforced on women with multiple severity, the liberation of sexuality and the de-alienation of love were, for her, a specifically feminist issue.

Finally, femininity includes the potential for motherhood, and here, Braun believed, lay the secret of women's superiority over men. Human beings may have different aptitudes and potentials, but, by and large, they are of comparable worth and dignity. The one most vital potential, however—the life-giving and nurturing capacity—belongs to women alone. The primeval human relationship, antedating all other relationships and being basic to all of them, is the tie between mother and child. This most human of all relationships men cannot share. But this relationship, too, Braun saw as being threatened by capitalism, especially in the working class, where the conditions of work made it impossible for women to be proper mothers; and even in the bourgeoisie, Braun saw the need for a career as interfering with the need for motherhood.

It follows from the above that in Braun's opinion the abolition of capitalism would solve some but not all of women's concerns. Hence socialism would be a precondition for women's liberation, but it would not bring it about; on the contrary, the real struggle for satisfying the legitimate concerns of women would only then begin, the principal issue being the reconciling of the conflict between liberation through work and liberation for motherhood.

Meanwhile, she argued that it was the duty of the socialist movement to make feminist issues its own. As a feminist, she was alert to the many major and minor modes of oppressing women through discriminatory laws and educational opportunities, through dress codes, language habits, and chivalrous courtesies. She herself was a militant fighter in a wide variety of causes. She was the first woman in the 1890s to demand for German women the right to vote, and before 1900 she called for an equal rights amendment to the German constitution. She agitated for reform in women's clothing and for coeducation, but much more actively for women's right to their own bodies and hence for the decriminalization of prostitution and abortion. As one of the leaders in the League for the Protection of Motherhood she agitated for equal rights for single mothers and their offspring and helped set up employment agencies through which single mothers might find work while keeping their babies. She tried to organize labor unions for domestics and suggested similar organizations for actresses, waitresses, and prostitutes. She demanded legislation to ban all health-destroying work or at least to protect women from it. In all these endeavors she believed that she was entitled to, if not active support, then at least passive approval by the party. In this hope, however, she was disappointed.

Two of her pet projects were designed specifically to attack the problem of reconciling the right to work with the right to motherhood or to an autonomous personality. One of them, which was later to become a staple of legislation in socialist countries, was her proposal for maternity insurance, which would guarantee pregnant women (married or unmarried) generous maternity leave with full pay, that they would get their jobs back, and provisions for infant day care. In the SPD this proposal was dismissed as injecting too much feminist concern into the workers' movement. Even more hostile was the reception given to her scheme for communal housekeeping by which she proposed to liberate wives and mothers from the deadly routines of housework while at the same time providing these necessary services more cheaply and more efficiently.

Braun made enemies in the movement by a wide variety of other ideas she advanced. For example, she was appalled by the low cultural level of the party and the working class—the sexism and patriarchalism in their daily lives, the nasty, uncomradely tone of discourse at party meetings, the vindictiveness with which they envisioned the socialist future, the contempt shown for the achievements of the past. In short, she decried the absence among her comrades of moral and aesthetic sensibilities. Her own upper-class upbringing had made her sensitive to the social functions of art and literature; she strongly believed in the role of art as a medium for raising consciousness; and, with Engels and Marx, she was convinced that this educational mission could not be carried out by an art that had been transformed into a popular propaganda vehicle. Great works of art, she thought, would have to speak their own language, not that of the party. Her sympathies thus lay not with the precursors of socialist realism or with those, like Plekhanov and Mehring, who promoted them, but with the avant-garde outside the Marxist movement, especially the German Naturalist school of the 1890s.

In contrast to prevailing orthodoxies around 1900, Braun was concerned not only with the contradictions in the base but also with those in the superstructure. She demanded the transformation not only of property relations but also of modes of daily intercourse and of human minds, a revolution not only in political economy but also in consciousness and in the culture of the proletariat itself. In criticizing the puritan humorlessness of the movement, in demanding that the party educate the working class not only politically but also aesthetically and morally and that it appeal to its members' emotions, to their yearning for pageantry and ritual, indeed in urging that a revolutionary movement must carefully foster utopian thinking, Braun expressed her belief that the coming transformation would have to be total. That was the essence of her Revisionism.

That such a program for total revolution is difficult to translate into a coherent political strategy was recognized by Braun herself, who repeatedly pointed out that she had not worked out—and probably never would work out—a coherent program of action to accommodate all these demands. All these many claims, she argued, were legitimate, though some obviously were more important than other. Freeing women from the corset or from having to assume their spouse's last name obviously was a less pressing demand than giving them the vote, freeing them for meaningful work and for motherhood, or abolishing private property in the means of production; and anyone investing all his or her energies in fighting for the pettier issues was a crank at best and in many cases a grotesque fanatic. But in Braun's opinion that still did not give anyone committed to human liberation the right to condemn such cranks or fanatics; on the contrary, all radical causes seeking to emancipate women and men from the many modes of alienation and oppression should be tolerated, supported, and pursued.

Braun was only too painfully aware that some of the causes of liberation contradicted and opposed each other; and she felt this most keenly in the conflict between women's need for self-fulfillment in motherhood and their right to a professional career. Revolutionaries, she suggested—perhaps somewhat lamely—would have to learn to live with such dilemmas. They would have to accept the notion that not all problems will be solved at once when the revolution occurs, and some may never be solved completely.

For Braun this was no reason to despair. Instead, it spurred her resolve to try fighting for liberation from all forms of oppression simultaneously, principally by raising her party's and her society's consciousness, alerting her fellow human beings to all inequities and alienations, combating laxness and insensitivity within the socialist movement, and continually criticizing the radical movement.

She also demanded, in effect, that the revolutionary socialist live according to socialist-feminist, humanist morality at all times, beginning now, not after some revolution of the future, and that all criticism should begin with self-criticism. The revolution, she seems to have suggested, must begin as an individual, personal revolution; the new consciousness and the new morality ultimately can be engendered only in and by each individual through revolutionary praxis. What she taught, and what she tried to practice, was that self-transcendence that according to Engels was the most basic precondition for a successful proletarian revolution. In her writings, the sentiment is expressed most often in Nietzschean terms of courage, heroism, and self-sacrifice, but the meaning is the same. And, once again, it was in her many writings on the meaning of motherhood that her resolve for self-transcendence appeared most clearly. For too long, she argued, parents have imposed themselves on their children, trying to relive their own failed lives through them, treating them as property and as an investment, trampling on their children's personalities and potentials. In fact, she argued, parents have no rights against their children, only duties toward them, most particularly the duty to rear them for autonomy. They must serve as stepping stones for their children, promoting their growth away from, and beyond, the parents.

Like her feminism, Braun's Marxism too was deeply imbued with Nietzschean idealism, taking from Nietzsche the idea of the moral, aesthetic, and political transcendence of humankind through heroic commitment. A humanist Marxism, it consistently looked beyond the abstractions of political economy to explore the many depredations to which men and women were subjected, and it preached a war on all fronts against them. It was feminist Marxism because it was imbued with the conviction that ultimately the human species could be saved from self-destruction only through the de-alienation of femininity and motherhood. She believed that all politics could be humanized only once they were feminized.

This mix of ideas alienated her from her bourgeois feminism as well as from the Marxist movement, and after her death she was forgotten quickly and almost totally even though in her lifetime she had been notorious and widely influential. Today we can readily recognize her as someone who anticipated many of the ideas current in the political avant-garde of our own time. Her urgings to raise the culture of the proletariat, including its aesthetic culture, its appreciation for the great minds and artists of the past, as well as her warning that the movement must not neglect the workers' yearning for myth and mystery, for satisfaction of their religious instincts, predate similar concerns of Bogdanov, Lunacharski, and the Capri school of Bolshevism, which in turn may have influenced Antonio Gramsci. Her writings on women's concerns were eagerly seized upon by Kollontai and many other women in the Marxist parties of Eastern Europe, and many of her practical proposals have become standard legislation throughout the world of socialist states. Her fight for sexual liberation and her criticism of patriarchal and traditional culture in the working class—and in the party—make her a direct precursor of Wilhelm Reich, that key figure in the transformation of Prussian and Russian Marxism into Western Marxism. Finally, her attempts to alert the movement to the consciousness-raising and revolutionizing effects of avant-garde art and literature make her an interesting pioneer of the ideas later advanced by the Frankfurt school. Altogether, as an unorthodox Marxist she seems to have recaptured and expressed the essence of Marx's ideas far better than those Orthodox Marxists who drove her out of the movement as a Revisionist.

With a few exceptions, the following pieces, all of which I have translated from German, were written between 1894 and 1912. I have grouped them thematically rather than chronologically, and each section is preceded by a brief explanation. I have omitted several categories of her writings from the selection: her monographs on Goethe and the women around him; her numerous essays in literary and artistic criticism, including her discussions of women's poetry and dramatic works dealing with women's problems; a large number of articles dealing with policy conflicts within the SPD, particularly the polemical pieces directed against Clara

Zetkin but also polemical essays directed against antagonists within the women's movement in Germany and abroad. In short, what is presented here is a highly selective sampling.

One word about Lily Braun's style of writing. I am tempted to call it Edwardian, or to suggest that it was a German analogue of Edwardian style. It is self-consciously elevated, at times to the point of pretentiousness, although every once in a while Braun laces her high-flown prose with a bit of colloquialism that may delight some readers and offend others. Like any author, she had her pet phrases, and like any polemicist she harped on certain points that are forever recurring in her writings. The repetitiousness may irritate some readers, but others may be impressed by the cumulative effect of Braun's oft-recurring ideas and may enjoy them as a listener delights in the recurrence of a simple theme in many variations. Many of the essays offered here originated in political oratory and should perhaps be read out loud so as to replicate their first form. In my translations I have followed the rule given me by my *Gymnasium* teachers: "as closely as possible; as freely as necessary." That is not always easy to do, and I may have erred in both directions, though I believe that I have rendered faithfully both her meaning and her tone of voice. In a few cases of doubt, my wife, with her precise knowledge of both languages, has been a valuable help, and I thank her.

I.

Women and Work

Braun had early expressed awareness of the hard plight of working women. With Friedrich Engels she believed that stepping out into the world of wage work and liberating women from boring household drudgery would make them economically independent. Wage work would therefore be an essential means toward self-liberation. But in the work performed by proletarian women she saw nothing liberating; instead, she saw it as oppressive, demeaning, exploitative, and health destroying.

In 1901 she published her major economic work, *Die Frauenfrage*, which dealt exhaustively with the problem. Since it is very long and because its statistics are outdated, it will probably never be translated. In its place, the following selections will give a flavor of Braun's treatment of the exploitation of female labor. As does her book, these articles stress the excessively long hours, the unhealthy conditions, the insufficient wages, the sexual harassment of workers, and the inadequacy of legal provisions and institutions to curb the worst of these conditions.

In these articles Braun goes beyond the policies of the German Marxist women's movement by concerning herself not only with women working in factories, but also with those in cottage industries, with domestic servants, with artists' models and actresses, waitresses and sales personnel as well as prostitutes. Her repeated urgings that the Marxist movement seek to organize these women always were repudiated.

In the sketch entitled "The Dog" Braun also shows concern for the lot of women without special gifts or skills and for the cruelty of the labor market that gives such women a sense of utter uselessness. Having a recognized function in society seemed to her to be a fundamental human right that is violated in a market system that wastes or frustrates a great deal of human energy and creativity.

Other pieces in this section deal with the double burden of wage work plus housework. In her opinion, housework was boring drudgery performed mostly by people who had no special ability for it. Her aim was to relieve women of it as much as possible and thus to liberate working women of all classes from the double burden. Note, however, that whatever housework would then remain to be done is inevitably described by her as *women's* work. Her favorite scheme for liberating women from this double burden was the creation of household communes; and she insisted that such a proposal was quite compatible with the political goals of the workers' movement.

WOMEN'S WORK AND HOUSEKEEPING

Preface

I offer this booklet to the public in the hope that the questions it raises will be discussed vigorously. In its last two chapters the work develops a plan that the Social-Democratic party has not, so far, advocated, and for which I alone bear responsibility. But the idea has been germinating in many heads for a long time, and I wish that it will turn out to be fertile and ripen toward its realization in practice.

The author

I. The Development of Housekeeping

It usually is assumed that housekeeping is the most conservative element in the life of society: It seems to be the rock against which the waves of economic development and disturbances break without ever loosening more than a splinter. Yet one glimpse into cultural history shows that this is not so, that in reality housekeeping, like a faithful mirror, reflects all the features of life outside the home.

In prehistoric times, when human beings had already won the fire from the lightning of heaven, but had not yet learned to generate it themselves, they used it for the first time to lay the foundation for the domestic hearth, around which the life of the family structured itself. The woman became the keeper of its flame; she was tied to it, for she had to take care day and night that the fire would not go out. The man brought her the game he had killed; she prepared it, fashioned warming clothes and

Frauenarbeit und Hauswirtschaft (Berlin:Vorwärts Verlag, 1901).

protective blankets out of the hides, and indeed learned to put them up as tents over the campground. Over the glow of the fire she roasted the meat. Then came the time when humans learned to make the fire themselves through friction; this may have coincided roughly with the point at which they no longer fought against only wild beasts but also against their own kind, when they had to defend their campgrounds and sought to conquer new hunting grounds from their neighbors. House-keeping now expanded. For better protection, large families moved to-gether so that three and even four generations lived with each other. They began to learn a primitive kind of agriculture which was done entirely within the framework of the household; they knew how to raise animals for milk and wool. They baked bread in solidly constructed ovens. Above them, there no longer hung hides drawn over poles to protect against the rain; now there was a firm roof built on top of firm walls. And the first spindle, thought so valuable by our ancestors that they ascribed its invention to gods, turned in the hands of the housewife who knew how to spin thread from the wool of the sheep and, later, from the flax of the field, and out of this thread she would weave fabrics in slow labor.

With increasing wealth and rising needs, housekeeping more and more extended its area of activities. Prisoners and subject tribes, over whom the master of the house assumed command, became the male and female slaves of the household. Their labor power was needed in order to carry out the increased housekeeping responsibilities. The spindles danced in their hands, the shuttle of the loom flew to and fro; artful embroideries were fashioned to adorn the garments of the lord and master; delicate lace soon was added, on which female workers labored for many months. Simple clothing increasingly gave way to ever more precious garments, the fashioning of which required much time and skill; clothing the feet likewise became a difficult part of domestic work. And how the hearth was expanding, how its functions increased! Not only meals had to be prepared, including dishes which became ever more difficult to put together, but also soap had to be boiled, candles made, corn roasted, beer brewed. People had learned to make cheese and butter from milk; but the larger the flocks and herds grew from which the milk was extracted, and the more the internal household expanded, the more it lost control over them: The roving hunter turned into the sedentary pastoralist who undertook personally to guard his greatest wealth.

In the castles of the early Middle Ages the household economy reached its peak. It comprised entire building complexes, in which male and female serfs carried out their manifold duties. Their labor not only created means to satisfy the needs of the moment but also those of generations to come: The well-stocked linen closets, the heavy garments, the rugs and tapestry testify to this. Meanwhile, to still the hunger of the numerous castle dwellers and the equally numerous guests, there were not only freshly prepared meals, but in cellars and pantries large supplies of smoked and preserved foods lay stored. Already in classical antiquity, cities had transformed houskeeping: the individual home could no longer produce all its own needs and had to procure part of its foodstuffs from the grocer; the weaving and even more the dyeing of fabrics was already assuming the forms of an independent craft. But the development of towns in the Middle Ages had a much more profound and lasting effect. One area of work after another was forcibly taken from the household and taken over by craft guilds: Spinners, weavers, cobblers, soap boilers, and chandlers—all helped to diminish the household. The countless female servants turned into wage workers; the housewife, like her distant ancestress by the first fire, had to do with her own labor power or with very few helpers. Cooking, sewing, knitting, and embroidering, laundering and ironing soon came to be the sole contents of the urban household. Only away from cities and major highways, in rural areas, villages and isolated homesteads, was the extended home economy to some extent preserved into even most recent times.

Its most dangerous enemy became the machine. Where with primitive tools people had worked only to satisfy their own needs, the machine made it possible to produce far beyond one's own need. Under its influence, the household of the poor shrank tremendously. Their rooms turned into workshops in which soon the entire family, adults and children, old and young, men and women, labored for scant wages. Nothing remained of housekeeping except the cooking range with a miserable meal hastily boiled together and the wash tub in which at night the poor mother in great haste would wash out the few rags owned by the family. But the machine, driven by the giant power of steam, led to even more revolutionizing developments. The factory arose. Human muscle power no longer was needed to put the machine into motion; it was replaced by mechanical forces of all sorts, and vast quantities of commodities were produced at a speed with which neither the workers in cottage industries—let me recall only the Silesian weavers—nor the workers in the household could hope to keep up.

What the craft guilds had done to a limited degree large industry did most extensively: Not only the urban household but also the rural one was almost forcibly deprived of work: Industry not only spins and weaves and cobbles, it also knows how to knit, to embroider, and to launder. It has rendered countless working hands of the home redundant and gradually draws them into the factory. Many a poor man's home stands abandoned: A small flame in the range still recalls the fire in the hearth of bygone days; on it at noon, when husband and wife return for a brief rest, a meal prepared the night before is warmed up; this, a bit of mending, and a bit of laundry, are what remain of housekeeping. Even in the homes of the rich, who primarily enjoy the benefits of everything the machine produces and who have become rich through it and its unceasing productivity, even in their homes the housekeeping functions have shrunk down to a minimum: Here indeed the cooking stove is almost the only thing that remains. And even that is no longer what it once was: No bread is baked here any longer, no meat is smoked in its chimney; even fruits and vegetables are only rarely prepared for conservation now. The stove, moreover, has taken on a new shape; the black coals and the fire crackling so long have given way to the quiet gas flame, at times even to electricity. This, too, means a saving in labor power, a decrease in the burdens of housekeeping, because it means an end not only to lugging the coals but also to kindling the fire and emptying out the ashes. In addition, as the stove disappears from the living room, with it goes the place around which in winter the family used to gather; central heating, heating the house with a single furnace, has replaced it. Meanwhile, in lieu of oil lamps, which are difficult to clean and have to be filled everyday, we now have gas or, to save even the effort of lighting it, the electric light, a jump in progress which roughly corresponds to the transition from the pine torch to the wax candle.

Yet another factor must not be overlooked: Next to the cooking ladle it was the sewing needle which according to the old traditions was the mainstay of the household. It was replaced by the sewing machine, which in the homes of the poor then became a means for wage labor, while in the homes of the rich it worked for the needs of the family, and was set in motion by the feet of servants hired for this purpose or of seamstresses employed by the day. This, too, however, is coming to an end. Mass production in textiles and their rapid transformation by means of the sewing machine has brought the garment industry into life, which has wrested the sewing needle from the hands of industrious domesticity.

Even the better situated worker, male or female, today can clothe him/herself more cheaply by buying ready-made clothing than by trying to make the garments by him/herself. The precondition of this, of course, is the availability of a sufficiently large labor force, preferably female. Nor is there any dearth of them: Unemployed domestics and redundant daughters, the children and wives of workers, provide more recruits than this call to service can use.

II. The Spread of Proletarian Women's Work and Its Consequences

The development of women's work has kept up with the changes we have traced in the household, from the extended domestic economy down to its remnant, the cooking stove; indeed, as we have shown, the two developments were closely coordinated. It was not only that very many labor forces formerly used for service in housekeeping became free and necessarily had to work for a living elsewhere; that furthermore the machine increasingly deprived the old crafts and trades of the very basis for their existence, thus forcing their female members into industrial work; but in addition the steadily declining income and the growing needs of the middle class drove hordes of women into the wide-open arms of industry. If we compare the results of the last and the penultimate censuses in different countries, we see clearly that their number is growing rapidly and that in fact it is growing at a comparatively faster rate than the number of male workers. Relative to the number of workers in the preceding census period, the number of male workers in Germany rose by 16 percent, as against 20 percent for the female workers; in Austria male workers increased by 19 percent, female ones by 47 percent, in the United States, male ones by 24 percent, and female ones by 40 percent. Since as a rule female proletarians enter the workforce at a very young age, it would hardly make sense to talk about a period that could be devoted to schooling in home economics, even if we disregard the fact that in their parental homes there is not likely all that much for them to learn. Once she gets married, she will know little about the proper economic allocation of money at her disposal and even less about the selection and preparation of a diet that would conform with our knowledge of hygiene and nutrition. Moreover, she has been disaccustomed to domestic life too much to find pleasure in it, and the miserable dwelling in which workers almost always are forced to live cannot have any attraction for her either. Thus in most cases she will be glad to go back to the factory and the workshop. But all too often it is bitter necessity rather than force of habit which drives her back to work. The increase in the employment of married women is a fact which glaringly leaps into view everywhere. In Germany in 1882, of every 100 working women 13 were married, as against 16 in 1895. Of industrial women workers in Austria, according to the last census, 24 percent are married; in France as many as 30 percent. And, at that, there can be no doubt that these figures are much too low; many women who are not permanent wage workers but seek employment only when the husband's loss of his job forces them to do so may not have given any hint of their occasional work in the census questionnaires, and many more—I am thinking particularly of the wives of men working in the cottage industries—may not have considered it worth mentioning that they assist their husbands significantly.

Under present conditions, the consequences of wage labor by married women are as unfavorable as they could possibly be. These consequences hit those the hardest who are the weakest, i.e., the children. Later generations will think it sheer lunacy, and yet it is a fact: The more children a woman worker has, and thus the more her presence at home would be required, the stronger is the necessity which drives her out of the home to work. To her small infants she cannot give the drink of life which flows from her breasts because she has to provide bread for the older ones: The four or at most six weeks of rest provided by law is a totally inadequate attempt to help her. And as a consequence death mows away the little human flowers as if they were worth no more than wildflowers in the grass. If they do survive, the dangers do not lessen. The street is their playground and their educational institution. I am sure I need not adduce any evidence that, especially in the big cities, it does not always exercise a favorable influence, that the physical and moral filth it exudes can stick to the children. The poor mother is not blind to these perils. Wishing to protect her children against them, she often uses strange means toward that end: She locks her children in until her return, she ties them up in their little beds, she becomes cruel from anxious and caring love. And then those terrible disasters happen about which the newspapers report so frequently, and which give the fat and comfortable bourgeois no end of opportunities to scream about the cruelty of proletarian mothers. The poor little tykes get too close to the stove and burn to death, or they grab into the washtub, lose their balance and drown; they climb up on the window sill in order to drive away their boredom by looking outside—since they have no toys, after all, which might keep them busy—and break their necks falling into the courtyard; they get entangled in their bedding, and when the mother comes home she finds her youngest one choked to death under the pillow.

These are the internal and external dangers threatening the children of proletarians when the mother is gone, and in addition there are others to which they are subject when the mother comes home. Then, too, she has no time for her children. She has to do cooking and laundry, must clean the home and mend clothes; she is much too harassed to think of anything else. She can play an educational role for her children only in the most superficial fashion. She does not have sufficient leisure to observe their personalities, and as a result of her ceaseless labors she has become too dull intellectually to fertilize the children's minds with her own. Once the children leave the house, she will most of the time have given them nothing that might fill their inner lives or arouse their enthusiasm as they go their own ways. She was a good mother already if she did nothing more than keep a clean and orderly home, feed them adequately, and did not send them out to beg. But only in the rarest cases would she have been able to function as the friend of the children while they were growing up. And yet a good part of the development of the young generation is based on the mother's intellectual and moral influence. None of life's storms can totally blow away the seed she has sown in the children's hearts and minds; out of this seed that strong tree often grows which alone gives protection to the adult human being. Thus the multiple burdens placed on the mother turn into a curse for her children and for the society in which they are members, and favorable or unfavorable development depends partly on them.

But the man also must suffer from his wife's wage labor: She has no time for him. The few short hours she spends at home she must devote to housework and to the children. Once her work is done she falls into bed dead tired, unable to take an interest in anything except the daily worries crowding in on her. She gets more and more estranged from the man, does not understand his interests, and opposes them as soon as they cost only a few dimes. He gets bored and angry, disgusted by the messy household and the poor food; and many a man will seek refuge increasingly in the saloon and in drink. If he loves his wife with that love which is more animal than human in nature (the only love which he can muster for her as long as she can be no more to him than the object of sensual lust), then all too often he will subject himself to her influence. He will abandon the principles that guided him in his youth: He will alienate himself from his work comrades, will lose his interest in the workers' movement. The union no longer holds him; at times he will become without hesitation even a strike breaker to make sure that his household will not lack the things to which it has become accustomed. The political struggles have lost their attractiveness for him; he has sunk to the level of his spouse instead of drawing her up to his.

For the woman herself, the excessive work load means physical and intellectual destruction; first of all, she ages unnaturally fast—just look at the women workers: How often they are already old women at 40! Furthermore, she loses all her resistance against disease and threatening decrepitude. She cannot afford to grant herself any rest even when she is badly in need of rest, and therefore all kinds of ailments begin to trouble her which either poison her entire life, render her incapable of working, or lead her to an early death. But what illness or even disability mean for her can be measured by the blessings of workers' disability insurance: It gives the poor invalids* of labor too little to survive and too much to starve.

The excess burden of work hits her intellect as cruelly as her body. Already in primary school it was fed only the very most essential nourishment—the treasures of learning, like all higher enjoyments in life, are primarily at the disposal of only those who can weigh them with gold. Once out of school, she can give her mind even less; to be sure, she too thirsts for the fountain of knowledge, but she has no time to drink her fill. And with that, she gradually loses her thirst. But even the questions that ought to constitute the woman worker's vital interest, those concerning her own working conditions, arouse her interest only with great difficulty. To begin with, the voices of those who wish to enlighten her often fail to reach her, or do not reach her insistently enough; further, she lacks time and leisure to go to meetings or to organize and be active in the trade union movement. It has become apparent in all countries that attempts to organize women workers encounter virtually insuperable obstacles; one of these, and certainly not the least important one, consists in the double work load of the woman. As a consequence, the percentage of women who are organized in unions is amazingly low everywhere. Of 3½ million women workers in Germany (including domestic servants) a mere 15,000 or so are organized; in France, of almost the same total number, about 30,000; in England, of little over 3

---

*"Invalid" here has the connotation of "wounded war veteran." (Translator's note.)

million, 120,000. Those are figures which are tiny in comparison to the great mass of female labor, and they make any fight for better work conditions almost hopeless. Thus from the very beginning, women find themselves paralyzed in developing an interest for what should be most pertinent to them, because back-breaking toil and ceaseless rushing day in and day out actually seem to be drumming the facts into their consciousness. Even less can it be expected that they will be able to get interested in local government or larger political problems. In fact, much of the time they live in that dumb and dull state of contentedness which is the biggest obstacle on the road to enlightenment and progress. There are exceptions. There are women workers who despite their excessive work load still have enough physical and mental energy to continue educating themselves, to take active part in the trade union and political movements. These exceptions more than anything else attest the indestructible and fundamentally healthy nature of the people and demonstrates that the many others could also be awakened from their lethargy.

III. Bourgeois Women's Work

In recent times, a small group of wage-earning women who must endure hardships similiar to those endured by the female proletarian, albeit in very much milder form, has come into being alongside the large number of industrial working women. Among them should be counted all those women who carry out bourgeois professions, be it as book-keepers, teachers, or writers, as scholars, physicians, artists, actresses, and so forth. To be sure, against the millions their number carries little weight. In Germany there are about 190,000, in Austria 61,000, in France 220,000, in England 269,000, in the United States 480,000 women, who occupy the above-mentioned professions. Typically, how-ever, a large percentage is already married now, when women's work in bourgeois professions is still in its very beginnings; in Germany it is 15 percent, in Austria 36 percent, and in the United States 8 percent. This lets us conclude that here too the development favors and promotes work for married women. The reasons for this are not hard to find: Middle-class incomes have not kept pace with growing demands; marriage, still today seen in bourgeois circles essentially as an institution to provide support, has become more and more unattainable for the growing number of girls without independent means. Add to this the fact that a justified striving toward freedom and autonomy has developed in them, and that its fulfillment became possible when universities and many new professions opened up for women. Once these wage-earning girls enter marriage, their labor power today is often their most valuable dowry, just as in the case of the woman worker. At the same time, they want to stay with their work for reasons of their own, because they love or enjoy their profession, or because of the driving force of their talent which begs to be put to use. But even in a marriage like that of the bourgeoisie it happens once in a while that the wife must begin to contribute to the earnings because the man's income is not sufficient. Yet anyone who today enters the struggle for existence in bourgeois professions, where excessive demands are made of intellectual workers and where all too frequently they must be satisfied with miserable remuneration for long hours of work, must be able to invest all of his energies in this work. The conflict between domestic and professional duties which is very evident in the female proletariat exists also in the world of the bourgeois woman; a painter cannot spend her time in the kitchen, a writer cannot jump up every moment to see whether the soup is boiling over; not a single woman who is seriously devoted to her science or her art and who wants to eradicate dilettantism, that most dangerous enemy of her sex, has the understanding, the time, or the interest which would be required if she wanted to be a really good housewife. If her profession takes her out of the home, her children are just as much without supervision as the children of the proletarian woman, unless she can afford a nursemaid. If she works at home, she needs total rest for several hours every day if she wants to be successful in her work. As long as the children run around her noisily, as long as she is responsible for the cooking, she can do wage work only by overtaxing herself in a manner which will sooner or later take its revenge on her physical or mental health. Even if the intellectual worker has a servant maid, she has not really got rid of her burden, because it is only in the rarest cases that these simple girls understand housekeeping so thoroughly that the housewife becomes superfluous. Instead, she must still assume the role of teacher for the maids, and often she herself does not know all that much more! Even the daughters of the bourgeoisie do not get initiated into the secrets of efficient housekeeping all that often, and when they do get such training, then often they get it in a manner which later, when their circumstances are limited, cannot be of much use to them. About the proper budgeting of expenditures or about kitchen hygiene they do not understand all that much. The result often is such a boundless waste of money, material, time, and work that any earnings she might make can hardly compensate.

The men of the bourgeoisie show an irritability, sometimes intensified into the most bitter hostility, against women's endeavors to claim their right to work: This reaction can be explained essentially by these domestic problems, and it is sheer stupidity—and can at times have an actually damaging effect—on the part of so many representatives of the women's movement if they want to deny the reality of the enemies' arguments by pointing at some fabulous female physicians or attorneys in America who in addition to their professional practices allegedly run a large household all by themselves and possibly even are rearing a bunch of children in model fashion. In fact these arguments are irrefutable and will become weightier the more bourgeois women's work spreads.

There is one other circumstance which must be considered here for those groups of the population where the above argument applies: The domestic servants issue. Without going into details here, let me emphasize only that indeed the lack of female domestics has increasingly made itself felt, and in progressive countries like England and America it has become a veritable calamity. Class consciousness has at last been aroused even in our female house slaves; they are neither willing to sell all their time and energy for a miserable wage nor satisfied with the quarters they are provided and with the other work conditions to which they are subjected. In most cases, however, the not-so-affluent middle class is not in a position to satisfy the justified demands the maids make: They cannot pay much higher wages, they cannot keep two maids and therefore often must overburden the one they employ. Their budget is strained too much already by high rental costs; hence they cannot afford to take a larger apartment to provide a better room for the maid, and they are too deeply stuck in old prejudices to sacrifice the often rather superfluous "drawing room." But even higher wages and better work conditions are often scorned these days because these children of the people have come to value their freedom above everything and therefore prefer the career of a worker to that of a domestic servant: The worker may be leading a miserable life, but at least she is her own boss for a few hours a day, while the maid, however well she may be fed, is under perpetual control. Now it is not only to be hoped but can be assumed for certain that this entire movement for the liberation of domestic servants will spread rapidly. Bourgeois housewives like to talk about the terrible need for domestics— and particularly those housewives who stubbornly refuse to acknowledge the actual need of the domestics. This need for domestics will increase more and more and may go so far as to render wage work by married women in bourgeois professions impossible.

IV. Private and Governmental Remedies

It is clear from what has been said that the increase in women's work contributes significantly to undermining what little still remains of domestic housekeeping, with results that are so sad at times as to make us doubt the value of women's work. This has not remained unnoticed, and there has been no lack of good folks who thought they might patch up all the bleeding wounds with a few little Band-Aids. They created soup kitchens where for little money every woman worker can receive a hot meal, not worse than she could prepare herself, but hardly any better either. They instituted kindergartens and day care centers where the little ones can find shelter during the day; they even tried to combine a people's kitchen with a workers' tenement house, in hopes that the inhabitants might give up cooking their own food and obtain their meals there. These institutions to some extent got stuck in their infancy; but those whom they were designed to serve also met them with a degree of distrust that rose to the level of outright rejection. The self-conscious worker will scorn anything and everything offered to him in the shape of charity; before accepting alms he has to stand hard at the edge of the abyss from which destitution grins at him, for, as a person who spends his hard life in honest labor, he is *entitled* to nourishment, clothing, and living quarters and does not need to receive them as a charitable deed. He senses what those who provide charitable gifts have not yet learned to sense: That offering the poor worker compassion instead of justice means adding insult to injury. But there are still other reservations, especially from the point of view of the women, which one could adduce against these products of charity: The woman worker has no influence whatever in the creation of these soup kitchens; she must accept whatever, and in whatever manner, may be offered her. Meanwhile in the kindergartens her little ones are taught Bible verses and bigoted religious songs; they get all sorts of chauvinist mischief drummed into their heads and often are trained to be murdering flag-wavers; in short, they are systematically alienated from their parents.

These palliatives are to mitigate the damage done by women's work.

Whoever recognizes their worthlessness can easily become convinced that only radical action will be of use here: Do away with work on the part of married women—for them that is the slogan. By doing that, they suggest, family and home will regain the woman; female competition will disappear, and as a consequence the men's wages will rise to a level where they will be sufficient to feed the family. Too bad only that all these beautiful and seemingly so logical deductions are false! Such impeccable informants as official German trade inspectors have in their reports declared almost unanimously that a reduction of married women's work by law is impossible because the very existence of the family is made possible by supplementing the man's earnings with those of the woman. The woman must work so that she and her loved ones can survive. If there were a law preventing her from working in a factory, she would be compelled to switch to cottage work, and the entrepreneurs would profit from this. They would at once exploit to the utmost those cheap new labor forces that lack virtually all legal protection. If she wanted to escape this, the woman worker would be left without any recourse except that of circumventing the lawful wedding rite and living in concubinage. Without the certificate from city hall, no official agency would recognize her as a married woman, and the doors of the factory would once again be open to her. Very obviously she would, as a woman, be fair game far more blatantly than before, totally abandoned to the man's arbitrary cruelty, aware that from one moment to the next he might kick her and her children out into the street.

No law, however draconian, would be able to prevent the pattern of modernization. It would just be overrun. Whoever wishes to be genuinely useful will want to mitigate the hardships which progress inevitably entails and will want to remove the obstacles piling up in its way.

In all countries, workers' protection legislation has made more or less timid efforts in this direction. Such laws have limited the hours of work for women to eleven or at best to ten hours, so that, setting aside eight hours for sleep, five to six hours remain for the home. In fact, it is rarely even that much. Not only does the worker use a lot of time for the walk to and from her place of work, she also has to work overtime much too frequently, and if she works at home she is altogether without protection and can work her fingers to the bone in ceaseless toil. But she has been granted time off for her noon meal: At most they have given her 1½ hours in which to go home, prepare a meal, and eat! What a mockery of the highly touted jolly and genial German family table!

Against these unsatisfactory provisions the Social-Democratic movement, and primarily its female section, has set itself as one of its aims to make proposals for the thorough-going protection of women and to agitate for them by the spoken and written word. And since the movement is aware that there is nothing more important in the eyes of the woman worker than to provide her with time so that her body and her mind can gather strength, it lays the main emphasis on the struggle for the eight-hour day. If she had this, even the married woman would be able to take care of her household chores in greater leisure, and the children, too, would not be motherless all day long. But even assuming the fulfillment of this demand something would still have to be done to take care of the children during the eight hours of their mother's work. The aim of our agitation furthermore must be to get local authorities to make sufficient provisions for kindergartens and day care centers so that all workers' children are in safe care during their mothers' absence. There is yet one other matter to consider: As long as there are women working in cottage industries, as long as cottage work, this cancer eating at the body of the people, has not been eradicated definitively, the legal limitation of work hours will benefit only comparatively few women. Even an army of trade inspectors would not be able to sniff out this kind of work in every garret, every kitchen corner, every lonely mountain hut where it might be hiding, and to prevent violations of the law. I am told that there are still some queer ducks who think that cottage employment is a blessing for women, especially for married ones, because it ties them to hearth and home. What they do not realize is that, given the starvation wages paid in the cottage inustries, the woman must work much more intensively than in the factory and that her home and her children suffer even more under this arrangement. For not only does their mother have no time for them, but furthermore the wretched small home is transformed into a workshop and mocks the most modest needs for clean, healthy air in the most horrible way. Many women who before their marriage worked in factories turn to cottage industry afterwards because they can then be close to their children and because they think they will be able to keep their household in better shape. After only brief and painful experience, they would love to go back to the factory if only they could see their children taken care of during the hours they themselves are away at work.

State and society have taken a very different attitude toward bourgeois women's work than toward the work of proletarian women: They accepted the latter serenely as given and at most sought to outlaw wage work by married women; but against the former they fought tooth and nail. Quite understandable! The work of proletarian women is the basis on which the very existence of the bourgeoisie rests, but this existence is undermined by the work of women from its own class. "The woman belongs in the home" is the battle cry of those opposing bourgeois women's work—frequently the same men who employ a whole number of women in their own factory or business. Above all it was the majority of physicians who from the beginning took a hostile attitude toward female colleagues. For this purpose they fired all available artillery, from the fairy tale about the woman's intellectual inferiority to the pathetic reference to her "sole profession," which is to be wife and mother, and down to the thundering indignation of the students in Halle who in the name of imperiled morality demanded the exclusion of female students from the university. And the bourgeois women's movement, forcefully and skill-fully fighting for the right to work, had no better defense against its enemies than the constantly repeated argument that professional work would not in the least threaten the "sole profession" of women. It was right in so far as, in the world of bourgeois women, wage work in most cases is no more than a substitute for the "sole profession" and is abandoned as soon as the girl gets married. But, as we have seen, it is totally wrong when it believes it can speak in the name of women who are married and nonetheless continue to be wage earners. As long as women's work, like that of men, is not regarded as a lifetime career, it is condemned to get stuck in dilettantism; if that is to be prevented, the bourgeois woman, too, must be freed from the excess burden of her double duties.

V. The Household Cooperative

We have seen that the married white- and blue-collar woman worker aches under the load of double duties. She is unable to carry either of them out fully and satisfactorily. Neither existing nor desired workers' protection laws can fully relieve her of her burden. And if she is not independently wealthy, the bourgeois woman cannot pursue her profession either. The task thus is to create institutions that make this possible for both of them.

Such an institution is the household cooperative. I imagine it to look about as follows: A housing complex enclosing a large and prettily laid out garden of about fifty or sixty apartments, none of which contains a kitchen. There is only a small gas cooker in a little room which can be used in case of sickness or to take care of infants. In lieu of the fifty to sixty kitchens in which an equal number of women usually are busy, there is a central kitchen on the ground floor which is equipped with all kinds of modern labor-saving machines. Among the things that exist already are even automatic dish washers in which twenty dozen plates or bowls can be washed and dried in three minutes! A pantry and a laundry room with automatic washing machines are located nearby, also a large dining room that can also function as a meeting hall and, during the day, as a playroom for the children. A smaller reading room adjoins it. The management of the entire household is in the hands of an experienced housekeeper who is a specialist in home economics; she has one or two kitchen maids under her supervision. The quarters of these household employees are on the same floor as the housekeeping premises: They also include the room of the woman who takes care of the children; like all others she is employed by all inhabitants jointly. Depending on wish and inclination, meals are either taken in the common dining room or are carried to all the floors by special food elevators. Heat is provided to the apartments by a central heating system, so that here too one furnace replaces fifty stoves. While the mothers are at work, the children play under adult supervision, be it in the dining room or in the garden, where playground equipment and sand boxes give children of all ages something to do. In the evening, when their mothers have put them to bed and the parents want to chat with friends or to read, they go down to the common rooms, where they need not purchase their entertainment with the consumption of alcohol, if they do not feel the need for it.

This plan could be modified or elaborated in all possible directions. In order to simplify it, one could omit, say, the elevators and the reading room; the women would then have to go to the food-dispensing counter to get their meals. It could be expanded by centralizing, say, the cleaning of the apartments. For that a crew of chambermaids would have to be employed. By introducing electric light, setting aside tastefully furnished rooms for social occasions, putting in bowling alleys, and other such things, the plan could be elaborated even more. All this would more or less automatically conform to the needs of the inhabitants who—and this is an essential precondition—would all have to be on more or less the same income level. Absolute equality of income would not be necessary, if only because it would not create difficulties if those less well-off wanted, say, a smaller apartment or a meal lacking one particular dish.

This entire plan is by no means as new as it may appear. The beginnings of it can be found in many places. Thus, because of the lack of servants, many families in America live in boarding houses or hotels where they get their meals furnished. In a suburb of Chicago a number of families have got together to run their household communally; in England similar steps have been advocated quite a bit; in Manchester a society was founded recently which wants to set up food kitchens in various parts of the city from which all families could obtain good hot meals. Here too it is the scarcity of domestic cooks which provided the occasion for this initiative. There are houses in which single working women live and get fed in common; they exist in large numbers especially in England, but even in Berlin something like this is being started right now. All these institutions, however, with hardly any exception, are begun by, and designated for, bourgeois circles.

Indeed, at first sight it seems virtually impossible for workers with their limited means to establish and maintain household cooperatives. They have never been able to hire any kind of help, and now all of a sudden they are supposed to have the means to pay a housekeeper, nursemaids, and the like? And yet this is in no way outside the realm of possibilities, for not only would these expenditures be distributed over fifty to eighty families, but they would be amply recovered by the advantages of quantity buying of groceries, by savings in fuel, and by a rational household economy in general. Let us assume for instance that fifty families hire three persons for a salary of 125 marks a month; let us budget 156 marks for their room and board (board 1.40 marks, room 10 marks per person). Then every family would have to set aside 5.62 marks per month, which could very easily be recovered by the savings. Moreover, since the individual apartments would need no kitchen, the rent for the central kitchen and the other common rooms could also be made available without difficulty.

All that is the least difficult part. The greater difficulty is posed by the question about the practical methods for realizing the household cooperative for the working class. The existing tenement houses are not suitable for this. They usually are designated for tenants from a wide variety of income and property strata, where the worker is assigned any old wretched, dark rooms in the back, and often he cannot afford to pay rent even for those. Many very important features would be impossible here, and their lack could easily mean failure for the whole scheme. But is it too much to hope that those who make speculative investments in the construction industry might take up the practical idea and build houses for housekeeping cooperatives at the latter's risk? For reasons I will adduce below that might be a rather attractive idea for bourgeois circles, but the proletariat ought to proceed by a different route. Such a route is indicated in building cooperatives whose purpose it is to build houses, not for individual ownership but on the basis of cooperative property and joint administration. In new houses built to the proper specification the desired reform in housekeeping could be accomplished, and in addition building cooperatives would offer all those workers who are capable of helping in their formation the advantage of escaping from the housing shortage. In many places, including big cities like Berlin, Hamburg, Altona, Hanover, Kassel, and elsewhere, building and savings cooperatives have been able to develop very fruitful activity, and the participating comrades enjoy almost all the advantages offered by a house of their own without the disadvantages of house ownership which hit the modern industrial worker doubly painfully. The apartments in the houses of the building cooperatives fit the needs and the income level of the workers. Even though they meet hygienic and other requirements better, they are cheaper, as a rule, than the local average of comparable quarters in rental houses. But there is an advantage which can be considered much weightier: A member of the cooperative, as long he fulfills his obligation, cannot be removed from his apartment whereas he in turn is free to leave any time. As co-owner of the cooperative's building he has sure possession of his apartment as if he had sole property of it, but that does not tie him to the soil; instead, he can take his leave unhindered, if, let us say, a change in employment should require it. A member who lives in a cooperative-owned home will never know raises in the rent that hit the individual most painfully and often rob the working class of wage increases won by the greatest possible efforts. Protected against such danger, secure, and independent, he is master within his own four walls and has the uplifting consciousness of owing these advantages to his own and his comrades' initiative.

The cooperative movement, which otherwise has flourished so richly, has paid least attention of all to cooperative construction activity. That is understandable because the difficulties here are particularly great; and in contrast to consumers' cooperatives they presuppose considerable initial cash outlay, especially in the large cities where speculation has caused real estate and building prices to rise sky-high. Nonetheless, the existing savings-and-loan and construction associations have demonstrated that it is not impossible to succeed even under these circumstances. Of course, one should not indulge in illusions about the overall significance of such ventures. A complete solution of the housing question is possible only through comprehensive and trenchant laws that have the purpose of transferring all real estate, primarily in towns and cities, to societal ownership. Yet even though construction cooperatives will never be an acceptable substitute for necessary legislation in this direction, and if particularly they cannot be of any help to the large mass of the most poorly paid workers, they might still mitigate the worst excrescences of our housing misery for the better situated groups of workers.

But even these workers will not be able to create amply financed construction cooperatives with financial means of their own. Even so, a large number of them will be able to lay the financial foundation through the instalment purchase of cooperative shares, usually issued in 200 to 500 mark denominations. Beyond this, they have at their disposal a large fund which they can claim on grounds that are based on good juridical and moral arguments. I am speaking about the pension fund of the disability insurance administrations. Article 164, Disability Insurance Law of 13 July 1899, which regulates the administration of the insurance administration pension funds, specifies that the administrations may invest half of their funds for any programs which exclusively or primarily benefit that part of the population covered by the compulsory insurance. The preamble of the law explains this expressly by stating as follows: "Raising the portion of the fund to be thus made available to one half is to respond to those desires which aim for increased participation of the insurance administrations in endeavors to improve the workers' housing conditions." No doubt working-class pressure will soon impel the insurance administration, which so far still resists compliance with the provisions of the law, to invest their funds in loans for workers' housing. Such use of their money would be in conformity with the task given them under the law: Improvements in housing would lead to improvements in the workers' health conditions; meanwhile, the insurance administrations would be investing their funds safely, would realize adequate interest, and would at the same time be giving rise to gratifying social effects. Everything really speaks in favor of this kind of action—the law, the needs of society, and financial interest. If the insurance authorities have not lived up to their obligations, then it is only because the workers have shown neither the correct insight nor the necessary action to assert their claims energetically. The workers have failed to make the necessary sharp demands for support in trying to obtain housing reforms not only vis-à-vis the insurance administration but also vis-à-vis local and national authorities. That is the reason why practically no new legislation has been written and no serious administrative measures have been taken in this matter even though the opinions here are much more clearly developed than in many other areas. Indeed, the conviction that effective measures are urgently needed is quite widespread by now, as shown by, among other things, the decree issued by four Prussian ministers on 19 March 1901; hence powerful agitation which mobilized the great mass of the people would very likely lead to serious response both in legislation and in the administration; national and local authorities might be compelled to proceed with the construction of numerous workers' dwellings, with guarantees against any dependency relations that might result from this, and to support building cooperatives with loans or loan guarantees, by providing inexpensive construction sites, and the like. About building cooperatives particularly it is essential to point out that under today's circumstances the major precondition is clarity about their value and the energetic will on the part of the workers to create them; against this the procurement of the necessary financial basis recedes into the background. Wherever large consumer cooperatives exist, as for instance in England, they constitute the best point of departure for the formation of building cooperatives, but they could also be created independently by the better situated workers. They are a splendid method of self-help within certain limits. Workers should make maximal use of it, and working women should participate with all their strength in an agitation on the success of which the creation of household cooperatives will to a large extent depend.

For bourgeois circles, as mentioned above, the question is a different one. For them, too, there are no obstacles in the way toward the creation of building cooperatives, but the procurement of money is not regulated at all; and since it can be assumed from the beginning that there will be no rich people among those who wish to set up a household cooperative, the latter could not think about building with means all of their own. Either they would have to find someone willing to provide funds because the venture itself appears to provide sufficient guarantee for him to risk his capital, or else the house would have to be built by some entrepreneur as a speculative venture, like any other apartment house. This would eliminate some of the advantages offered by a cooperative, but it would still be better than nothing at all as the basis for further elaboration of the project.

VI. Effects of Reforms in Housekeeping

The reform in housekeeping I have in mind would have very important results, since the work of the housewife or the cook to which we cling with so much expenditure of sentimentality is nothing else than pernicious dilettantism. The dilettantism would be eliminated so that it can no longer wreak havoc in an area as important as human nutrition. For the children, including even the youngest ones, communal life would be of incalculable advantage. Not only would they be protected against the influence of the street and the deplorable precocity of city children, but they would at the same time learn to develop the spirit of brotherliness in themselves. For the women, however, the housekeeping cooperative constitutes one of the foundations of their liberation. As Peter Kropotkin writes, "To liberate women means not only to open the doors to the university, the court of law, and parliament for them; rather it means to free them from cooking stove and washtub, it means creating institutions that will permit them to raise their children and to participate in public life." Women will never win the fight for emancipation they are waging today if they do not first win time and leisure and bring their lives into harmony with their aims. The woman's aptitude for productive work is something one will be able to evaluate only when she has ceased to groan under double obligations which ruin her physically and intellectually. As things are today, the married working woman will always have to be inferior to the man because unlike him she does not have any opportunity to gather new strength during hours of rest. The very same thing is true for the woman who does intellectual work. Filled with a thousand petty household worries, her head cannot at the same time make clear ideas ripen that go beyond the narrowest range of interests.

Moreover, a restructuring of housekeeping would promote a whole number of additional important reforms. For instance, it seems to me that a solution to the domestic servants problem cannot be expected as long as today's private households continue to exist. A solution will be in sight only when domestic servants quit the now prevalent personal relationship to their employer and come closer to the status of the factory worker; and that is possible only in housekeeping cooperatives where higher wages can be paid, better quarters can be provided, the work hours can be regulated more equitably, and the housewife's control over everything her servants do at all times is eliminated.

There is another problem, discussions of which have barely begun until now, that might also receive a powerful push toward its solution, though only as a result of a large-scale spread of household cooperatives. I am speaking about the problem of cottage industry. We will be able to combat this cancerous sore with all the necessary decisiveness only when the worry over her children and her household need no longer chain the woman to her home permanently, and when this pretext can no longer be used even by those who regard any legal interference in the home as sacrilege.

Does all this spell "revolutions," "dissolution of the family," or whatever those nice slogans may be that send shivers down the philistines' spines?

We have seen how changing economic circumstances and technological progress subjected housekeeping to continual changes until today it has shrunk to near-insignificance. In the depth of our hearts we are aware that the nuclear household already is a thing of the past; if it is now replaced by the communal household, then this is part of the inevitable pattern of development. To declare the kitchen to be the foundation of family life, as it were, to declare that the family stands or falls with the kitchen means to descecrate the concept of the family. If it were indeed only the cooking stove which keeps it together, it would deserve to perish. In reality matters are as follows. The outer form of the family has undergone perpetual change. What remains firm in this continual transformation is the relationship between man, woman, and child. The relationship becomes deeper and more loving, the more it can free itself from external conditions. In ancient times the woman was the man's submissive slave, the first administrix of his property. In modern times he esteemed her primarily as his housekeeper who, after he had sown his wild oats in his youth, created a comfortable home for him. In the future she will be both his lover and his friend with whom he shares his joys and his sorrows and in whom he finds full understanding. But for the children, to whom in their infancy she was only a nursemaid, she shall turn into their educator and their friend.

Is that the dissolution of the family? Is this not rather the dissolution of today's circumstances which force the wage-earning woman to ruin her health and her mind, while driving the man into the saloon and the children into the street?

But it is not only the enemies of women's liberation who are against us. Even some of our friends voice all kinds of reservations. They argue that the wives in the cooperative will not get along with each other; wrangling, bickering, and gossiping will write a miserable finish to the venture. I do not wish to deny the justification for this objection. Poorly educated and overburdened, women simply have not had the possibility to get themselves interested in the more serious questions of life; and it is no wonder that, as a consequence, they have been sticking their noses into their neighbors' affairs. No household commune will be able to change them from one day to the next. But it certainly will eliminate a great deal of the cause for gossip and bickering by preventing the one from finding fault with the other's method of housekeeping and from poking their noses into their pots and pans. In time, moreover, it will exercise an important educational influence precisely in this direction. Of course, whoever wishes to organize the first housekeeping communes and set them up as models for others ought to be fully aware of the seriousness of this matter and of the responsibility they are assuming, and should not jeopardize its success by acting frivolously. In all similar endeavors among workers, in trade unions and cooperatives, it has been shown that the participants were quite capable of rising to the importance of the matter in everything including their behavior. In fact, there are few sentiments more apt to influence people's moral behavior than a sense of responsibility; this experience would surely not betray us in this case either.

The fluctuations in workers' incomes have also been used as an argument against the idea of household communes, and not altogether without justification. Against this it must be emphasized that, for the time being, only workers who are somewhat better off than the average will be able to join such a cooperative, but that for them the ever-present threat of unemployment is less threatening inside the commune than outside. Not only will a commune be more willing than any landlord to grant a delay in rent payment, but also it will be able to protect its member from the worst possible disaster by not letting him go hungry. Precisely here can the spirit of cooperation most clearly demonstrate its vitality.

Of course, many a man will ask, "But what is the woman to do if she does not do the cooking?" and many a woman herself will cling to her kitchen with genuine affection. That leads me to point out that, after all, the household commune is designed to unite primarily those families whose female members are pursuing independent professions. Nobody who is unwilling to part with the individual family kitchen can be forced to do so.

This still does not exhaust the arguments raised against housekeeping cooperatives. Among the objections are those which particularly the most advanced ranks of the workers raise against any and all cooperative endeavors. They will deflect the workers from their principal aim; they will absorb energies which ought to be at the disposal of the political movement; and there is the danger that members of cooperatives get to be so content with their own conditions that they forget the misery of the others, and that solidarity within small communes is promoted at the expense of total proletarian solidarity.

These arguments need not frighten us, for they have been disproved by the course of events; the retarding elements in the workers' movement are always those who have been rendered apathetic by misery. Conversely, it is the better situated workers, who were able to develop higher inner needs, who have always been the pathbreakers. Moreover, it should not be overlooked that the workers' movement poses a wider variety of tasks the more comprehensive it becomes. Like the trade union movement, the cooperative movement is but one of its many different elements which carries out important functions in the fight of the proletariat for liberation.

I would also reject the argument that pressing for reforms which will benefit only a small number of people is a waste of our energies. All reforms, even the greatest ones, grew out of small beginnings, and whoever recognizes the natural laws of development of social life will have to admit point-blank that even great revolutions usually began with almost imperceptibly small movements. For instance, the giant English consumer cooperative movement grew out of the little grocery store of the poor Rochdale workers.

In his book *Women and Socialism*, August Bebel writes: "Like the workshop of the petty master craftsman, the small private kitchen is a thing of the past, an institution which senselessly squanders and wastes time, energy, and material." He then depicts a kitchen which was exhibited at the Chicago World's Fair in 1893, and in which the heating, cooking, frying, and dishwashing was done electrically; "our women," he suggests, "will grab on to this kitchen of the future with both hands when it can be had in lieu of today's kitchen"; but he places the communal arrangement of food preparation into the "society of the future," as Bellamy, among others, has done also. Now I do share the view that the definitive victory of the household commune over the private household is possible only when the socialist economic system has replaced the capitalist one; but just as the one will not disappear all of a sudden, the other one will not suddenly come into being; instead, like a butterfly within the pupa, the society of the future will develop gradually until, having matured, it will slip out of the dying husk. Just so the replacement of the individual household by the housekeeping commune will be able to occur only gradually. The first step taken will not conquer the entire country all at once, but it must be taken if the country is to be conquered at all.

More than before the male workers ought to remember that winning the women over to their ideals can be a life-or-death matter for them. The number of women workers is growing rapidly, as we have seen; the moment might come when the men will sense this mass of women with all their intellectual backwardness as a chain that ties their feet. In order to prevent this, in order to wake the women from the leaden sleep weighing on them, they must be liberated also from the slavery of the household.

That this liberation alone will not solve all problems is self-evident. Only quacks will give the patient medicines allegedly curing all the body's ills.

The housekeeping commune is designed to help bring about the reign of that spirit of fraternity without which the development of better conditions is not even conceivable. It is to be no more than one stone in the proud structure of the future in which some day a happier human race will live.

COTTAGE INDUSTRY

Legislation affecting cottage industry can be divided into three categories: One set of laws based on the principles of workers' protection, which therefore treats cottage industry workers similarly to factory workers, hence seeks to protect the weak against excessively reckless exploitation by the strong and to put limits on the exercise of economic selfishness; another set that arises out of consumer interests and is limited to sanitary controls; and finally a third one that aims at the suppression of the cottage industry. We will have to look at the relevant legislation and its effects from these three points of view.

The extension of workers' protection to the cottage industry is the most popular demand, often repeated rather thoughtlessly, by which, according to widespread belief, its harmful abuses can be effectively combated. Indeed, such laws have been passed, but they fulfill their purpose only in part because in Europe as well as in some states outside Europe they do not cover the cottage industry or the family workshop.

In England, France, and Austria, workshops are regarded as equivalent to factories with regard to workers' protection laws; English law even dares to intrude into the otherwise well-protected family workshop as long as children and juveniles are employed there; French law even covers the workshops of religious congregations and those founded by charitable organization, while Austrian law excludes them. In Switzerland, workers' protection legislation embraces all workshops employing more than six people, and all workshops in which dangerous work is done, regardless of the number employed. Finally, New Zealand has extended workers' protection laws to all family workshops employing two or more persons; Victoria has done the same, except that the critical number is four rather than two. Against all this, let us get a clear perception of the situation in which cottage industry finds itself: It is spread over big cities and small towns, over the plain and the lonely little village as well as over the most

"Hausindustrie," *Die Zukunft*, 37 (1901).

inaccessible alpine valleys and high meadows. It is quartered miserably in basement nooks and in garrets, it hides behind the splendor of bygone better days in ladies' drawing rooms in the bourgeois world. Especially in the big cities it has no fixed abode, because no immobile machines like those in factory production tie it to the soil. Its workshops are opened as quickly as they are closed. Against this, do laws for the protection of workers have any prospect of being effective? Not even a whole army of officials would be able to enforce them. Among other things, it must be this consideration that caused family workshops to be placed outside the regulatory law in those countries in which domestic industry occupies a particularly broad area. Of course, with this the range of those covered by supervision is narrowed considerably; the poorest and the most miserable, among whom women and children are by far the largest group, thus are abandoned to exploitation without any protection, and meanwhile those employed in workshops do not get much help either. For the difficulties of satisfactory supervision are intensified by the apathy of those who are supposed to get the protection. The existence of cottage industry is based essentially on the fact that human labor power works more cheaply than machine power; but the inevitable complement of the low wages is the long work time. The people, especially the women, who have always, so far, been subject to such conditions, do not have enough insight to help support compliance with the laws. On the contrary, save for scattered groups of enlightened big city workers, they are likely to regard a decrease in their hours of labor as an unwelcome diminution of their wages, which are scant already, and they will seek to circumvent the law. Moreover, they are not very capable of organizing, not only as a consequence of their low living standard and their being overburdened with work but also because of their isolation, so that it is only in rare cases that a unified strong collective can replace the separated weak individuals.

The legislators are not ignorant of these facts. Hence they have made repeated attempts to find out, first of all, the identity of the people working in home industries, whom the law was supposed to cover. As far as workshops are concerned, the Australian states of Victoria and New Zealand [sic] have prescribed annual registration for them, and specify that a workshop can be put to use as such only after the labor inspector with whom it must be registered has given a permit. This measure is supposed to give the authorities knowledge of existing workshops and is also supposed to make control by the health inspectors possible from the very beginning. But measures that are possible in a small state become almost impossible to carry out in a large society with widely extended home industry. For in the final analysis yet another control would be needed to determine whether in fact the prescribed registration for control is always made. In this connection the English labor commission suggested that the owner of the home, or possibly the one commissioning the work, be made responsible for timely registration. But even if by such a measure registration could be assured, one major disadvantage would remain: The labor inspector could not always be available for inspection at once, and the work stoppage caused by this would always imply a painful loss of earnings. In an attempt to cover all those working in home industry of all kinds, a number of North American and Australian states have made it incumbent on the employers to maintain precise rosters of their workers and to submit them on demand to the labor inspector. England has gone one step further by demanding, though only of a limited number of trades, that shop owners and suppliers must twice a year submit the names and addresses of their workers to the trade inspector. This is a noteworthy regulation which deserves to be imitated; yet it will be effective only when the officials are able to supervise all workers adequately. But under present conditions that is altogether hope-less. Hence a better means to guarantee that the protective laws are in fact carried out seems to be that of extending responsibility for them to a larger number of people and thus to create some sort of volunteer inspectorate to supplement the governmental one. English lawmakers have made this a rule for certain trades and have made the entrepreneur liable when his workers are employed under health-endangering condi-tions. But even this provision can be effective only where matters like the sanitary conditions of the workshop are concerned. The most important things, however, secure work hours, rest periods, protection for pregnant women and new mothers, etc., cannot be guaranteed by anything be-cause even the employer cannot exercise continual supervision and will scarcely feel obliged to try, as he knows much too well how rarely any violation of rules would be noted. Thun relates about a Rhenish indus-trialist who had to pay a fine for violating the law for the protection of children and who exclaimed: "I'll work the children so hard that I will have the money back in a week!" The same thing would happen here, in some variations, and therefore it would be a mistake to make the employers alone responsible for enforcement. Beatrice Webb suggests that one ought to make the owner of the premises and the landlord of the workshop liable also. In New York, this demand has partly become law, in that in some trades the owner of the premises is made responsible for seeing to it that the merchandise is manufactured only after the workshop has been registered with the authorities. Beyond this provision, it seems to me, it would not be practical to expand anyone's liability because otherwise the law might give rise to intolerable harassment of the shop owner and his family by the landlord. Once the landlord or his agent—and one ought to realize clearly what kind of people they often are and how suspiciously they confront the poor worker from the very beginning—has a right to supervise his tenants, he can make life miserable for all those whom he dislikes for some reason or other, to say nothing about abuses of various kinds which would necessarily result from this; moreover, this kind of supervision would never be possible anywhere except in the outskirts of cities, because cottage industry workers in the countryside and in the mountains frequently own their miserable work premises themselves and may also live far away from the contractor.

One more method deserves mentioning, which is to help secure the legally prescribed work hours for a limited group of workers. It is the prohibition against giving work material to factory or shop workers on their way home after their regular work period. England has blazed the trail in this but expressly specified that taking work home is prohibited only if the female worker has been kept busy in the shop full-time. This opens the door as wide as possible to abuse because it is impossible to determine whether or not she is being given too much home work for the remainder of the time legally still available for her employment. The law was formulated that way in the belief that this would show proper consideration for women who, having children to rear and a household to manage, would have no more than a few hours of time for work in the shop. The lawmakers did not want to deprive these women of the opportunity to add to their meager wages by work in the home. But to this consideration they sacrificed the far more important concern for hundreds of other women, whom the paymaster can now load up with so much work that at home they have to work until deep into the night without finding time to care either for their children or for their household. If indeed the female worker is to be protected against exploitation, even if only in this relatively small area, the prohibition against taking work home must be absolute.

The upshot of all that we have observed about the extension of workers' protection laws to the domestic industry is that all efforts to make them fully effective remain fruitless. The basic reason for this is that the waters of domestic industry disperse in countless small hidden rivulets which by necessity are immune to supervision. With pained feelings of resignation in the face of this realization, many legislators have limited themselves to drawing up general sanitary rules so as to mitigate the effects of domestic industry. Originally, their point of departure here was not the interest of the workers but that of the consumers, whom they wished to protect against the harm done by commodities made under unhygienic conditions. This system has been instituted most extensively at the state level in the United States. Epidemics originating in the sweatshops of the domestic industry gave the impetus for it. In order to prevent dangerous crowding in smaller work premises, they decreed that in tenement rooms that were used for eating and sleeping, outside labor forces were not allowed to be employed in the making of saleable commodities. That was at the same time a first and highly promising step toward requiring the creation of separate workshops; but at the same time it was an indirect support of family shops, in which exploitation could celebrate orgies. Industry will always go after the cheapest labor; and thus the law contributed more to promoting the spread of domestic industry than to preventing it. However, to facilitate the supervision also of the family shop and its hygienic conditions, it was made obligatory to register it with the health authorities and to obtain a license from them. For compliance with this law, the State of New York made the landlord responsible; and Massachusetts, the firm for whom the work is being done. In this manner work premises are made subject to inspection by the health authorities, in some states, such as Massachusetts, only when they were used for the manufacture of garments; in other places, when merchandise of any kind is made in them. Specific rules such as the prohibition against making merchandise in dwellings harboring infectious diseases, which England passed, are natural consequences of this. Many more steps, however, have been taken to protect the public. In New York, Massachusetts, and New Zealand commodities known to have originated in workshops or family enterprises without a licence, or known to have been made under unsanitary conditions, must be labeled by the health or trade inspector with a tag containing the term "tenement made," thus scaring both retailers and consumers from purchasing them. Merchandise made in premises in which infectious diseases prevail must be disinfected after being tagged; and these rules apply also to goods imported from abroad.

BACKSTAGE

The child who for the first time sees the colorful curtain rise and then watches with breathless wonder the fairy tale being played on the stage believes that the wondrous world behind the scenery could not be any different from that in front of it. As the human being grows into adulthood, he will gradually lose some of his illusions, but nonetheless he may often think with concealed envy of the "free and jolly artists' life" of the men and women who are not forced to stand behind the lectern or the store counter. The experienced roué does not share these ideas; for him the theater is a place of entertainment, and every female who enters the stage appears to him to be indicating thereby that she is in a mood to lend a willing ear to his wishes. Not dissimilar is the judgment of the virtuous bourgeois housewife who, however, not only holds the "theater princess" in contempt but also harbors an irrepressible feeling of envy when she sees the actresses wear costly modern gowns on stage and when she attributes to them a carefree life commensurate with such luxurious clothes.

Who has ever looked behind the scenes except with prying or lascivious eyes?

Who has tried to judge fairly whatever he saw?

Not many people; and whatever they said has gone without echo. The majority of women wrap themselves in the cloak of their virtue, close their eyes and ears, and pay no attention to those not walking on their own straight and narrow path. The actresses themselves, however, are groaning under the yoke of the worst kind of slavery without being able to shake it off by their own effort alone; every single attempt to do so results in its becoming ever more oppressive. I am here appealing to the hearts and the reason of fair-minded men and women by reporting facts about the life of artists; as soon as such people come together in order to help

"Hinter den Kulissen," *Ethische Kultur,* 2 (no. 46, 1894); ibid., 3 (no. 14, 1895).

those who are being sacrificed to penury or to shame for the sake of their enjoyment and delight, then—I hope—the actresses' feeling of solidarity will stir also and will give them the strength to shake off the yoke of slavery by *joint effort*.

The theaters in which the female personnel occupies the best position are the small court theaters. Provincial theaters usually pay very low wages, on the average, so that the only actresses finding employment there are very young, very old, or mediocre. Every ambitious talent who wants to have a future must have worked, at least for a few years, at one of the larger Berlin theaters and cannot afford to be deterred by the deplorably low moral climate of the Berlin stage which is generally known in artists' circles. The general public does not know much about the vast extent of this corruption. Only once in a while a particularly tragic case lifts the veil with which the producers, in alliance with agents and unscrupulous representatives of the *jeunesse dorée,* cleverly know how to cover up all this misery. Let me recall only the suicide of one of our most charming comedy actresses; she had been unable to face the destruction of her bridal happiness by slander of the most wicked kind. Rumor had it that the director had demanded to see her in the nude before signing her contract; that she had consented; that he had allowed other people to watch, hidden behind the scenery; and that years later these people told about what allegedly they had seen. Only after her voluntary death did the hapless woman receive that justice which she had demanded as the most beautiful decoration for her grave.

Requests like that made by this director are by no means to be relegated into the realm of fairy tales. An actress who was made the same demand and who refused to comply with it was dismissed by the director with the words, "I am sorry, but I won't buy a pig in a poke." Another lady rebuffed the advances of her director with the words, "But, sir, I am a decent girl!" whereupon she was told, "For God's sake, don't say that so loudly, otherwise your career will be ruined forever!"

The director who said this to her was right, alas, for a poor decent girl will only in the rarest cases be able to get ahead, given the situation on our stages today. To begin with, the expenses of an education at a theater school are considerable. Most students there take a one-year course for which they have to pay a fee of 75 to 100 marks a month. Besides that, the student will have to have sufficient cash to pay for adequate food and good clothing, for in the competition with her colleagues what ultimately counts most of the time is the external appearance. Once the training is finished, the actresses rush out of the schools, and since their number increases from year to year, they bid against each other more and more fiercely. Like beasts of prey, the agents stalk these novices of the theater. To be sure, the young actresses often are told that it is their own fault if they allow themselves to be exploited by their agents; after all, they could get in touch with the directors directly. But that is possible only if the actress has excellent connections and is financially independent enough to spend a long time fighting against the intrigues of the agents who use all their resources to keep theaters from hiring a girl who does not put herself into their clutches. Most of the time, moreover, directors have a regular business arrangement with certain agents so that they procure their "merchandise" only through these middlemen. The actress is obliged to pay 3 to 5 percent of her wages to the agent who got her the engagement. In the case of guest appearances, the cut is 10 percent. The poorer a girl is, the more urgently she wants to find a position; in her anxiety, she often will turn not to one but to two agents. If the two get together and obtain one and the same engagement for her, she must pay the agreed upon percentage to both of them. Let us assume an actress is hired at first for two years, then she must pay the percentage to the agent or agents all that time; if her contract with the same theater is renewed, this usually is done without any further action by the agent, simply because her talents are being appreciated. Nonetheless she continues to owe tribute to the agent who got her the initial engagement until she leaves that particular theater. Since in most cases her wages anyhow are not sufficient to cover her expenses, this tribute to her agent is a heavy burden on her.

In a later article I will go into precise figures on income and expenditures. Today I will deal only with actresses in Berlin, and those of first rank who despite their prominence are not able to get by without substantial financial support from their parents. They get a salary of 200 to 500 marks a month including stage money. The last term refers to the salary they receive for each evening on which they actually appear on the stage; it too is agreed upon at the time of hiring, but often is limited further by arbitrary deductions made by the director. It may happen, for instance, that a lady is prevented by illness from attending a rehearsal, and for this 15 marks will be deducted. In order to get a proper perspective on the expenses of actresses we have to realize what demands are made on them with regard to their clothing. It is a well-known fact that even outstanding talents fail to get some role or another just because their clothing is not sufficiently resplendent and expensive. If the actresses are not elegant enough, the directors reproach them much more than if their acting leaves something to be desired. Of course, the public would undoubtedly rather see pretty figures in pretty dresses than the opposite. But why do so many actresses spend an inordinate amount of money on their clothing so that the demands made on their simpler colleagues to keep up with them rise continually?

Recently a director harshly reproached an actress because of her clothing. She reminded him of her earnings, which made it impossible for her to dress more stylishly. "What," he cried with irritation, "you have been in Berlin for four weeks and still have not got a rich friend?"

With this he touched the cancerous disease afflicting our whole theater system and which I will not hesitate to uncover again and again.

At many of our private theaters we will find ladies employed who are distinguished by great elegance and who are given the best roles to play and who nonetheless receive no wages or a very low wage. They are the "girlfriends" of rich men. Their "patrons" not only support them but also quite frequently pay the directors for hiring them, in order to give them public status. Most of the time the directors have no reason to be unhappy about such an acquisition: The lady in question lures the most affluent men into the theater and lends it a certain glamour—and she costs nothing. The task therefore is to keep her with the theater as long as possible. Should the director ever wish to place a budding talent with unblemished reputation in front of the footlights, it may very well happen that one of the ladies discussed above will prevent him from doing this by threatening to quit. Frequently a gifted actress is assigned a role which doubtless suits her competence. But then it will be taken away from her and given to a colleague who compensates for lack of talent with glamorous clothing. Let us place ourselves in the situation of a girl who enters into a stage career with a lofty conception of art, uses all her energies to make something of herself, and then has to realize on repeated occasions that prudence wins out over purity, toiletry over talent. If under such conditions she does not lose her enthusiasm for her calling and preserves her purity, she is worthy of our admiration. But if she falls, we must not throw stones at her because it is we ourselves, by tolerating such conditions, who are responsible for her fall.

She is protected against it most effectively if her family is supportive and keeps her out of real economic disaster. Her life will be entirely different if she has no parents or poor parents. By chance I became acquainted with the career of such a girl, which in many respects can be regarded as typical. She was desperately poor and an outstandingly pretty young thing. As a chorus member at a small theater, her wages were barely enough to pay the rent for a narrow chamber in which a bed, a chair, and a table constituted all she owned. In her threadbare little dress she was miserably cold; a piece of herring in the evening often was her main meal. Hungry as she was, she did not hesitate to ask the neighbors for a bit of food. At that she was a cheerful girl with a soft good heart. Suddenly she showed up for rehearsals in elegant clothing, and with shining eyes told about the "wealthy acquaintance" she had made. "And how he loves me—oh, it is too beautiful!" She cried happily; until then she had not experienced a great deal of love. Four weeks later she was living in a fancy apartment and was wearing the most attractive clothing; a few months later she enrolled in a theater school; within a few years she was a star of the first order in her profession. This ending of the story, to be sure, is not typical, for girls of this kind much more frequently land in the gutter after a short period of glamour because their lovers leave them, and their talents were smothered in luxurious living or, linked to a weak character, were not strong enough to come to the fore.

A much more somber story is the following episode from the life of a decent actress. She was poor and therefore saw herself obliged to accept a position with a summer theater during her summer vacations. Since her contract provided for vacations, she got in touch with a summer theater, and with the offer of a contract in her pocket she went to the director to find out whether and when she might take her vacation. He told her that at the time set aside for the summer theater she was urgently needed. Of course, she declined the temporary engagement because she much preferred to work on the same stage and at the same salary as in winter. Shortly afterward the director told her that on the next day she was free to start her vacation. When she complained, the director told her, "If you don't like it, you are free to go and not come back at all." Thus she saw herself kicked out on the street without means and, in order to escape the worst, asked once more to see the director. He asked her to his residence for a personal discussion, and she went. What happened there is not known. Rumors talk about a cry for help. The one thing which is sure is that the girl immediately quit her job and is today struggling against the most abject destitution.

Schiller, as we all know, talked about the stage as a moral institution. He believed that a profoundly moral movement might result from the works which the stage presents to the public. Our contemporary literature is not poor in works of this kind; but I cannot put great stock in the moral effect it may have as long as it consists in momentary compassion or indignation and nobody asks how those people live who stir those feelings in us. I would rather see all our theaters closed down than have our delight and our uplift purchased at the price of misery and shame. And even if our greatest writers produce the best works, the stage will not be a moral institution as long as immorality is promoted backstage.

THE DOG

She has poor eyes and wears glasses, does not hear all that well, walks with a bit of a stoop, and is neither one of the smartest nor the most soft-voiced of her sex. Everyone calls her The Dog or The Oaf because of her marvelously developed ability at every single moment to do just the opposite of what would have been appropriate. She has tried all sorts of things. For factory work she lacked the necessary strength and skill. For house work she was not strong enough either. For years she tried to find employment as a maid. Everywhere they dismissed her after one to three months, handing her friendly letters of recommendation. Good friends suggested she should work as a children's nursemaid; the work would be easy, the wages not too bad; and hadn't she always liked kids? And yet she gets fired month after month; she means well but turns into a terrible affliction for the children. When she wants to joke with them she shouts so loudly the kids get frightened and start to cry. When they are supposed to run and jump and romp, she gets out of breath; and excessive cleanliness is something she herself was not taught as a child; so how can she teach it to the children?

All her life she has heard few friendly words. She has been pushed around, sent away, and looked for new jobs, again and again without a steady home of her own. Now she is twenty and looks like thirty. Her energy is leaving her, she is beginning to lose interest, to say nothing about punctuality. As soon as she is alone, she stands by the window and enjoys the quiet: at last no one is giving her hell! Of course, this does not make her work go faster, and so afterwards there will be hard words, loud voices, and fighting. And she meant so well!

One thing she is good at: She sews and darns quite well, a bit slowly perhaps, but neatly and with a certain aesthetic devotion. But a twenty-

"Der Trampel," *Neue Gesellschaft*, 2 (no. 23, 1906). The German word "Trampel" that Lily Braun uses for this sketch is untranslatable. It denotes a good-natured but clumsy, slightly oafish, female *shlemiehl*.

year-old girl cannot live by sewing and darning! And that is the reason why she always gets into jobs she cannot do. Live she must, and earn wages—that is the iron law of capitalism, the whip which keeps driving her month after month to look for new jobs. But those who know her are aware that this is destroying her. She simply has not been born with the skills and traits which are needed to make it in the competitive rat race of capitalism; she is doomed to go under.

An over-enthusiastic Nietzsche disciple would say at this point: Let her starve! Kill her! No sentimentality! She only spoils the race. But Zarathustra himself, who buried the tightrope walker with his own hands, would argue even in this case that it should be possible for her to find a source of a life of her own, if only the poor girl could be placed wherever she might make a contribution. If Nietzsche had learned to think as a political economist, which he had not, he would say: Capitalism ruins the species, for it pushes the weak into the struggle in which they are bound to go under. Capitalism is the enemy of the survival and evolution of humanity.

In a different environment even The Dog would be able to develop her energies in the service of the whole; small energies, perhaps, but energies nonetheless. Now she is only a burden to herself and others.

II.

Women and Politics

In the Wilhelmine empire women did not enjoy citizens' rights or indeed the rights of adults. The conventional reason for denying them all rights to participate in public life was that politics was a rough game, participation in which would demean women and, more important, defeminize them.

From the very beginning of her career as a publicist, Braun vehemently argued against this condition and asserted that it was not only women's right to take full part in public life but indeed their duty. Voicing these demands placed her on the radical left wing of the German women's movement, and from this position she proceeded to accuse her fellow feminists in Germany of timidity in pressing their legitimate demands. A leading figure in the German Ethical Culture movement, she was on the farthest left wing there also and increasingly criticized the movement for voicing lofty moral sentiments while shying away from meaningful radical action. In one of her first public speeches she demanded the passage of an Equal Rights Amendment to the Imperial German constitution.

One of the chief obstacles to the mobilization of women, in her opinion, was the deep gulf of suspicion and antagonism that divided the middle-class women's movement from its analogue in the Marxist party (SPD), and to both she suggested that there was cause for concerted action. She repeatedly exhorted the bourgeois women's movement to concern itself with the plight of proletarian women, and she criticized its leaders as well as those of the Ethical Culture movement for excluding socialists from their ranks.

At the same time she criticized the women of the Marxist movement for refusing all and any cooperation or communication with their bourgeois sisters. In "Left and Right," written in 1895, she chided the women of the Marxist party for their narrow partisanship and criticized the bourgeois women's movement for its timidity. If they could work together, she implied, German women might win the right to vote, which Braun saw as the key to their liberation. At the time, she had words of praise, though hedged with reservations, for the SPD and its women's auxiliary for being the only organizations that were at least making the right kinds of demands. Once a member of the Marxist movement, she remained committed both to the cause of women's emancipation and to the belief that militant women of all parties and classes ought to work together for aims they shared. She continued to deplore the unwillingness of both bourgeois and proletarian feminists to collaborate and tried hard to define issue areas in which they might fruitfully work for common goals.

Women and Politics shows Braun in her most orthodox Marxist phase. It is a pamphlet she wrote in 1903—an agitational piece explaining why any thinking woman, whatever her class, ought to become a militant member of the socialist movement. The final piece in this section was written in 1912 as the Introduction to a large collaborative volume on the theme of motherhood. Here again the stress is on what bourgeois and proletarian women's movements have in common and on what separates them. Again Braun stresses the limitations of both movements, but by now the definition of the problem that a united women's movement would have to solve has changed from education and political rights to the issue of the double and triple burden, that is, the difficulty of reconciling the right to work with the right to be feminine.

LEFT AND RIGHT

I.

The German women's movement is split into two camps; on one side, the "class-conscious proletarian women" are standing in closed ranks, on the other side, the female representatives of bourgeois society in separate little detachments; on one side, many thousands of women are fighting, shoulder to shoulder with their male comrades, a joint fight for equal rights, on the other side, hundreds of females, accompanied by a few men, fight for equal education, often against the men. From both camps I have heard voices sounding rather challenging which, were I King Stumm, would have compelled me very decisively to engage in a duel. But since I am neither a man nor a millionaire, I will have to do without the dueling privilege. At this time I am somewhat like a war reporter trying to arrive at an objective judgment about the battle tactics of both armies.

Hardly had *Die Frauenbewegung* been launched into the world when Mrs. Klara *Zetkin* in her journal, *Die Gleichheit* (Number 1, Wednesday, 9 January 1895), shot off a shower of arrows against it in an article entitled "Women's Libbers' Stupid Dreams about Harmony." I assume that not many of our readers know *Die Gleichheit* and its editor, even though I would wish that it were otherwise; for whoever is interested in the women's question and wants to guard against one-sidedness can do no better than to read the organ of the Social-Democratic women workers. He will find in it a wealth of important material offered by no other women's paper; to be sure, he will find not only many justified attacks on the bourgeois women's movement, which are very useful for us to hear, but also those which will offend him not so much by their factual contents as by their tone, and which therefore defeat their purpose. An

"Nach links und rechts," *Die Frauenbewegung*, 1 (no. 5, 1895); ibid., (no. 7, 1895).

attack of this sort is that on our journal. Mrs. Zetkin says that *Die Frauenbewegung* was guided by the "most uncritical stupid dreams about harmony," which she deduces from the fact that in our program we have stressed our neutrality. To her, as to all those who serve one political party exclusively, the journalistic principle manifest in our paper, according to which the editors let all opinions be heard without personally being nonpartisan, is alien and beyond understanding. I know that there is no harmony between the bourgeois lady and the proletarian woman, but I can nonetheless publish the proletarian woman's views together with those of the bourgeois lady in one and the same paper. Only through this can all readers arrive at an independent judgment which side represents truth and justice. *Die Frauenbewegung* is no party paper but a review for women's interests. It does not wish to exert its influence through polemics as much as through the reporting of facts; it does consciously what in my opinion *Die Gleichheit* does unconsciously, for the latter's news and notes about women's wages, the treatment of female workers, etc., etc., have a more lasting impact than its editorials.

In our program we have acknowledged that equal rights for both sexes are the aim of the women's movement. Against this Mrs. Zetkin argues:

> Contrary to the character of the bourgeois women's lib movement, the proletarian woman's struggle for the right to become a total human being is not at all primarily a women's movement but a socialist workers' movement. It is directed not against the privileges of the male world, but rather against the power of the capitalist class. The proletarian woman cannot attain her highest ideals through a movement for equal rights for the female sex, she will gain salvation only by fighting for the emancipation of labor.

The Social-Democratic movement has adopted the emancipation of women as one of its political aims. With this it has recognized the fight for this aim as justified, and it is a contradiction when a member of this party attacks those who struggle for the emancipation of women. Were I to try to put myself into Mrs. Zetkin's place, I would say: "In this struggle we are united. But we Social-Democrats have an entire large party behind us and therefore do not need you as allies; for, after all, we help you more than you with your feeble powers are able to help us."

Our program further states that we want to do our share in women's struggle for equal wages. On this our antagonists comment as follows:

> We regret that *Die Frauenbewegung* does not say a word about the means through which the women's libbers are to support this particular struggle

of the proletariat. The way we figure out our German women's libbers on the basis of their past and their social and political insight, we are convinced that in the case of powerful wage conflicts not even ten of them would support the struggling working men and women openly and without reservation. Let us not forget one thing: In every larger and thoroughgoing fight for better work conditions, the whole power of the state takes sides against the rebelling male and female wage slaves . . . And another thing should be kept in mind: The petitioneering of our bourgeois women's movement, its humble and plaintive servility before princely thrones, its hurrah-shouts to crowned heads and noble bodies, its cowardly aversion to anything that looks the least bit like politics or perhaps socialism! In confrontation with His Honor the Mayor and all the authorities, the women's libbers' goodwill for their "poorer sisters" would melt like snow in the March sun. Their enthusiasm for the principle of equal rights would soon be routed by their cowardly sub-missiveness, their loyalty to the government, and their revulsion against "rebelling mobs," against "dissatisfied, greedy, crude strike agitators," etc.

Our journal displays the motto, "This paper is open to all opinions." If Mrs. Zetkin were to send us a calm, factual article about the struggle for equal wages, written from her own political point of view, we would accept it and thus live up to our principle. But just as we would reject an article from the bourgeois women's movement if it contained sneering and baseless attacks on the proletarian women's movement, so it would be also if the reverse were the case.

Whoever thinks he is fighting for a good cause should fight for it with clean methods. Convincing the antagonist seems to me to be a greater victory, and more valuable for humanity, than "smashing" him. With unjustified and exaggerated attacks one puts oneself in the wrong against him, one throws dirt not only at him but also sullies the cause one is advocating.

For instance, Mrs. Zetkin speaks generally against the "bourgeois women's libbers," accusing them of insufficient social and political in-sight, cowardice, personal ambition, submissiveness, etc. I personally concede that she is not *totally* wrong; but has she really looked into the heart of everyone of us, examined our intelligence, observed our work, to be entitled to deny us all our human dignity? With these generalizations she commits the same mistake of which she accuses us when she cites expressions by which many representatives of bourgeois society describe the workers in general.

She jeers at our "petitioneering." I myself am opposed to humble and plaintive petitions because I know very well that we have the right to *make demands.* But in many cases we German bourgeois women have no other means except petitioning, if we want to be heard at all; for *behind us there is no political party making our demands its own,* as the Social-Democratic party is doing with the demands of the proletarian women. In the beginning of her article Mrs. Zetkin states that the German bourgeois "women's lib movement is externally and internally weaker, more colorless and gutless than its sister movement in other countries." I have stated the cause of this fact above; in England, for instance, the bourgeois women's movement is as successful as it is because the Conservative and Liberal parties support it. When Mrs. Zetkin speaks about the "cowardly fear" of politics and socialism, I would like to remind her that she subscribes to the materialist conception of history and therefore should understand the reasons for this very prevalent "cowardly fear," and that she should pity those who have it rather than ruthlessly condemning them. The bourgeois woman is the product of her conditions, is dependent on her husband, her father, her brothers and sons. I know many who in private recognize the most ambitious demands made for the female sex but would endanger the position of those nearest and dearest to them, might perhaps deprive their families of their livelihood, if they advocated these views in public. If it only involves their own person, if it is a matter of personally renouncing their status and reputation in the class to which they belong by birth, great characters may indeed assume martyrdom and find compensation in the awareness that they are struggling and suffering for humanity; but when it is a case of dragging her nearest and dearest ones into disaster for the sake of convictions *which they do not share,* then it is not proper to cast stones at the one who sacrifices herself for the happiness of her husband and children.

Strangely enough, Mrs. Zetkin demands that the program of a journal give its entire table of contents at once, for she argues:

> It is typical, in this connection, that the program does not even hint at the shameful way the laws concerning association and assembly are applied to proletarian women, even though this treatment always is defended by reference to the lack of rights of the female sex. The most liberal possible right to form associations obviously is the basis, the life-giving atmosphere, for any struggle for better work conditions. If the women's libbers want to help the women workers win better wages, they therefore must come out in favor of an unlimited right of association and assembly for the working class. But this demand gives off a bit of the "abominable smell of revolution"; hence no word about it in the women's libbers' program, nor any word regarding the right to vote.

Now it so happens that not long after the appearance of Number 1 of our paper, the editors together with Mrs. Adele Gerhard were the ones who circulated a petition to collect signatures for changes in the laws concerning association and assembly as they apply to women. Remembering Mrs. Zetkin's arguments quoted above, I thought we would get at least some brownie points from her for this procedure, which, by the way, had nothing in it of "cowardly fear", and which caused great indignation in good "bourgeois" circles. But nothing of the kind! Instead, Mrs. Zetkin unleashed a polemic against us in a large portion of the Social-Democratic press, which could have made one think that the party was in danger. I have been thinking about this; for even if I now try to put myself into Mrs. Zetkin's place and concede some formal mistakes in the wording of the petition, then I might still have argued something like the following: "You are pretty naive if you think you will get many signatures, because we Social-Democratic women have no need to petition, since our party is proposing a resolution on the same matter in the Reichstag." I would have smiled while writing this. As a member of a party counting millions of members, my time, my pen and ink would have been too valuable for me to waste on a campaign against a small troop of "women's libbers." If Mrs. Zetkin does not possess this sovereign assuredness of behavior, this shows me either that she is so filled with blind party fanaticism as ill befits the leader of a party which according to its program wants to liberate all humanity, or that she is not sure of her "goal-conscious" proletarian women. In fact, in an article in *Vorwärts* she admits this quite frankly, when she writes:

> As for the sharp tone I have used, and of which *Vorwärts* does not approve, I consider it *necessary* for a very *special* reason. The appearance of the most recent line in the bourgeois women's lib movement, which I would like to designate the "ethical" line, has had a *confusing* effect here and there among our female comrades.

But let us return to the *Gleichheit* article. Its author will meanwhile have enlightened herself about another point—the demand for the right to vote; for *Die Frauenbewegung* not only published an independent article about this* but continues to report about women's struggles for equal political rights. It almost seems to me as if this fact were disagrea-

*Georg V. Giżycki, "Frauenbewegung-Stimmrecht," *Die Frauenbewegung*, 1 (no. 3, 1895); ibid., (no. 4, 1895).

ble to her. Up to now she was proud that the Social-Democrats were the only ones to demand the right to vote for women, she was fully justified in jeering at the bourgeois women's movement which shied away from the word political as if from the live devil. Now she has to acknowledge exceptions to the rule. Our successes have only intensified her anger at us. Even the subscription invitation of *Die Gleichheit* contains a warning against us; and in some form or other every issue of *Die Gleichheit* contains an attack against us. Perhaps it will help calm down my excited antagonists if I tell her that the number of those she is attacking still is rather small. Nonetheless I repeat what our program states: "The woman's cause is not the cause of any party," even though Mrs. Zetkin has tried to contradict me in the following sentences:

> If *Die Frauenbewegung* is telling itself and would like to tell others that "the woman's cause is not the cause of any one party," this is sufficiently explained by the fuzzy stupid dreams about harmony to which the paper has given birth, and on which, in turn, the little baby is to be nourished. Yet, even though the statement can be explained, it nonetheless remains fundamentally wrong. The "woman's cause," to the extent that it means the emancipation of the female masses, the proletarian women, is indeed the cause of a party, and of one party only—the Social-Democratic one."

The Social-Democratic movement has made the women's cause its own; but that is no proof against the assertion that it is the cause of humanity, it only proves that no other party in Germany was far-sighted and fair enough to make its own cause. But the motive behind our actions, regardless of which party we belong to, should not be the maximal well-being of *one* community, *one* class, or *one* gender, but the *maximal possible well-being of all.*

In its program, the Social-Democratic party identifies this goal as its own; but I doubt that humanity can be led closer to this goal when those in the vanguard turn around and beat with sticks against those who do not step exactly into their footprints; and I particularly doubt whether the example thus given by the leader is a fruitful one. As the most outstanding female leader of the Social-Democratic women, as far as I know, Mrs. Zetkin has assumed a very heavy responsibility. Through the influence of her paper she could have a tremendous educational effect by using a calm, objective, and fair tone to accustom the thousands of her readers to the virtues of calmness, objectivity, and fairness, virtues which are disappearing more and more from political life. The conflict between political parties should be a conflict for and against principles much rather than a fight against individual persons. It seems to me, for example, that Mrs. Zetkin would succeed far more by challenging her antagonists' principles with hard facts than by attributing base motives to their actions and by casting suspicion on them personally. By her present method she will satisfy her opponents, for she not only hands them weapons against herself, but she also prevents earnest people seeking truth and justice from identifying with her cause unreservedly.

II.

Let me now turn to the right and survey the various troops composing the German bourgeois women's movement. The sight reminds me painfully of the North German Federation, which to the outside was supposed to confirm the unity of the states belonging to it, whereas inside they were more or less disunited. We too have a Federation of German Women's Associations which was supposed to bring about united, well-coordinated tactics in the women's movement. Indeed it has produced a number of important petitions, among which I would stress particularly the plea for the appointment of female factory inspectors. Regrettably, however, in the formulation of the petition an attitude became apparent which leads to the conclusion that in the choice of the wording not a single woman worker was consulted. The first petition was directed at municipal authorities and discussed the question of juvenile care centers to be created next to every school. The demand for juvenile centers was argued by reference to the growing neglect of teenagers: "Unruliness, laziness, pleasure seeking, lying, and dishonesty are difficult, and at times impossible, to eradicate among youth beyond school age"—and now let us note the sentence that follows—"as will be confirmed everywhere by apprentice masters, factory managers, ladies in charge of youth homes, and housewives."

This last clause would have been made impossible by a more refined empathy, by the ability to step into the souls of those who are supposed to benefit from these youth shelters, for it expresses the opinion, perhaps without the authors being conscious of it, that the children of the poor must be reared in youth shelters for the specific purpose of providing better apprentices, workers, and maids to masters, factory owners, matrons, and housewives than those they are getting now.

This shows total ignorance of the so-called "lower" classes. The same ignorance is the reason for a sentence in the second petition, where the argument is made about how embarrassing it is for women workers to make complaints to male supervisors about grievances, especially those touching on moral matters. The sentence then adds: "The female work force has not yet entirely lost the innate reticence of the female." I would like to know whether a similar sentence would have been incorporated in a petition for the employment of female physicians, and I doubt it, even though a woman undergoing a medical examination would have to give up far more of her "reticence" than the one who tells her grievance to the factory inspector. And I would like to know also whether the women who drafted and signed this petition can justify their giving such a poor moral report card to the female work force.

These two petitions are the only accomplishments of the Federation in the first year of its existence. It has not, however, attained its real aim, which was to gather the splintered forces, to promote mutual acquaintance, and to create unity. In a city like Berlin, for instance, the several associations belonging to the Federation to some extent exist in a state of bitter warfare with each other. This warfare is caused primarily by personal motives. Because of their upbringing, because of the artificial narrowness of their intellectual horizon, the women of bourgeois society have become so used to having a mind and an understanding for only the most obvious, the pettiest, and the most personal matters that they have almost totally lost the vision for, and the comprehension of, the large picture. It is precisely the task of the women's movement to free them from this straitjacket and to open their eyes, and only those women should be recognized as leaders of the women's movement who by their good example are leading the others. But there is not very much we can expect from the German bourgeois women's movement as long as they give each other's achievements the silent treatment or try to diminish the successes they have won, be it through individual effort or through the activity of their associations.

Why is the German movement so far behind its sister movements in America, Australia, England, and Norway, or even behind the Austrian women's movement? Why is this movement, like the bourgeois woman, concerned only for what is most obvious and petty? Because from the very beginning it was not given a great aim for the attainment of which strong characters and farsighted human beings might fire their enthusiasm. "Nobody leaps into the fire for small aims." Reflecting on the women's question and studying the women's movement in other countries has led me to conclude the opposite of what Miss *Helene Lange* said recently in her lecture on "Women's Work in London," where she argued:

> If today English women sit and vote in county councils and school boards, if they work next to and with men in universities and hospitals, then this is because, clear-eyed and practical, they started by aiming for intensified education, because they concentrated on attainable goals and did not fritter away their energies in the blind chase after all sorts of utopias. Precisely in this respect their activity should be a model for German women. *

In number 2 of this journal, Mrs. Eva MacLaren surveyed the progress of the English women's movement and added:

> There is no doubt that the concessions made to women are due to their demands for political rights. Many men who refuse to give them these rights concede minor rights to them in order to show that they are not altogether deaf to the women's complaints; moreover, lively agitation for a great cause, the justice of which is demonstrated again and again, renders resistance to lesser demands virtually impossible. Several important reforms have been introduced in this way. . . .

> The most outstanding women in England are convinced that the right to vote is the key to everything and therefore must be demanded first of all. By demanding the right to vote or, in other words, equal political rights, you are *ipso facto* demanding all subordinate rights. It may be that they will be granted you first, as was done here; but we won them by demanding the right to vote.

Great aims are needed to drive the masses of people forward. Another convincing instance of this is offered by the development of the women's movement in Norway. (See Number 3 of this journal, page 20.) It was born there only eleven years ago; from the very start it wrote equal political rights for women on its banner; under this banner it has conquered the universities and presumably will conquer parliament before long, because only a few votes are lacking to make women's right to vote into a law. Miss Lange talks about the "blind chase after all sorts of utopias." I do not know whether she calls utopias those goals that England and Norway soon will reach, that New Zealand, South Australia, Wyoming, Colorado, and Utah have reached already, and for

*From a report by M. Mellien in *Neue Bahnen*, no. 4.

which Condorcet, a century ago, and, decades ago, men like Wendell Phillips and John Stuart Mill fought enthusiastically. Just today I received an interesting news item from Kentucky, according to which an association was created there in 1888 which demanded equal status for women in areas of economic and political life and proclaimed the right to vote its most important aim. In the seven years of its existence the association has achieved the following: Women now have the full right to dispose of their own property and earnings, they have the right to write a last will of their own, and they inherit their husbands' estates, just as the husbands inherit theirs. The universities are open to them; boys and girls together receive the same education. The report concludes with the words: "But these are all but way stations on the road to citizens rights, and we will not rest until the women of Kentucky possess the right to vote, which alone gives them power to influence the laws they as well as the men have to obey."

Against this, what are the achievements of the German women's movement, which did not "blindly chase after utopias?" It will soon celebrate its 50th anniversary, and still stands almost in the same place as in the beginning. If since its beginning numerous charitable organizations have been created and a few professional schools and *gymnasiums,* etc., were founded with private endowments, that does not gainsay this statement. *Charity toward the poor and the miserable may be the cause of women, but it is not the cause of the women's movement.* The women's movement demands *not alms, but justice* for the female sex. It demands open access to universities, changes in the laws that treat women as second-class people, and constitutional recognition of the woman as a citizen with equal rights.

In December of last year, when I spoke in public meetings in Dresden, Breslau, and Berlin, positing the demand for citizen's rights as the most important demand of the women's movement, I was anticipating not only strong opposition but also jeers and mockery. I was pleasantly surprised to note that the press reported my lecture almost without opposition and without mockery, and that later, too, in private and public discussions, opposition to my arguments did not make any headway. I later learned that those who were frightened by my demands or indignant over them avoided confronting me as honest antagonists in public discussion. But in the same month a meeting of the Berlin women's association discussed the German women's movement which strives only for "attainable goals." According to newspaper reports, the discussion concluded as follows:

> Our women would be acting foolishly and rashly if already today they were to demand rights of participation in public life which were granted to the men only decades ago and which, as possible results of further progress, still lie in the hazy distance of the future!

Whoever said this has put down the Germans, and especially German women, in a manner which could not have been more demeaning. After all, she has suggested that what Americans and Australians, the English and the Norwegians have partly attained or soon will be attaining is, for us, part of the hazy future! In the name of my fellow countrymen I formally protest against this humiliating point of view. I reject the insinuation that German women who already today are demanding the right to participate in public life are acting "foolishly and rashly." That they are neither foolish nor rash is demonstrated by the fact that the question concerning women's right to vote was treated seriously by the German Reichstag on 13 February of this year. For the German bourgeois women's movement it is a cause of profound humiliation that it was not its own spokeswomen who first demanded of the Reichstag equal political rights but that they left this task to the men, and indeed to those men who, as we like to say in our arrogance, represent the "uneducated" masses of the people. Humiliating, too, is it for the men who call themselves "liberal" and "freedom-minded," but who leave the advocacy of rights for one half of the human race to those against whom they like to muster all the forces of "religion, tradition, law and order."

In all countries where the women courageously and frankly outlined their strategy plans, they did so before any political party adopted their demands into its platform. Thus it happened that, say, in England the Conservative and Liberal parties seized upon the women's cause and made it their own. The German bourgeois women's movement from its very beginning has been very timid and has not had the courage to demand full equal rights for the female sex. The Social-Democratic party has taken the lead in this, and this fact, it seems to me, has contributed a lot to the stagnation of our bourgeois women's movement. For ever since the demand for women's right to vote has been written into the Social-Democratic program, anyone openly demanding the same will quickly be considered an adherent of the "party of revolution" in these times corrupted by partisan passion and partisan blindness. In many circles it is regarded as shameful to agree with the Social-Democrats on even one single point. And since the bourgeois woman usually is dependent on her father, her husband, her brothers and sons, it is easy to understand and, often, to forgive if she prefers to remain silent about her views in order not to destroy peace in her family. Those women, however, who want to be leaders of the women's movement must, like all reformers, belong exclusively to their cause and must free themselves of all considerations that stand in their way. They must not look to the right or the left but only ahead; they must be able to say someday what the noble American, Abby Kelly, once said: "Sisters, with bleeding feet we have smoothed the path along which you are now striding upward."

The German bourgeois women's movement will receive any uplift worthy of a great cause only when it stops focusing on minor aims for which only a small fraction of women can muster enthusiasm. What good is it, for instance, for the large mass of women if universities are opened and a few sisters, privileged through property and education, can study? What good is it if female factory inspectors are appointed who will uncover many evils with regard to the female work force, as long as the remedies for these evils depend on the insight and the good will of men alone? To be sure, both are worth aiming for, but, as the women of Kentucky put it, these are only way stations. It will be child's play for us to take these outer fortifications as long as the heated and glorious battle for the main fortress which is still ahead gives wings to our steps, rouses our courage, and makes our enthusiasm flame high.

The young generation is our hope; the future belongs to them. In them a spark is glowing which only needs to be fanned if it is to shoot up in a mighty flame.

WOMEN AND POLITICS

1. Once upon a Time . . .

It was a gray October day in the year 1789. Dark and heavy hung the clouds over Paris as if in their compassion they wanted to cover up all the misery spread out underneath them. For Paris was starving. And from all the streets and all the corners the women crowded together. They were looking for bread for their children. In their narrowly encircled homes they had felt little so far of the revolutionary hurricane that was beginning to shake all of France from top to bottom. But now when starvation was knocking audibly at their doors and spoke to them in the narrow, pallid faces of their little ones, they were waking up as from oppressive dreams. Mothers whose hearts were rent by the wailing of their loved ones, daughters whose souls were cut to pieces by the unspoken misery in their old parents' eyes, women who suddenly had gained their sight when they saw the starving people—they all met in front of locked bakers' shops and on deserted markets. They were one in their desperation, one in their resolution, one also in their hatred for the grain usurers who not only had made bread prices rise but also had been unconscionable enough to sell spoiled flour, so that the poor children of the people died away like the flowers of the field. Meanwhile in Versailles the National Assembly was meeting and fighting with the stubborn king for recognition of the paper rights of men, even while in Paris the real human right, the right to obtain nourishment and bodily necessities, was being trampled underfoot. Suddenly a shout, "To Versailles!" rang out from out of the ranks of the women; the call spread as if borne by the wind; hundreds of women heeded it, and their crowd swelled in every street through which they marched. In the end it was eight thousand women who moved toward the royal residence in a long procession, in storm and rain,

Die Frauen und die Politik (Berlin: Vorwärts Verlag, 1903).

through the muck of the streets, jeered by the bourgeoisie. These were not old slatterns or young whores, even though that is how the representatives of reaction preferred to describe them afterwards for shuddering later generations; these were poor women of the people to whom stark need lent heroic stature. What the glib orators of the National Assembly had not succeeded in doing, they did achieve: trembling before the revolution they were threatening, the king signed the Declaration of the Rights of Man; fearing the will of the people, which through their mothers, their wives and daughters manifested itself dictatorially, he followed them back to Paris with his entire court and the National Assembly. Along the same road they had come to get bread for the starving people they now walked back with the king in their midst.

Their hands that had grasped swords and rifles with gloomy resoluteness now were swinging colorful autumn branches in triumph: they had wanted to destroy starvation and had destroyed the royal system. With the lashes of whips their need had driven them forth, now the victorious revolution marched at their head with waving banners.

2. The Revolution of the Machine

More than a hundred years have passed. Two closely allied partners had been the midwives of the revolution: women and poverty. But now the revolution had forgotten about them; its human rights were only men's rights, its liberty and equality did not apply to the slaves of labor. Women withdrew from the stage of political life as quickly as they had once entered the scene. But it was no longer their own home that received them. For in the meantime a power had come to life in the world which drew them as the magnet attracts iron: the machine. Its power began to replace human muscle power and made it possible to employ people without muscle power in increasing measure. And the owners of the machines, anxious and eager to squeeze the maximum profit out of them, chose the weakest labor forces, which at the same time were the cheapest, for their service—women and children. Each stage of technological progress drove hordes of men out of the workshop and drove hordes of women and children into the factories. If a man did not want to succumb to the horrors of unemployment, he saw himself coerced into lowering his wage demands to those of his female competitors; but as soon as he did that he was no longer able to support his family from the returns on his labor, and thus his wife and daughters were compelled in their turn to work for wages. This is the incessantly recurring cycle of the depressing effect women's work has on the men's wages and the stimulating effect of insufficient men's wages on the development of women's labor. Something like a law of nature which heretofore had tied women to the home and had also confined their earning capacity within the four domestic walls seemed to have been subverted, and with all the rage that grips people when somewhere the foundations of old habits and conveniences begin to crumble, the male workers began to fight against their female competitors for jobs. Yet neither raw force nor the power of labor union organizations was able to drive them away. For social progress cannot be contained; whoever tries to stem it will be trampled down by it. And it was not irresponsibility or dislike of carrying out domestic duties that made women succumb in droves to the seductive wiles of the great tyrant machine; it was need, bitter need, the need that made them grasp into the wheels of world history at the time of the French Revolution, which drove them into its arms.

As early as 1839 more than half of the textile workers in England were women. Twenty years later the total number of male workers had doubled, but that of female workers had tripled. And after another thirty years the number of male industrial workers had grown by 53 percent, but that of female workers by 221 percent. In all nations where the machine moved in, women were following it quickly, and in the hundred years of its rule its influence in this direction has increased steadily. On the basis of demographic and labor censuses from all civilized states we know that still today female labor grows faster than male labor, faster indeed than the female population itself. Germany alone accounts for 6-1/2 million women wage earners, and of these 6-1/2 million more than 5 million are proletarian women. Today, of all workers of both sexes more than 36 percent are women, i.e., more than a third.

The revolutionizing power of the machine shows even more, however, in the special area of married women's labor than in the general observations made above. One would think that married women should be freed from the compulsion to earn a living; one would think that they should continue to take care of the home and the children as before. But the development of capitalism (for only the capitalist—and this in ever-increasing measure—can have the means to acquire machines and keep them running), which has followed closely on the heels of technological progress, does not interest itself in moral considerations. It takes labor power wherever it turns out to be the most profitable. In America a

survey was done once of entrepreneurs for the purpose of investigating
the reasons for the employment of married women. And the answers
were unanimous: because they are more reliable and nimbler (they
usually have had more practice than the young girls); because they are
more interested in their work (unlike the young girls, they do not regard
it as merely a transitional stage before marriage); because they make fewer
demands (only too often they are compelled to work for any kind of wage
for the sake of their children); because they are less ready to go on strike
(at times their worry about their children is stronger than their loyalty to
their colleagues). German entrepreneurs have made similar statements to
officials of the trades inspectorate but stress in particular that industry
cannot do without its most skilled female workers. The needs of the
women coincide with the wishes of the entrepreneurs.

With the increasingly seasonal character of proletarian lines of work,
men are more and more subject to weeks and months of unemployment.
Recessions like the present one intensify this condition. But who will
then provide support for the family if not the woman? It is cruel mockery
to preach to her about the duties of the housewife and the mother, to call
her derelict in her obligations if she goes to the workshop or the factory
instead of cooking or taking care of the children; is it not precisely her
children's hunger that compels her to do this? But it is not only during
interim periods that she must make up for the husband's wage losses. The
large mass of married women workers is compelled all the time to go out
for wage work, because even the frequent rises in the men's wages have
not in the least kept in step with the rate of price increases for the
essentials of life, especially for rent, and with the rise in expectations for
material and intellectual needs. Even the reports of the German trade
inspectorate officials for 1899—a year, moreover, that was not yet affected by economic crisis—show clearly that sheer need was the cause of
married women's wage work. In many districts this has been demonstrated by the statistical data. In this connection it is worth pointing out
that people, especially those who have everything they need, can see
misery only where it shows us its grimace in ragged clothing and hollow
eyes. But there is a kind of misery suffered by people who are on a higher
stage of civilization than coolies and slaves, and that misery is every bit as
painful as being cold and hungry. The modern worker no longer is blind
to things that can beautify life, elevate the mind, or widen the heart. He
demands an opportunity to participate in the attainments of civilization,
which are results of his sweat. He wants to learn to enjoy and understand

art and science and is no longer satisfied with crumbs that fall from the tables of the Lords. But a golden magic wand is needed to get to the treasures that humanity has stored up in thousands of years of industrious work. Alas, human greed has enclosed even free nature, forests and meadows, mountains and oceans, behind walls and fences that open only for those who pay with bare coin. But in the best case the worker's wages are just about enough to still his and his family's physical hunger. If he is so insolent as to think himself higher than the dead machine which demands no more for the maintenance of its productive capacity than that its belly be filled every day, or if the woman worker is uppity and wants to better herself and her children so that they become richer in their understanding of the higher joys of life, richer in intellectual possessions, then she must create the means for this by the labor of her hands.

Now there are a lot of people who do indeed recognize that female labor had to spread so rapidly under the pressure of the prevailing conditions, but who believe that this has now reached the peak of its development and that either women's wage labor altogether or at least the energy married women bring into the struggle for existence would have to diminish. Whoever makes that assertion can base his statement on no arguments other than wishful thinking. Because as long as the reasons for female wage labor have not been removed, the phenomenon itself will not disappear. All its reasons, however, are still effective today. The possibilities for technological progress are unlimited. Just consider, for instance, how the honorable shoemaker's craft is crowded out increasingly by the shoe factory where ingenious machinery makes it possible to employ weak women in large numbers, or how the male garment cutter to whose strong hands the scissors used to be entrusted can be replaced by a woman as soon as a cutting machine has been introduced and one push on a lever is all that is needed to cut a whole number of pieces. One could add to these examples ad infinitum. At the same time, the entrepreneur also needs women, particularly in times of economic prosperity and in those enterprises where particularly intensive work is done only seasonally. In those cases, the available female labor force constitutes the great inexhaustible reserve army from which he can always fill his needs.

Most particularly, it is but vapid dreaming to believe that economic misery, the chief motive for women's work, could possibly diminish. To be sure, the unspeakable squalor of the kind that prevailed around the

middle of the 19th century in English factory districts has disappeared.
The ruling classes have learned by now that the life and health of their
workers have to be protected at least up to a certain point, if the safety of
their own possessions is not to be threatened, if he is not to lose the
whole basis of his existence. But it is equally certain that economic need
will affect ever wider circles of the population. As long as the capitalist
system prevails, we will not be able to rid ourselves of periods of economic decline during which factories often employ only half of their
usual workers, while many close down entirely and instead have the work
performed, mostly by women, in the cheaper home industry. Nor will we
be able to abolish the regularly recurring weeks during the year when
work stops altogether. Nor is there any prospect that out of the goodness
of their hearts the entrepreneurs might perhaps raise the workers' wages
to an adequate level. Their interest in the continual and uninterrupted
accumulation of capital is diametrically opposed to the workers' interest
in attaining living conditions fit for human beings; and the entrepreneurs' interests will maintain a determining influence on the structure of social relations as long as it is their power, and not that of the
workers, which prevails in the state. In addition, as the influence of the
large estate owners—the "agrarians"—keeps growing, the necessities of
life will continue to become more expensive all the time: bread will be
smaller, meat will cost more, all food staples carry indirect taxes. Finally
the house owners join this unholy alliance, because the percentage of his
wage that the worker must pay for renting his home gets larger all the
time. Further, the demands that life itself makes are growing. The worker
learns the simplest rules for protecting his health, and no longer cares to
live, cooped up with many others, in some hole without light or air,
where his and his children's vital energies are used up prematurely. The
young woman worker's most ardent wish is to have a room of her own
instead of that disgusting dormitory bunk, and the wife and mother
wishes to have a comfortable little room where after work she can sit with
her family, can relax, chat, or read without being smothered by kitchen,
laundry, and work smells. And everywhere the enjoyment of nature is
awakening: it is manifest in the clusters of little gardens that the luckier
ones among the proletarians have created on the outskirts of the great
cities, and in the trek into the country as soon as a holiday makes it
possible. Almost as strong are the expressions of the urge to education:
with admirable zeal men and women, hardly back at home after a day of

heavy labor, study serious books and attend all sorts of learned lectures, often only to reach the painful realization that they lack the key to all this wealth—a good elementary education. In order to spare their children this same deplorable experience, it is necessary to provide for the possibility of a thorough school education. Then another need develops, even though very timidly at first: that is the need for beauty; and quite surely a time will come when the proletarian learns to see with a different eye, a time when the cheap rotogravures, the crummy furniture, the miserable dime store junk, the ugly nickel picture books, the smoke-filled dirty saloon insult his newly developed aesthetic sense, a time when theater and concerts will be part of his leisure-time activities.

Those who speak for the present social system tend to be unanimous in condemning these rising expectations of the laboring people. What we gladly hail as a sign of awakening human dignity and developing culture looks to them like pleasure seeking and wastefulness on the part of morally corrupted people. They cannot have any other point of view: for whoever believes that society will always be divided into rich and poor, masters and slaves, will have to try to nip in the bud every attempt to break their chains made by the hapless people who carry humanity's burdens, because this could only lead to useless discontent and pernicious unrest. We, on the other hand, know that there is such a thing as steady progress of humanity, that the earth produces goods sufficient for all, and we therefore have the duty to investigate what would bring us closer to this goal. Rising expectations, however, are one of the strongest driving forces of progress. But they are also one of the reasons why there is no going back in women's wage labor.

Yet there is another reason that must not be overlooked: it consists in women's wish for independence that began to develop when economic necessity forced them to stand on their own feet, and then they gradually learned to appreciate the value of independence. Why do more and more girls shy away from becoming domestic servants? Because quite rightly they prefer autonomy to dependence, even if the latter secures them food and shelter. Why do so many girls leave the parental home at an early age without much regret? Not only because the misery at home drives them out, but often because a dim yearning for freedom comes into play as well. And how many married women are there who painfully feel the scourge of being dependent on a husband they do not love; they too seek freedom and autonomy by way of their own work.

Thus the revolution of the machine brought all kinds of revolution with it, and societal as well as personal factors collaborate in bringing about the ever wider expansion of wage work by women.

3. The Transformation of Women from Workers into Citizens

All the talk about women's liberation from the economic, legal, and moral chains into which past periods had confined them would be nothing but hollow phrases if economic need, that cruel teacher, had not engendered wage labor, that great emancipator.

As long as women were tied to the home, their intellectual horizon was usually as narrow as its four walls. The windstorms of history roared by them, but they were hardly aware of them. Profound respect for crosier and crown, fanatical faith in authority, repression of their own personality—all those cancers grow exuberantly between the walls of narrowly confined domesticity under the protection and management of women. They had to be forcibly yanked out of this oppressive atmosphere into the windstorm of the struggle for existence in order to test and develop their own strengths, in order to develop their own capabilities of collaborating in the working of human civilization.

The vast mass of women in previous times had no interest in the political processes within their country. Only after they entered the workshop and the factory, after men had been transformed from their dance partners, lovers, and marital masters into their colleagues at work, and when one and the same need oppressed them all, did it become possible for them to think about its causes, consider means for its abolition, and learn about the forces that make the world move. And just as it was joint labor with men that first got them in touch with public life and awakened political interests in them, so also only after they were dismissed from the exclusive protection of the home and had to enter the struggle for existence as independent individuals just like the men were they entitled to claim special consideration under the law. To say nothing of the recognition of their equal political rights.

Today women have entered virtually all occupations. They have been able to hold on to the traditionally female callings—although the factory spinning jenny has replaced the domestic spinning wheel; the self actor has taken the place of the primitive weaving loom, the hosiery knitting machine has been substituted for the industrious housewife's four knitting

needles, the bobbinet machine has replaced the lacemaker's artful nee-
dlework, and in the entire field of garment manufacture the most thoroughgoing changes in work methods and work conditions have come
about. But new occupations became open to them almost every year.
Women's work is concealed in virtually everything that surrounds us,
everything that helps to maintain and beautify our lives or educates and
gladdens our minds. Not only do they spin, weave, and sew; the bricks of
the house in which we live have passed through women's hands, women's
hands may have planed its boards or forged its nails; women worked as
glaziers and plumbers, locksmiths and carpenters, have whitewashed
walls or painted and pasted up the wallpaper; furniture and furniture
coverings, carpets and drapes attest to their industriousness. The weary
eyes of tired working women have rested on the pens with which we write
and the needles we use for sewing. With sore fingers they have sorted rags
to have them made into paper; in an atmosphere polluted with nicotine
they have rolled cigars, have sacrificed their strength and their health to
work in the boiling heat of sugar refineries, in the phosphorus vapors of
the match factories, in the mercury-poisoned atmosphere of the mirror
plants. They dig peat, lug stones, pour molten ore, and work as black-
smiths, filers, and in machine construction. They bind our books, fold
our newspapers, and are typesetters and printers. They stand behind store
counters and bend their backs sitting at writing desks in offices. They
mow the grain and load it into wagons. As gardeners they provide us with
flowers and fruit. They decorate the tables of the rich with the porcelain
they have painted and the silverware they have etched. To the necklaces
and bracelets, the rings and the broaches that lend glamor to happy
women at merry festivities clings the sweat of those who made them in
long hours of work. Everywhere it is women in growing numbers who
staff post and telegraph offices, compete with the men as pharmacists and
physicians, as lithographers and photographers, who enter the sacred
halls of art as writers, painters, and sculptors. Indeed, they are increasingly beginning to conquer the press, that superpower of modern
life. They are beginning slowly to influence public opinion as journalists
and politicians.

It is said that all they reap from their work is misery and poor health,
that they have sacrificed their beauty and their youth to it; that labor,
which ennobles the man, has abased them. There is much truth in this:
dust covers their hair and their clothing from endless toil—but even more
does it cover their male companions. Their backs are bent from loads

they have to carry—but equally the backs of the men at their side. Their youth faded even before it reached its full blooming—but how long was the woman's comrade ever young? It is said—and what woman's heart does not tremble when she thinks of it?—that wherever women work for their daily bread the children go to ruin in body, soul, and mind. And yet it is precisely for the sake of their children that thousands of poor women are compelled to work, even when the highest wage they can get for their labor guarantees them no more than a piece of bread for their hunger, a piece of clothing against the cold.

Wherever we look in the world, need teaches people to think. Need and work have torn women out of their isolation and segregation, have acquainted them with fighting comrades. Hence it was only in the 19th century that an organized women's movement could develop. Its leaders at first were only women from bourgeois circles, relatively affluent intellectuals. The deepest misery saps people's sensibilities, their energies, and courage and does not let the ideas of struggle and resistance come up at all. Hence a movement of women workers could not develop until its vanguard, the male proletariat, had torn the women workers out of the darkest depths of contemporary slavery. Now the women workers in all industrial countries began to enlighten themselves, to organize unions, to struggle for better work conditions like the men. Today we can point with pride to the masses of women who not only constitute a loyal following of the militant working class but frequently provide them leadership. The history of the proletariat can tell about many poor women workers who during strikes encouraged workers who had begun to vacillate and showed themselves their superiors in endurance and willingness to sacrifice. Their labor had matured them not only for a recognition of their immediate circumstances but also for the understanding of political processes. This is demonstrated by the fact that in Germany it was women speaking for the proletariat who first had the guts to take positions on political issues and to witness for their political views in speech and in print. Because still today it requires guts, much more guts than needed by the man, particularly for a German woman to have her own political opinion and to express it in public.

Custom and law still today have not kept up with social and economic development but in fact lag far behind it. A classic example of this is the social and juridical position of women. It still is considered immoral for both sexes to work together, even though myriads of men and women came together every single day in workshops and factories. It is considered unfeminine to choose so-called male occupations, even though the overwhelming majority of them was long ago captured by women, as we have seen. We are told that it mocks all decency and femininity if women speak up in public and participate in public life, even though they have been part of public life as workers and government officials for well nigh a century. Women are even worse off with regard to their status under private and public law. According to the new civil code the man has the sole right of decision in all matters pertaining to the marriage, even though all too often it is the woman who is and must be the one who supports the family. The husband can prevent his wife from signing a labor contract if he does not like it; indeed, he possesses the means to force her into the immediate cancellation of the contract. And yet more and more often it is she alone on whose labors her children's welfare depends and who therefore ought to be entirely free to decide as she will. If there are differences of opinion concerning the rearing of the children, the father's opinion decides; yet how often is the mother the man's intellectual and moral superior and understands her children's individuality better! Unlike the widowed mother, the mother who has never married does not have full parental authority over her child; but often the jilted woman who, full of loving trust, surrendered to the man of her choice is more capable intellectually and morally of rearing her child alone than those whose undisputable moral probity has been publicly certified, as it were, by city hall and church.

Public law is in even sharper contradiction with women's position in contemporary economic life, and the police and the courts always interpret it in their disfavor, especially where proletarian women are concerned. Women are not allowed to belong to associations active in politics or to form such associations of their own. A large number of working women—rural laborers and domestic servants—have no right to form any associations whatsoever. And the fuzzy definition of politics permits the authorities to create the most serious obstacles to even legally recognized and permitted union organizations or to make them impossible altogether. For instance, any discussion of issues relating to workers' protection, which are of tremendous importance of them, often is interpreted as being political. Many flourishing associations for women workers' education have fallen victim to this and similar interpretations of the law that mock all modern progress.

It is as if the legislators had no idea of the 6-½ million women who are involved in the struggle for existence; as if they did not know that women just as well as men have an interest in whether they must work longer or shorter hours, for poor or good wages, under tolerable or intolerable conditions; that they, and particularly the most efficient among them, cannot be indifferent to the way in which the government and parliament decide about their lives. Therefore they must have the right to form associations in order jointly and publicly to defend their interests. Every other means to this purpose is denied women even more severely. They do not have the right to vote. They do not have the power possessed by any man 25 years or older, even a lazybones, to cast their vote and make it count in electing the people's representatives to the legislative assemblies. Nor can they vote or be elected to the trade courts where, after all, their grievances are to be heard just like those of the male workers. Not to local assemblies either, whose deliberations and resolutions touch women's interests as closely as those of men. The kind of health care provided, the aid given to sick and poor people, what kind of taxes to raise—all this is of utmost importance to women. And how crucially important for the peoples' mothers are all the issues touching the welfare and the physical and mental upbringing of the children! If there were no other issues than these about which women were capable of making decisions, merely for their sake they ought to have seats and voices in local administrations. Who better than the mother is able to judge what the child needs, who suffers more than she when the child is oppressed by poor school systems, who has more love, more energy, more good judgment than a mother when the task is to secure a happy youth without dangers for her darlings?

The popular representative assemblies of our various constituent home countries, the regional diets, are no less important in the way they affect women's and their children's conditions of life. In particular, it cannot be a matter of indifference to them whether or not they are composed primarily of people who were elected due to the power of their purse on the basis of the three-class franchise. It cannot be a matter of indifference to them to see that the worth and importance of various interests are measured by this standard; they cannot sit by quietly when the vote of a man whose sole merit may consist in that he has inherited hundreds of thousands from his father counts for more than that of a worker who earns his living by the sweat of his brow from dawn to dusk.

The more widely the jurisdiction of legislative bodies has been defined, the more women's concern over their composition and activities must grow. The Reichstag is the ultimate determinant of justice and law, taxes and imposts. But women are without rights here too, even though they help create the nation's wealth and through their work have become autonomous citizens of the State. Nations with tougher civilizations—America and Australia—have granted them citizens' rights. Europe in its gray age fears everything new; it is still dreaming about the women of long ago: princes' whores who from the backstairs and boudoirs held the threads of politics in their hands; female slaves without voice or will who toted all of humanity's loads; the goody-goody motherly homemaker whose ideas and whose work never strayed beyond pantry and kitchen, home and farmstead. It is our task, women, to shake Europe out of its sleep. It is up to us to help unleash the storm that is to blow the dust of centuries out of its eyes. Then it will look around in amazement: standing at the threshold of the 20th century it will see the female full of strength and dignity, demanding to be admitted to the great council of humanity, on her head the crown of the martyrdom of misery, in her hand the palm of victory of labor.

4. Women's Interests and Politics

More loudly, more insistently than ever our period demands women's interest and women's collaboration. The world is bristling with weapons on land and on the sea as if we were headed for a men-murdering war. The masses of the people go without necessities in order to produce guns that are to defend a social system in which the poor must deprive themselves of nourishment to fill the ample pockets of the rich. Abundance displays itself conspicuously before them; the millions of human beings whose hands and heads produced all that splendor stand before the shining plateglass windows of happiness suffering cold, hunger, and thirst.

That's how it is everywhere. Should that not arouse all those primeval women's energies—love and hatred, compassion, and a sense of justice? Indeed it does. There are temperance and morality preachers, peace advocates and women's libbers in large numbers among them, and the causes they represent certainly are nice and good ones. But our time demands more than noble sentiment, moral sermons, and general humanitarianism. From this lofty level we must descend into the dark valleys of everyday work, duties, and demands.

Acquaint yourselves just a little bit with the issues of domestic and foreign politics now on the agenda that continue to dominate the attention of the German people and especially its representatives in the Reichstag in the coming period, and you will not be able to dismiss the impression that women have no valid reasons to give for their indifference with regard to these issues, and that they are guilty of neglect of duty as long as they remain in this indifference. And that applies particularly to women wage workers, especially those who work with their hands, whose life and work conditions Germany's domestic and foreign policies affect very deeply.

Of the issues being discussed and decided in the Reichstag the ones that are easiest for them to understand are those dealing with social legislation, which includes *workers' protection* as well as workers' insurance. As is well known, all people living by the exploitation of other people's labor praise Germany as the classic country of social legislation; indeed, they go so far as to speak of "giant steps" taken in this area and to warn against "excessive haste" in this rush. But let us take a look at the extraordinary things that have been done with regard to the protection of women workers. We will have no difficulty summarizing their essence in a few sentences: 1. For female workers over 16 the law establishes the 11-hour day; on days preceding Sundays and Holidays, the 10-hour day. 2. The law prescribes a lunch pause of one hour which can be extended by half an hour at the demand of women workers who have to take care of a household. 3. Nightwork is outlawed. 4. Women who have given birth must not be employed for six weeks after delivery; that can be reduced to four weeks on the basis of a physician's certificate. These provisions apply to factories and workshops where the machinery is motor driven but have at last been extended to the workshops of the garment industry as long as nonmembers of the family are employed in them. There are additional regulations, as follows: 1. The ban against work below ground (in mines). 2. The nine o'clock closing time for shops, and regulations concerning rest periods, midday pause, and sitting facilities for commercial employees. Finally the Federal Council has authority to bar or limit women's work in health-endangering enterprises. Those by and large are the accomplishments of more than three decades of German workers' protection legislation! Even they should not be considered insignificant were it not that almost every single regulation is robbed of its effectiveness by a large number of exceptions. Thus all too often the 11 hours turn into 13, and night or Sunday rest are canceled. Moreover, even the best laws are inadequate because means and personnel are lacking that would ensure their enforcement. On one hand, the number of trade inspectors is too small to warrant any satisfactory supervision, and on the other, the workers themselves are prevented from standing up for their own rights because they are disenfranchised politically. And the nicest legal provisions turn out to be insignificant when we remind ourselves that their blessings are shared by only about 1 million out of approximately 5 million women workers, i.e., not more than one fifth! Rural women workers and domestic servants are totally without protection and are exposed to arbitrariness and exploitation. The various laws about master-servant relations, which still reflect the spirit of the darkest Middle Ages, certify the employer as a feudal lord with practically unlimited authority. And the majority of Germany's people's representatives was cowardly enough to bring this unworthy relationship with them into the twentieth century through the new civil code! Like the servants, the legions of our poorest women, who as workers in home industries represent the darkest side of the workers' existence, remain unaffected by workers' protection laws. The scope of their labor reaches from the huts on mountain tops into the most hidden valleys and down to the darkest caves of the big cities. Endless hours of work, the lowest wages, workplaces that defy all rules of hygiene—those are their trademarks. Neither illness nor old age protects anyone from exploitation here; the youngest child as well as the worn-out grandmother must work—work without rest or letup, so as to maintain their bare existence, in the best case. The lawmakers pass them by; are they afraid to peer into this abyss because it might defy and mock all their bridge-building tricks? They pretend deep respect for the family, for the sacredness of the hearth and home where no unwanted person may trespass; did they not long ago allow trespass by the most unwanted stranger, by capitalism? Are they not silently permitting it to trample the last remnant of family life and family bliss with its iron heel? In cottage industries the entrepreneurs discovered the way that makes it possible for them to circumvent even what little there is of worker protection legislation. At times they even close down their factories and farm out the work to people working in their homes—for the human machine is still cheaper than the one made of steel and iron, and fuel for it costs less money. And women in particular are only too willing to serve as tools.

The solution of the problem of cottage industries can be considered almost a life-or-death issue for women workers. It gains additional significance because it is intimately linked not only to the issue of women's work but also to that of *children's work*. The trades laws valid until recently outlawed the employment of children under 13 and made that of children under 14 difficult. For young people between 14 and 16 the ten-hour workday has been established, some insignificant pauses in the work have been decreed, and work at night, on Sundays, and underground has been prohibited. But here too the law stopped halfway in that, just as in the case of women workers' protection legislation, it allows for all kinds of exceptions and fails to apply to the vast majority of working children. After long and tremendous efforts it was at last possible to move the government to undertake a special investigation of children's work. In these efforts energetic cooperation was rendered by the teachers, next to parents the most competent observers of children: they know only too well that unwillingness to do schoolwork and mental sluggishness almost always are but consequences of physical overtaxing. But even these investigations were marred by incompleteness, because they restricted the scope of inquiry to include only the children employed for wages, excluding the countless juveniles in domestic service and agriculture. Despite this unjustified limitation, it was found that the huge number of more than half a million children under 14 are obliged to sacrifice their weak strength to the struggle for existence outside the factories; within factories, trade inspectors discovered their number to be about 9,000. Out of the figures misery cries loud enough, and yet it took another four years before the lawmakers dared take a new step by proposing a bill which the Reichstag passed into law. In one direction this act constitutes significant progress. For the first time German lawmakers had had the courage to climb over the walls of the family circle that had until then been considered unsurmountable, by seeking to protect not only other people's children but also people's own children against exploitation. Nonetheless, the whole thing looks horribly like wretched patchwork. Not only that, there is no mention at all of extending protection to all working children, if only in the future: the gentlemen estate owners fear they might be deprived of their cheapest and most willing rural workers and mask this fear in pretty phrases about children's work as an educational necessity. Moreover, for many occupations the age limit has been set extraordinarily low. In workshops, except a very few in which children's work is outlawed, children from age 13 may be employed. In commerce and in show business (theater, circuses, etc.) children are barred from work only up to age 12, and for delivery and messenger service only up to age 10. In restaurants and pubs other people's children may not be employed at all, but one's own may without any age limit, and that includes children related to the owner in a third degree of kinship. All these regulations appear all the more inadequate when we realize what the vast majority of those 11-, 12-, and 13-year-old proletarian children actually look like, who according to the new law are admitted to various kinds of work: all too often they are smaller and weaker than the 7-, 8-, and 9-year-old children from bourgeois families. Legions of poor children, cheated of the only happiness they expect in life—the happiness of their youth—still today are exempt from any kind of protection!

Consider the errand boys, marked by tuberculosis from early on; the set-up boys in bowling alleys, their eyes tired from staying up deep into the night, who all too soon succumb to the devil alcohol; the pastry and newspaper delivery boys who chase upstairs and downstairs before thaw and daylight, in the grim winter cold, clad in thin rags, their stomachs growling; the peddlers and flower vendors who with avid eyes peer into the deepest morass of the metropolis, gilded by a thousand seductively glittering lights; the young circus artists who with faces made ugly by fright, and for a few pennies, contort their limbs that are emaciated from hunger and from beatings; the many, many miserable slaves of the cottage industry! And all those children who grow up to form a generation of people feeble in mind and body and morally corrupted, all these children shall be left without adequate protection for their future because the politicians tremble before the wrath of entrepreneurs anxious about their profits! More yet: let us remember that it is children, children at an age when they require the gentlest treatment, who are always commanded to render feudal service wherever the labor is heaviest and conditions worst, and therefore no grown-ups can be found any longer who are willing to do it; let us remember that every year agriculture devours countless children in its labor force: their weak backs bent, lungs and hearts and stomachs compressed unnaturally, feet in dung and muck for hours, their overheated bodies exposed to all winds and weathers—thus the children of the poor crouch on potato and turnip fields in order to garner the harvest for the rich! Our legislation passes by all these children with blind eyes and untouched hearts!

A vast unplowed field here beckons to women. There is no doubt that they, the nation's mothers, are called to act on the children's behalf, that coming generations will curse them if in cowardice they stand aside. The children are silent in their misery. And yet the cry for help that comes from the hearts of hundreds of thousands of joyless children clearly reaches the ears of those who gave birth to them. O, that they may not be deaf!

Do we really have to waste any more breath to demonstrate that women's interests are at stake here and that it is the duty of women to take action here? Should it still be necessary to tell them what every day they experience with their own bodies: that the existing workers' protecton legislation is in no wise sufficient to secure family life and health; that even the eleven-hour day and the hour-and-a-half midday pause are a mockery of the idea of domestic bliss, in the name of which, according to the myth, they were instituted; that the prescribed furlough from work for women who have given birth is practically worthless for the mother and even more so for a child; that the laws for protection merely paste a Band-Aid over the wound even while the insidious disease spreads through the body? Could there possibly be a woman of the people who might claim that the existing laws on workers' protection are doing enough and there is nothing more to be done by her and her comrades?

The characteristic picture of one-sided measures and timid restraint repeats itself in all areas of social legislation. So with regard to workers' insurance. Nonetheless, even in its present form it is quite significant and represents the first step on a road that could indeed bring about essential improvements in the conditions of proletarian life. The precondition is that the people directly involved must help pave this road. In one area, that of *health insurance,* this applies particularly to women because, as we will see, they are forced to have an especially keen interest in it. In this case they also have the power, because here they possess a right which has been granted them nowhere else in Germany: for the health insurance law granted them the active and the passive franchise. In other words, they can not only participate in elections to the administrative boards, they can also be elected to them. What that means for women can be seen from the functions that the health insurance funds are to carry out. These are, in brief summary, the following: they have to grant the insured free medical treatment and medicines for a maximum of 13 weeks—the new proposed bill raises this to 26 weeks—or, instead of this, pay sickness support up to 75 percent of the wage and maternity support up to 6 weeks—in the new bill, a full 6 weeks—recovery care that can be extended for a year, and to the survivors a death benefit amounting to 20 to 40 times the day's wage. All that is doubtless better than nothing and yet does not in the least come up to what is required. If a sick working woman or a worker in childbed receives between 4 and 6 marks a week, that does not, of course, cover the loss of her wage to the family, whose principal support she may be; and even less does it enable her to take proper care of herself and feed herself adequately. There can be, of course, no thought of her hiring help to take care of the household and the infants; in addition, women in childbed have no claim to free treatment by a physician, and the health insurance funds do not have the right to place pregnant mothers in birth clinics or women who have given birth in shelters for new mothers or, with their babies, in infant homes, even though only too often their conditions at home often make this necessary. Hence, despite the much-touted German social legislation, women workers continue to be compelled to pursue wage labor until shortly before delivery; indeed they must do so with even more intensive use of all their strength, because concern for the expected child demands extraordinary expenditures. In addition, they are obliged, in most cases to get up as soon as possible after delivery to take care of their household and to look for some earnings on the side even before the period prescribed by law is over. Meanwhile the infant, so urgently in need of being nursed and cared for by his mother, already in the cradle gets acquainted with the misery that goes with poverty: to be abandoned, to be starving for nourishment and for love. The scanty blessings of health insurance are severely limited further by not being available at all to the vast majority of proletarian women, just like the workers' protection. To be sure, the system could be extended by special decree to women working in cottage industries and in agriculture, but this has so far been done only for part of the former. In the case of female agricultural laborers, the fictional stereotype of the "rosy-checked sturdy country lass" seems to make any health care scheme superfluous. But no, even our lawmakers are not that sentimental; what makes them so nervous and scared is rather the wailing of the Junkers in their economic distress. It is such wailing that is responsible also for the fact that so far domestic servants have been excluded altogether from the health insurance scheme. Obviously the servants' never ending hours of work, standing by the stove and the wash tub, scantily allotted hours of rest, inadequate food, and nasty treatment are so good for their health that any and all illnesses are thereby prevented.

A wider circle of workers is covered by *accident insurance,* even though here too a lot of lowly self-employed people and virtually all workers in home industries remain uncovered. That is particularly weighty because, as we discussed earlier, many entrepreneurs employ home workers in increasing numbers in order to avoid paying the insurance premiums; in a sense, they are repudiating all responsibility for their workers' economic security. For the insured, however, the support they receive from the insurance funds is terribly important. It consists in free treatment and institutional care, an accident pension, up to 66 percent of the annual wage, which can also be paid to dependents if the patient is hospitalized, a death payment up to twenty times the daily wage, and a survivors' annuity that can go up to 60 percent of the victim's annual earnings. This last provision is the most important, for it marks the beginning of a much-needed great reform: welfare provisions for widows and orphans; and for the few who are covered by it it is already today a great help. Here too therefore interests are at stake whose importance every woman should realize clearly.

This is even more the case for *old age and disability insurance*. With regard to the number of people covered, this is the most comprehensive scheme, and is similar to the others only in leaving it to the decision of the Federal Council whether or not to include small entrepreneurs and home workers. Still, however comprehensive it be, however grandiose the conception on which it is based must appear, its realization lags far behind the ideal of providing a worry-free old age to every worker who ate his bread by the sweat of his brow, to take from him the fear that incapacity for work would condemn him to beggary or the poorhouse, which—and this is typical of the moral views of our times—would immediately disenfranchise him politically, as if poverty and crime were one and the same. But for women, incapacity for work is the beginning of a much deeper fall: all too often they then become victims of prostitution, even if heretofore they remained steadfast in the face of grave deprivations. One of the aims of the social security legislation ought to be to protect them against this extreme outcome. But even this it does not accomplish. For instance, a woman garment worker who in periods of good health and under most favorable circumstances was able to earn 700 marks a year but due to many years of sitting at the sewing machine has ruined her ability to work to such an extent that she can earn no more than 350 marks does not receive any compensation for the loss of earnings, and therefore if she does not want to starve to death she must try to eke out additional income. Once her earning power has declined to the point where she is entitled to a pension, that does not mean her liberation from worry and need. For the amount of her pension is determined by the number of weeks she contributed premiums and by the wage bracket of the insured pensioner. Given the general low level of wages paid to women, that is rarely high. Thus after fifty years of hard work she will at the most be able to claim 330 marks per year! But what if disability comes earlier and for someone in a lower wage bracket? Should a poor creature prematurely worn out by toil be able to live on 116 or 150 or 220 marks a year? Matters are even worse with regard to old age pensions. A woman worker has to live to the age of 70 before she can count on a pension of 110 to 230 marks! She rarely reaches this age, and if she does she will have been a spent old woman long before. And so she is not even sure she will have a quiet evening of life when she might rest from a burdensome life. Her life, which began with poverty and hard work, will end with poverty and begging.

Workers' social security comprises the proletarian's entire life from the cradle to the grave. But its accomplishments seem like groping attempts, like the first timid steps on an unknown path. There is something unfinished and amateurish about it; it also shows, without any particular need to tell this in detail, that it was originally meant to be no more than some sort of pacifier that you stick in the mouth of a hungry baby to keep it from crying. But neither working men nor working women ought any longer to be equated with a child that can still be satisfied with fairy tales. To be sure, most of the time they know nothing of their rights. In school they teach them about the laws of the ancient Jews. But they tell them nothing about the laws of their own times and their own country. If they did know them, they would not have remained so silent and impassive.

Many may be easily persuaded that workers' protection and women workers' social security have an impact on the vital interests of women and that therefore they have the duty to concern themselves with them but that their interests do not and must not extend beyond that. Yet it is easy in regard to every single issue to demonstrate that the lives of women are touched by them just as much as those of men. Let me demonstrate this by adducing just a few of the most important issues.

Since the creation of the German Reich, the government and the ruling parties have deemed it necessary to clothe it in annually more expensive armor, to arm it to the teeth. Current spending for the army, which in 1872 amounted to 250 million marks has risen to 569 million marks, that for the navy from 12 million to 87 million for the year 1902. If we add extraordinary expenditures, the total *military budget* comes to no less than 1,016 million marks. There is no reason to assume that this rise in expenditures will end in the foreseeable future; on the contrary, nations behave toward each other like the little boy who thinks himself the greatest among his playmates because he has more tin soldiers than they. And each of them wants to top the others. Sure, they preach peace and in sentimental speeches from the throne talk about "good relations" with neighboring countries, and in moments of inflated feeling they even spread the gospel of general disarmament, like the emperor of Russia. Yet, every year the people are presented bigger bills for new murder weapons, new ships, new uniforms. Hardly has one country replaced its old rifles with new ones when the other seeks to top it with even newer ones. Hardly has one country added a new ship to its fleet when the other country has to add at least two to its own. This intensive growth of navies automatically supports a tendency toward a global political reach that seeks to extend the power of Germany over foreign continents. Colonies are created, and the mailed fist forcibly interferes in the destinies of foreign countries, and with guns and whips "civilization" and "Christianity" are spread among black and yellow nations. The bill presented to us for this runs to almost 30 million marks. And who pays these huge sums? Who else but the German taxpayers whose money is sucked out of their pockets by the millions in the form of customs duties and excise taxes on the most important consumption staples. Are our women so stupid that they do not feel this burden imposed on them just because these taxes are not taken in bare coin but are contained in their daily household expenditures? Alas, they do feel it; they do know that their little household costs more and more money despite all their careful economizing; then they probably denounce the small shopkeeper next door and the woman in the basement who sells vegetables and blame them for getting fat on their hard-earned pennies. But when the guard changes and the soldiers march by or even ride through the street on proud horses and with the band playing, they run out and gape and have a good time. The young girls come out from their shops and factories, the kids run out of their schools, and they all march in step behind the troops, their eyes shining, their pulses throbbing, greatly enjoying the colorful spectacle and the loud noise. That they have to deprive themselves miserably in body and mind for the sake of the billions spent for this splendor and these blaring bugles—about that they have never thought. They would quickly lose their romantic infatuation for the pretty uniform if they knew, if women—all women—had the faintest idea that the inadequate nutrition and the substandard intellectual fare their children receive, the overcrowded schools, the shortage of teachers and their insufficient salaries, are, all of them, prices they pay for "our magnificent armed forces." But there are even more direct reasons for women to take an interest in the issues of *militarism* and *the cult of the navy.* They take sons away from their mothers and all too frequently return them physically and morally ruined. Moreover—and here is yet another indication how wrong the people are who say this is a just and equitable social system—if the young man is the child of poor parents, he will be taken away from them for a longer period: he must serve for two years, whereas the one whom fate happened to place in a warm nest needs to serve only for a year. That is not all: we do not always live in times of peace; our distant colonies are often the cause for minor engagements; for the sake of the Chinese adventure legions of young lads had to take up arms, and if it is not warfare itself, then harsh climates and all kinds of diseases demand the sacrifice of flourishing human lives. And for what? Perhaps because our country is endangered, because our lives, our honor, our freedom need to be defended—values for the sake of which every man will risk his life? The people have no interest in the world power ambitions of those in power, and a proper mother who taught her son to be brave and fearless, to place honor and freedom above life, must rebel when they want to force him to shed his blood for the sake of other people's avarice or romantic dreams. But she must fear even worse: the army is considered to be the strongest prop of the existing social system. The young soldier is taught obedience to his superiors as his first duty; he must obey not only when the task is to fight against Kaffirs and Chinese but also in case the ruling classes should arrange war against the "domestic enemy."

No female can say that militarism, navy obsession, and global power politics are of no concern to her. On the contrary, she is derelict in her duties, a poor mother, if she closes her eyes and ears to what goes on outside, to what decisions are made about her and her children's lives.

There is another issue that is no less likely to excite women most profoundly: the *raising of protective tariffs,* as it was decided by the passage of the customs tariffs law by Reichstag majority. After all, its consequence is nothing else than a rise in food prices, a price rise which must hit the poorest most sharply. Often they must spend more than half of their income on food and, in order to be able to do that, must curb all other expenditures most severely, e.g., those for clothing, living quarters, education, and leisure activities. The more affluent a family, the smaller the percentage of its income spent on food. After all, even the gourmet cannot exceed a certain limit in his food consumption. From this we see that tariffs on foodstuffs are especially a burden for the poor. This is particularly true of grain tariffs and the rising bread prices to which they lead.

With the number of children and the decline in income, bread consumption rises demonstrably. When the old tariff of 3.50 marks was in force, a worker's family spent about 32 marks annually for bread. Now with the minimal rate at 5 marks this sum rises to 45 marks. Given annual earnings of less than 500 marks found to apply to 2 1/2 million Germans, this represents a substantial portion of the annual income; if that money is not available, this does not mean what it would mean for the affluent—doing without a few luxuries—it means misery and a lack of essentials. This sum, which the Junkers allege to be petty and paltry, deprives the proletarian family of the little bit of meat that they still enjoyed, robs their children of the protective clothing and the last remnant of life-giving sunshine that could still penetrate into their chambers. These sums spell weeks of hard work that must be done for the big lords as in the period of feudal service. Let me bring out the crying injustice of the *grain tariffs* even more sharply: these sums have been squeezed out of the sweat of the poorest. They have no other purpose than that of filling the pockets of the rich, for the more affluent the large estate owner, the more he profits from grain tariffs, whereas the small farmer who needs to buy additional grain to cover his needs gets no or little benefit from them; on the contrary, he too must contribute his little bit to the people's blood tax.

It is not these tariffs alone that will necessarily depress the workers' standard of living. Already meat prices have been raised by closing our borders to livestock from abroad and by aggravating this exclusion through a meat inspection law. As a result, meat prices on both sides of the German border often differ by 20 to 39 pfennigs a pound; at the Russian border, for instance, pork costs 20 to 25 pfennigs a pound; and even horse meat, the consumption of which rises under these circumstances, has become more expensive. Of course, this state of affairs once again benefits only the large estate owners who are able, as soon as the import of livestock is restricted, to sell their own animals at the highest possible prices. They can do this in particular because in proportion to the number and growth of our population the number of livestock in German agriculture is much too low, and it is not possible to raise it in a short time to a level corresponding to the demand for meat. In light of this fact it is irresponsible to curb any possible import of livestock by means of *livestock tariffs*. If all import is stopped that could mean for the German nation a deficit of 7 million cattle and swine which could not be made up by German agricultural production very quickly; it took us 40 years to up our animal production by 3 1/2 million head. Even so, it is well recognized that the German population consumes little meat per capita. The statistics report a per capita consumption of 34 kilograms a year, while the people of England consume 52 kilograms. Today the large mass of proletarians can afford meat only on Sundays and holidays; and most of the time its quality is wretched, its nutritional value minimal. The consequences of the inadequate supply of nourishing materials are becoming apparent already; military recruitment, which yields poorer results every year, testifies to this. But the squires, the landed interests, the large estate owners, who always orate with ringing words and great hullaballo about their worry for the preservation of the State in its present form, show that in the final analysis they too dance around the golden calf: for it is they who are aiming to lower the effectiveness of the army, that most valuable prop under throne and altar, by their screaming for high grain and livestock tariffs. They have attained their goal: meat will disappear altogether from the worker's table and will have to be replaced by additional potatoes. But for these insatiable people all these tariffs are not yet enough. To prevent the people from obtaining the lacking nutrition in other forms—e.g., by greater consumption of sugar, fruit, butter, and eggs—the government in its loving kindness has placed tariffs on all these foodstuffs as well. Even when fruit could be imported duty-free, it was always a luxury item for workers' families, even though because of its food value it ought to be a basic part of the diet, especially for children; now, under the new and very high tariff rates, it will be out of reach for them. In vain the yearning eyes of proletarian children will be glued to red-cheeked apples. Even the most innocent pleasures will be denied them so that the children of the rich may enjoy even more. The emaciated and anemic bodies and pallid cheeks will testify without effect about the weak nourishment the sons and daughters of workers are condemned to eat; already in their youth they have to turn old, sickly, and worn out so that the limbs of the luckier ones may all the more exude good health and their youth may not be marred by any unhappiness. And all that should really be a matter of indifference for women and mothers? They should really be capable of standing there with folded hands as the bread is being stolen from their children's mouths?!

A bourgeois scholar, Professor Flugge, has calculated that the daily income of a worker's family must amount to between 3 and 4 marks if it is to make possible the minimum of necessary nutrition. But even now there are 8 million families in Germany, i.e., about 38 million human beings, whose income does not come up to this minimum and who are thus suffering from permanent malnutrition. Under the reign of the new customs tariffs their number will have to increase considerably. Of course, there are those who defend the tariff because they think that under its influence wages will have to rise and with them the people's purchasing power, since the entrepreneur will be compelled in his own interest to feed his human labor machines adequately. Too bad that historical experience concerning protective tariffs gives the lie to this opinion. For the more high tariffs curb the import of commodities from foreign countries, the more these foreign countries in their turn use tariffs to close themselves to our commodities. High food prices and low wages, grain tariffs and unemployment, always go hand in hand. And this tendency for wages to go down is reinforced by yet another phenomenon that accompanies high tariffs.

The poorer a person's nutrition, the weaker his strength for work will be; his energies flag, his attention gives out, physically and mentally he is spent more quickly. This state cannot but have a profound influence on his productivity. A healthy, vigorous labor force is a necessary precondition for flourishing and competitive industry. But as soon as the quality of the goods produced goes down, the possibilities for selling them will diminish. Also, exports will drop, other nations with a better standard of living will step into our place; then, the less our commodities are in demand, the fewer hands will be needed for their manufacturer. Here too therefore unemployment and a drop in wages are inescapable consequences. With this the decline in purchasing power goes hand in hand. If the worker has to spend most of his income for food, he is obliged to curb to the utmost the satisfaction of all his other needs. The effect of this on industry would be disastrous because its development and prosperity depend not on the purchasing power and purchasing willingness of the affluent few but on the consumption capacity of the vast masses of the people.

Unemployment and low wages, lack of the bare necessities in food, clothing, and shelter, repression of all desires demanding rest and enjoyment, intellectual and artistic delights for children and adults—who feels all these horrors more deeply than the female? Whose heart is torn more deeply than that of a mother? And who is imperiled more by the ghastliest consequences of all this misery than the girl who even in good times has to fight hard enough for her very existence?

It is an indisputable fact that vice and crime increase and decrease with the rise and decline of food and especially grain prices. For *crimes against property* that was demonstrated long ago by an outstanding scholar, Professor Georg von Mayr. For *alcoholism* it is true as well. Not only is the worker compelled to satisfy falsely his growling stomach and to whip up for a moment his flagging energies with beer and booze, he will also more readily reach for the bottle since every other joy in life remains unattainable to him, and, his misery being intolerable, he cannot overcome it. At least he would like to forget it. But it seems hardly necessary to describe what the man's drunkenness means for the woman: it destroys the last remnant of family happiness left by the sad conditions, it intensifies need into squalor and compels the woman to submit willingly to every degree of exploitation.

Hunger swings the whip under the lashes of which grow not only criminality and alcoholism but also *prostitution,* that worst curse of degenerate humanity. The female, "crown of all creation," representing the "beautiful, tender sex," of whom all poets sing, at whose behest all heroes endured the most perilous adventures, at whose feet the world is lying, and under whose heart the future of the human race is sleeping— the same society that celebrates her casts her into the muck of the street and compels her to offer her body for sale like a commodity on the open market. The holiest goods of humankind turn into sales objects, even love itself, the creator of all life. And terrible is life's revenge on her, because insidious ailments and disease are the inseparable companions of prostitution. They are transferred also to innocent wives, rob them of their health, make them infertile, or poison the unborn new life. According to assertions made by medical authorities, every fifth man in Germany who marries at the age of 30 is a carrier of a venereal disease through which he can ruin his wife and children and make his progeny into criminals or lunatics. Yet as soon as property advantages are at stake, the ruling society closes its eyes to these consequences and recruits ever more legions of hapless girls and women into this army which ravages more countries and destroys more nations than war, starvation, and epidemics.

This does not yet exhaust, however, the unholy effects of politics-for-profits. One menacing and frightening specter for every worker exposed to poisonous vapors, to the dust and dirt of his work place is *consumption of the lungs*. All scholars are agreed that there is no better way of damming its spread than a living standard conforming with the demands of hygiene, that is, in other words: bright, roomy dwellings and a nutritious diet. Either of them is attainable by only the most favored workers, though in the future not even they will be able to afford them; hence the murderous disease, this scourge of the proletariat, will demand increasing numbers of victims. This fate threatens men and women, but it is particularly a threat to children whose parents are hit by the disease and are rendered incapable of meeting the perils of life head on. And yet it is no more than a demand based on logic and on justice that people doomed from birth to a life of unending hard toil should at least be equipped with the strength and the skills needed for this.

It has been established that the percentage of proletarian children who die in the first year of their lives is incomparably higher than that of the children of the affluent. That will not astonish anyone. But that this state of affairs now is to be intensified must revolt everyone, particularly every woman, to the utmost; and it will undoubtedly be intensified as soon as the high food tariffs become effective. The less adequately mothers feed themselves, the more economic need forces them to work their fingers to the bone in the struggle for existence, the more will their ability to give birth to healthy children diminish and the fountain of life that nature gave them for their children dry up.

Is there indeed a woman who remains locked in apathy and indifference even when politics intrudes with crude hands into the sacred core of her being, her maternal love? Whom neither the humiliation of her sisters nor the misery of her children manages to shake out of her dumb and contented dream life? I do not believe it; if only we could get our voices to reach the ears of all women, we would win their hearts as well; and the millions who stand aside, ignorant and timid, hardly aware of what goes on around them, would form an army of self-sacrificing heroines, whose flag will lead them to victory.

5. The Parties and Women

The number of political parties in Germany tends to confuse the uninitiated. We have no less than fourteen: German Conservatives, Free Conservatives, the Farmers' League, the Peasants' League, the Center, the Poles, Alsatians, Guelphs, Anti-Semites, National Liberals, the Liberal Union, the Liberal People's party, the South German People's party, and the Social-Democrats. But despite this number the differences between the great majority of these parties are not so trenchant as to make it difficult to get to know them. In particular, they can be divided into two large groups: one of them comprises all those parties standing on the ground of the present social system and wishing to preserve it. There are 13 of them—an evil number! The other group, consisting solely of the Social-Democrats, fights against the existing—capitalist—order and wants to replace it with a socialist one in which the contradictions between the propertied and propertyless, between capitalists and pro-letarians, are to be abolished. The thirteen parties of the first group, generally known simply as the bourgeois parties, are united in their opposition to the party of the second group, representing the proletariat, but between each other display a number of important differences, which we will trace here only to the extent that they touch on women's interests. For as soon as we concede that women cannot be indifferent to the politics of their country, we will also have to demand evidence to show which political direction is consonant with their interests.

Conservatives of all shadings—German Conservatives, Free Con-servatives, Farmers' League, and Peasants' League—have so far paid little attention to women's needs and interests. They take the view that "the woman's place is in the home" and advocate it, blind to things as they really are. Hence they oppose any extension of women's rights and every attempt to loosen the bonds of dependency that tie the women to men and the female proletariat to the entrepreneurs. Thus when the draft for the new civil code was discussed they came out in favor of the principle of community property, i.e., for giving the husband the right to administer his wife's property. They also favored making divorce more difficult and that famous provision, which flies in the face of all healthy instinct, according to which the father of an illegitimate child is not considered related to him or her; and the mother, while allowed to raise the child, can never be appointed his or her guardian. They are the sharpest opponents of granting women the rights of free association and free assembly; they voted against giving women the vote for the trade courts; they jeer and mock every mention of the idea that women should be given the right to vote in politics, as if the millions of women engaged in public life, struggling for their existence just like men, did not exist. And with all this they still have the gall at every occasion to put on airs as the exclusive knight protectors of the "weak sex."

But they oppose women not only where specifically women's interests are involved. To be sure, they often voted in favor of government proposals dealing with laws to protect industrial workers, because they thought the laws might slow down the development of heavy industry, which to them, as representatives of farming, of agrarian interests and Junkerdom, is a thorn in their eye. But they bear heavy responsibility for the fact that the men in charge never even dared suggest an extension of workers' protection laws to rural laborers and domestic servants but still today exclude them—more than half of all the workers—from the advantages of compulsory health insurance, the domestic servants from even accident insurance. That accident and disability insurance schemes still managed to cover these poor stepchildren of social welfare legislation is a cause of perpetual resentment among the conservatives, and they have left no stone unturned to shake off this "burden that agriculture cannot bear." Where their profits are at stake, all their beautiful principles recede into the background. "Do as I say, not as I do"—that saying applies first of all to them. They talk about the sanctity of family life while in fact they work to destroy it. They not only compel rural workers, men and women, to work endless hours, so that their home turns into a mere bunkhouse; they also advocate the merciless exploitation of child labor, and it is for their sake that the new children's protection law stops short of covering children's agricultural labor.

That is not all. As stated, blame must fall to a large extent on the conservatives for the fact that the feudal system of master-servant relations still is in force and that domestics and rural laborers are still subject to exceptional legislation, thanks to which half of the workers in Prussia do not have the right of association; but all this hits women harder than men. And it gets still worse: even the existing law giving industrial workers the right to form associations they would like to see restricted as much as possible, because they need defenseless slaves, not free human beings. Their attitude toward all educational issues corresponds to this. "The most stupid worker is the best worker"—this statement by an honest conservative is the deep conviction of all his party comrades. To the proletarian child, therefore, the treasures of knowledge are to be as inaccessible as the world's material wealth. The workers are to live as eternal convicts in a fortified dungeon of disfranchisement and dependency; in order to complete this dungeon, the conservatives further seek to restrict their right to vote or to take it from them altogether. After all, their ideal is the era of serfdom when there were only lords and servants without a will of their own. It may well be that the good ones among them may want to take care of their subordinates like stern fathers of their children, but not a single one of them sees either in the worker or in the woman a free fellow human being with equal rights.

There are additional arguments for branding the conservatives as enemies of the proletariat and of women: militarism and the urge for a big navy get their staunch support. Every kind of indirect tax that takes hard-earned pennies out of the pockets of the people gets their vote. The tariffs on foodstuffs that will fill only their pockets but will expose the poor to the most abject misery are not yet high enough for some of the conservatives, especially the Farmers' League. The "mainstays of throne and altar," they threaten to withdraw their support from the government if it will not make the prices for bread and meat go even higher.

The female sex is called the conservative element in human society, and indeed women tend to cling to whatever is old and traditional. But is it the conservatives whom they ought to join and whose policies they ought to support?

The *Center party* is a large party which in the German Reichstag today determines the outcome of votes. It arose as a consequence of the "culture conflict" waged by Prince Bismarck against the Catholic church. On many points it shares its basic principles with the conservatives. But what specifically ties its members together is adherence to the Catholic church. For this reason its politicians represent the most diverse groups of the population: agrarians and industrialists, property owners and proletarians, and the most artful acrobatics are not sufficient to do all of them justice. Inevitable, therefore, are the contradictions in which the Center gets wrapped up all the time and which come to the fore especially glaringly where workers' interests are concerned. For years it has been trying, particularly during Reichstag election campaigns, to demonstrate its friendliness toward workers by demanding a maximum workday of eleven or recently even ten hours, and many a poor proletarian in his naiveté may have given them his vote; but as soon as the issue came up for serious debate, as for instance in 1897, the Center withdrew to a position where it modestly demanded no more than a "hygienic" workday, that is, it was to be left up to the Federal Council to fix the length of the workday wherever workers' health may be impaired; and in 1900 it went so far as to deny support to the Catholic Textile Workers Union, that is, to its own followers, who were petitioning for the ten-hour day. Further, with seemingly great eagerness the Center supports workers insurance and indeed advocates broadening of the coverage, yet in 1897, in deference to its agrarian party comrades, it moved to have the application of the disability insurance scheme limited to heavy industry only. In the discussions of the commission to draft the new civil code it voted for the abolition of the master-servant relationship, but in the plenary meetings of the Reichstag, where it really matters, the Center voted against it. In 1900 the well known *Lex Heinze* was being discussed. That bill was introduced by the government ostensibly for the protection of morality, although in fact it would have meant the gagging of art and literature; the Center, our principal guardian of morality and women's virtue, sought to make this bill palatable to workers by adding an amendment making indecent acts or proposals by entrepreneurs against their employees an offense subject to severe punishment and by raising the age below which girls would be protected against statutory rape to 18. But as soon as the decisive third reading of the bill came up, the Center unscrupulously abandoned its own demands. In moving words, it sought not long ago to protect the nearly empty pockets of the poor against the demands of the army and navy budgets—but only shortly afterward showed itself more eager than all other parties to approve the millions asked by the government. With regard to the customs tariffs, it solemnly vowed never to give them its approval—but in the end, the Center, this "friend of the workers," voted for this thieving raid of the propertied against the propertyless!

All these facts demonstrate clearly that women have no reason to regard the Center as representing their interests. Nonetheless it exerts a strong attraction for many, and not for just the ignorant. This is based primarily on its stress on religion, on the power of the confessional, but also on the stand that the Center takes with regard to women's interests. This can be summarized by saying that the Center wants to restore women to the home and mothers to the family and wants to limit women's wage work outside the home. What woman worker groaning under the double burden—work for her daily bread and housework—who has to leave her tenderly loved little ones to themselves will not regard this as the fulfillment of her deepest wishes? And yet little reflection is needed to understand that barring married women from wage work outside the home not only would not liberate them but would in fact drive them more deeply into misery. For by outlawing their work in factories and workshops we cannot outlaw the economic want that forces them to do this work. Women thus excluded would in large numbers become victims of cottage industries, where no protective legislation covers them, where they would be most grossly exploited and paid the most pitifully low wages; and the miserable little bit of family life they enjoyed due to the legal limitation on work hours would be destroyed as well. Thus the welfare provisions the Center proposes for women, once they are examined in the light of the day, turn out to be a pernicious Greek gift.

At first sight the *widows' and orphans' insurance* plan they have proposed recently looks more serious, but it too turns out to be a snare to entrap the workers and to silence them in case they rebel against the Center's tariff policies. At the first reading of the tariff bill the Center announced it would vote for it only if all additional tariff revenue resulting from it would be used to finance widows' and orphans' insurance. But in the committee deliberations, where it was moved that at least the additional revenue from agricultural tariffs be earmarked for this purpose, the Center voted against it. In the end the Center itself moved to exempt the revenue from tariffs on a whole number of foodstuffs from being used for the insurance. Surely we have a curious kind of social welfare when they slip a measly mark into one pocket of a poor widow or orphan after they pulled nine marks or more out of their other pockets by means of the high tariffs on foodstuffs; but the entire scheme turns out to be even more pitiful once we have discovered that the entire insurance benefit would amount to 80 marks for a widow—some want to make it as low as 23 marks—and 30 marks for every orphan. That is a drastic illustration of the Center's "friendliness towards workers," an illustration designed to open the eyes of even the most stupid. In its support of the women's cause the Center is totally dishonest and refuses to turn into an open enemy even when confronted from outside by women's demands that it opposes. For instance, with regard to both private and publc law it is adamantly opposed to making women even nearly equal to men, but, just like the conservatives, it masks its enmity to women under the cloak of chivalry. It not only wants to narrow women's freedom to act and to move but also seeks to enchain women's minds, to deprive their children of the treasures of science and enlightenment by placing all schools under the supervision of the church. Outside of reading, writing, reckoning, and religion, said a member of the Center, everything else is superfluous frill for primary school students. It wants to make the children into obedient slaves, physically and mentally, and women into slaves without a will of their own. Hence women, if they want to free themselves from need and servitude, can never, never become its rank and file.

But the *Liberals*, are they not the ones who hold the flag of freedom high? Let us take a closer look at them. They present a confused picture in all the colors of the rainbow, the sad remnant, now split into several ideological groups, of a party representing the once genuinely free-thinking bourgeoisie. Their right wing, the *National Liberals*, increasingly come close to the conservatives in everything they do and omit to do. The label "liberal," which means free, today sounds like a mockery of their reactionary aims because, camouflaged by this label, they have assisted every effort at gagging the people, from limitations on the right of association to the fight against the universal, equal, and direct franchise. It is they, in their eagerness to approve whatever the government proposes, for whom no army or navy budget is too high and who can hardly wait to see the new tariff enacted. Only rarely, and always against protests by many of their own party members, do they decide to support demands for workers' protection. Recently, scared by the approaching election campaign, which is likely to diminish further their numerical strength, they moved the enactment by the Reichstag of a ten-hour day for juvenile working men and women. How little they really mean this is shown by the fact that almost at the very same time one of their speakers spoke against this move by referring oh so touchingly to the poor mother who ought not to be debarred from working more than eleven hours. At the same time, as a faithful spokesman of the entrepreneurs who claim the right of unlimited exploitation of the workers and as the mouthpiece of his party, he argued against any limitation of working hours for men on the pathetic ground that workers should under no circumstances be deprived of their sacred right to work as long as their strength permits. In yet another aspect it is evident that the National Liberals have turned into the typical representatives of the entrepreneurial class: they fought passionately against the nine o'clock closing time for shops and would really like to do away with it still today, and they came out most decisively against any laws to protect children working in agriculture and in domestic service. Most of the time they reject demands, or pass over them with silence, the satisfaction of which ought to be a task that liberalism should take for granted, such as giving women equality of rights in public and private concerns. The only thing they managed to do not long ago was to endorse women's demand for permission to become members of associations dealing with social concerns. The total meaninglessness of this demand is obvious; for as long as it is up to the police to decide what is social and what is political, women will remain without any rights, whether this demand is fulfilled or not. Thus women have nothing to expect from the National Liberals, and concerning the beggars' crumbs tossed to them now and then they say thanks, but no thanks.

Compared with the National Liberals, the *Liberal People's party* might almost begin to look attractive. It usually is opposed in principle to excessive military and naval budgets, even though it unhesitatingly approves credits for armaments; it fights against protective tariffs, even though at the time of the last big grain deals in the Reichstag it took a position that was rather dubious, to put it mildly; it advocates the extension and protection of the rights to organize and to assemble, but in extending these rights specifically to women it has never shown sufficient energy. It does endorse measures to shorten labor time for women but joins the National Liberals in opposing the establishment of a general norm for the labor day. Its major contribution on behalf of women was its vote in favor of giving them the right to vote and to serve in the trades courts, but this was far outweighed by other votes opposed to the interests of the people: for instance, it is opposed to disability and old age insurance, and in its political primer for 1901 its leader could declare without fear of being contradicted that the motion made by the Center party to restrict compulsory coverage by social security to workers in heavy industry and to eliminate the contribution made by the Reich "was altogether consonant with the views of the Liberal People's party," and he added that the proper thing to aim for was "the gradual abolition of the entire law." Even the health insurance scheme, which in fact covers far too narrow a range of people, goes too far for this party with regard to the extent of its coverage. The party opposed the nine o'clock closing hour for shops; its ambiguous attitude helped maintain the laws regarding master-servant relations, and recently it opposed even a law regulating compulsory rest periods for waiters. But what should especially impress itself in the minds of women, particularly women whose own children are forcibly drafted out of their schools to work in turnip fields and on potato farms, is the party's negative attitude toward the demand that children be barred from agricultural labor. Indeed, one of its spokesmen had the deplorable nerve to wax enthusiastic in depicting the advantages of agricultural work for children.

Turning now to the *Liberal Union,* it is less prejudiced about class warfare, more benevolent and more honest with regard to women's special interests; and in its struggle against the tariff policy of the government and the right its energy has not flagged. Against this we must note that in its enthusiasm and its willingness to approve budgets for militarism and naval expansion it has gone almost as far as the National Liberals. Indeed it has allowed itself to fix the rate of growth of the navy for many years, committing future Reichstags; without reflection it approved a budget of almost 5,000 million for this—5,000 million that the German people will have to pay for a policy of pursuing power on a global scale for which the proletariat must be lacking every trace of personal interest.

Would women, particularly proletarian women, be able to decide that the policies of the liberals deserve support? To be sure, we are dealing here with the most progressive elements of the bourgeoisie; between them and the conservatives yawns an abyss; yet many bridges of mutual understanding span it in both directions. True, one represents big landed property, the other, big industry; their interests frequently clash head on; and contradictions between the parties can be traced in all directions, political and religious. But even a liberal democrat ready to support a Republican constitution, full legal and political equality of women and men, of workers and entrepreneurs, [one] against indirect taxes and protective tariffs, against warships and guns—regrettably we are not acquainted with any such liberal—would still be linked in some ways with even the reactionary parties as long as he fights only against the existing political constitution but not against the prevailing economic system. We will be able to regard him as a helper just as today we regard anyone as our helper who assists the working class to gain even a foot of new ground; but one will be able to be a supporter of his party no more than we can support the conservatives or the Center party. And why not? Because political freedom can lead to a life fit for human beings for all people only in connection with economic freedom.

As long as [productive] property remains in the hands of relatively few people and huge capital accumulates in the hands of individuals, the mass of the people, those without property, remain dependent on the owners. As long as the wage system exists, in which the worker does not receive the entire returns of his labor but only as much as is necessary to enable him to go on working, while the surplus serves to increase the wealth of the entrepreneur, as long as all that persists, the proletariat must remain oppressed and enslaved. This oppression abases the woman more deeply than the man, because under the pressures of dependency and need she often is forced to sell not only her labor power but all too often her body as well. But the capitalist economic system that has brought about this state of affairs carries the germ of dissolution within itself. The further it develops, the larger the number of dependent individuals who necessarily join forces for the purpose of rebelling with ever greater vigor against an economic system that oppresses the many for the benefit of the few. In this way, as a child of capitalist development, was born the *Social-Democratic* movement, the one party that is still to be examined.

An important trait distinguishes it from all other parties: it propounds a scientific ideology, socialism, and not just the interests of a class. Nor does it, like other parties, fight more or less planlessly for gaining discrete advantages or regaining some outdated privileges and liberties. Instead, it has placed itself in the service of the laws of development discovered by its great pioneers and therefore can advance toward its goal assured of victory. This goal, toward which economic as well as political developments are urging society, is the replacement of the capitalist social system by a socialist one in which the means of production—factories, mines, the land, etc.—no longer are the property of individual owners who exploit them in pursuit of their own personal selfish aims but are put into the hands of the community, which can then regulate production for the collective benefit and can make the blessings of human civilization, from bread to the enjoyment of the highest art, accessible to all. To reach this goal must of course be in the interest of all the dependent, all the disfranchised, all the oppressed, in short, in the interest of all those whom today we subsume under the name of proletarians. In consequence of their community of interests, they constitute a class, and the struggle they wage necessarily is a class struggle.

Consequently, as their political representation, the Social-Democratic movement faces a double task to ensure its practical effectiveness: within the present social system it must seek to attain everything that can secure and raise the material and intellectual life of the proletariat, and at the same time it must go further toward its ultimate goal, step by step. Both tasks, in the final analysis, are but one and the same, for the value of any partial gain must always be tested by its usefulness in promoting progress toward the final goal. For instance, if the Social-Democratic party argues in favor of highly developed workers' protection laws, it does this not only for the purpose of easing the worker's life at this time, but also because it knows that a proletariat impoverished, physically weakened, and mentally dulled by poor working conditions can never be the pioneer and flag bearer of socialism. And if it fights for women's rights like no other party, then it does so not only in order to liberate the female sex from a condition unfit for human beings but much more because it is convinced that only women who are strong and intellectually free can bear and rear a race of free men capable of leading socialism to victory.

The *Communist Manifesto*, that most important historic document that appeared in 1847 and marks the beginning of scientific socialism, already demonstrates the close connection between women's issues and workers' issues by describing how present production relations increasingly draw the women of the proletariat into the great army of industrial soldiers. On the basis of this recognition the Social-Democratic movement became the party of women by becoming the party of the oppressed and dominated class. Its program, which contains its basic principles, demands the abolition of all laws discriminating against women with regard to public or private life. And it has acted in accordance with its program in speech and print, by proposing bills of its own and by opposing all laws that might do injustice or harm to the female sex.

As early as 1877 the Social-Democrats in the Reichstag moved to amend the trades regulation law in a manner which dealt in detail with the condition of women workers and made demands such as the limitation of work time, the banning of night work, of work underground, on high constructions, and on moving machinery. At the time, these proposals were defeated, but thirteen years later the government itself endorsed some of them, and they were enacted into laws. Already then the party demanded laws for the extensive protection of women who had given birth, including a three week furlough before delivery. Thanks to incessant pressure and vigorous agitation by the party even the other parties saw themselves compelled to demand legislation for workers' protection, if they did not want to lose all their working-class followers; and the government, worried about the growing restiveness of widening elements of the population, resolved to introduce social insurance laws. Even Bismarck, the bitterest enemy of the Social-Democratic movement, was forced to acknowledge publicly that without its initiative there would have been no social reform legislation in Germany. On the one hand, it is fear of the proletariat which compels the rulers to make concessions; on the other, it is the conscience of bourgeois society that has been aroused by the warnings of the Social-Democrats and that has helped limit its narrow-minded selfishness a bit.

The most important Social-Democratic demand in the area of workers' protection is the eight-hour work day for all workers regardless of gender. A woman, especially one suffering under the burden of double or triple obligations, needs no special explanation of the trenchant importance such a limitation of labor time would have for everyone's health, family life, and intellectual growth. The limitation placed on daily labor time is the most important precondition for the physical and mental growth of the working class, it is one of the sources from which it derives its strength. The Social-Democratic movement wisely recognized that a limitation of women's work time was easier to obtain from the ruling classes and could then become the best point of departure for wide-ranging measures, and it has fought energetically for this. Today it demands the ten-hour work day in lieu of the present eleven-hour day, and there is some prospect that this will become reality. It would con-stitute merely one more step on the way to the universally valid norm for the working day.

It would fill an entire book, were we to list every individual demand, every position taken by the party toward proposals made by the other parties as far as specifically women's interests are concerned. The party has always led in expressing them: its fights for freedom and equality of the female wherever law and custom discriminate against her, for her protection wherever she needs it in her capacity as worker and mother. From her right to vote for trades courts to her political franchise, it has always fought on her behalf, unafraid of the jeers coming from the foes; it has led the fight against the laws concerning association and assembly that make women the equals of minors. Recently it once again raised its voice to advocate thoroughgoing revisions of the health insurance system to benefit pregnant women and new mothers. By placing domestic ser-vants under the same laws as wage workers and by placing cottage industry and home work under special protective legislation, it wants to provide effective measures against unlimited exploitation in these areas of women's work. And it functions as women's representative also when, by favoring a strict ban of child labor, it seeks to secure children an untroubled youth during which their energies for their lives' work can mature unhindered.

Nor has the Social-Democratic movement ever failed to work for the rights of workers in the widest sense. Every year it has proposed to the Reichstag separate measures for workers' protection, either comprehensive ones as in 1877, 1884, and 1890, or to cover special topics. The Social-Democrats were the first to introduce a number of issues of great importance such as special public employment agencies to regulate the job market, unemployment insurance, and others, and some of these topics were then taken up by the bourgeoisie. There is no evil in employment conditions to which it does not pay attention—understandably enough, since it not only represents the proletariat but is constituted by the proletariat and therefore is bound to know exactly where the shoe pinches. Hence it had to be the Social-Democratic party that vigorously protests again and again in the name of the toiling people against indirect taxes and tariffs, especially those on food staples, that opposes militarism and naval armaments not only because the billions paid for these by the people could be used much more fruitfully for civilizing tasks of a higher kind, not only because armament efforts stimulate competition with all other nations, thus becoming an endless spiral and seriously endangering world peace, but primarily because militarism on land and on the seas serves aims that are contrary to the interests of the people by constituting the main prop of the existing economic system. Abolishing the standing army is not just an aim for the Social-Democrats but also a means to a higher end: the replacement of the capitalist social order by a socialist one.

In this pamphlet we have been able to bring out only the most important points from the vast totality of its aims, but they suffice to demonstrate that for the moment it strives for nothing else than a rise in the living standard and the physical and intellectual life of the people, particularly of those who now are oppressed and without rights—the proletarians; and for the future, a new order of things that will guarantee each and everyone a life fit for human beings. But these aims can be attained only by curbing the privileges and advantages of the ruling parties, as regards the present time, and in the long run by the total abolition of their rule based on private property. Because of this the entire bourgeoisie regards the Social-Democratic movement as its most dangerous enemy which, depending on the degree of its insight, it seeks either to destroy with all the weapons of power, legal as well as illegal, or to deprive of influence by meeting the workers' desires halfway. From the antisocialist law through the subversive activities and penitentiary bills to the most recent times one kind of persecution or attempt at persecution follows another. At times it is heavy artillery that is aimed at the workers, at other times it is pinpricks that hit them in the form of restrictions of the right to organize, banning of associations, prohibitions against assemblies, and jail sentences for press offenses and insults to the sovereign. From the throne itself we hear proclamations to battle against the Social-Democrats as the "party of revolution"; its followers are labeled as "wretches," as "fellows without country," and as "a gang of people unworthy to bear the name of German." These many kinds of persecution prove its strength and its certainty of victory far more ·than all its successes, more even than the two million votes that rallied to the Social-Democratic movement in the last election.

Women have to fight under the banner of this party side by side with the male proletariat. There is no other party that appeals to them with such force—to their interests as women, as mothers, and as workers.

6. Women's Duties in the Political Struggle

Explaining their political duties to men is not difficult: whoever has the right to vote and by voting can help influence the composition of various public institutions would be acting irresponsibly if he did not seek to prepare himself by forming a firm opinion and then to express it by casting his vote. But when women are told about duties of this kind they prefer to hide behind their legal disfranchisement in order to conceal their intellectual laziness and their lack of interest. But even after they have clearly seen that every issue in public life directly affects them personally, and even if within their own four walls they follow events with keen interest, the idea that they have duties to fulfill is far from their minds. And if once in a while it does occur to them, feminine shyness and insecurity hold them back. Many a poor overburdened working woman, many a slaving factory girl, thinks herself much too lowly and insignificant to think that her energy might make any difference at all in the great struggle of the proletariat. And yet precisely in this struggle we must count on every single individual, and on women more than ever.

History does not show us any instances of large masses of women participating in political and social struggles. As the example of the French Revolution indicates, it was always no more than small groups, momentarily excited by some shocking event, that emerged suddenly and just as suddenly disappeared from the political stage. In fact, there was as yet not the precondition for maintaining women's interest; that precondition was the emancipation of women from the confinement in the domestic sphere through wage work outside the home. Only now a hitherto unknown force grasps the wheels of progress, and only now is it essential that this not be done in an unconscious manner but with full awareness of women's responsibilities.

The first duty of women is to educate and enlighten themselves. That is no easy task for those without formal education, who have no newspapers or books at their disposal, who have neither time nor money to obtain them, and whom their daily toil saps of their freshness and receptivity. But almost everywhere there are meetings costing nothing or very little where all kinds of lectures present needed information to the listeners. For that, women must find the time even if it means sacrificing a few hours of gossiping with neighbor women, some fun on the dance floor, or the like, or the husband staying at home and taking care of the children. That too is the man's political duty, for he is principally responsible for seeing what kind of upbringing the mother will give to his children! In many cities there are self-education associations that women can join if other means to enrich their knowledge are lacking. That will also enable them to exchange views with like-minded people. But the most important means to attain all this is the union organization. Whatever the woman worker is obligated to know is best learned within the circle of her colleagues at work. Here too it is easiest for her to master her shyness, here she practices speaking without fear, here for the first time she feels herself a member of a collective, a fighter within the rank and file. Thus, apart from the fact that the union organization must carry out great tasks for its specific purposes, the woman worker must not exclude herself from it with regard to her political duties either.

In some of the German states the law makes it possible for women to join political associations. This they must do as soon as they think they have political views of their own. Neither the ill will of the men, which regrettably still exists a lot, nor the urge to economize must keep them from doing so. The few pennies it requires are part of the sacrifice women will have to make: one colored ribbon, one new hat that a woman foregoes buying, is that too much in the light of the lofty aim she helps all of us attain?

Further, under the protection of unenlightened women we get that lush growth of dime novels that poison the imagination and divert the mind from worthwhile concerns, that spread of newspapers feeding crime and gossip stories to their readers, gradually paralyzing their judgment and making them into thoughtless fellow travelers of capitalism. It is up to women to make some thoroughgoing changes here; no enlightened woman worker ought to tolerate such reading material among those around her. It has to be replaced by a decent, orthodox party newspaper, a union periodical, and occasionally a book recommended by the paper.

With all this, however, women fulfill only a part of their political duties toward themselves. There is much more to fulfill: duties toward their husbands, their children, toward their friends, their party, and toward society as a whole.

Many women, and by no means the worst of them, wail about every penny of his wage that the husband does not bring home. That is understandable enough in view of the meager proletarian fare. Or else they complain about the long evenings he spends away from home; even without this the time he can devote to his wife and children is scanty enough. Nonetheless here too the rule must be: be brave, hold back your tears, forget your sorrow when the husband has joined the ranks of the fighting workers' army. Indeed, this is not enough: even though her heart is constricted with pain, she must drive him out if he does not go on his own initiative. Many a worker has sat in a warm corner with his narrow-minded, unenlightened wife and adoring children, forgetting and denying his duties and deserting his colleagues outside. But others, urged on by their brave wives, have thereupon become aware of their duties and have found their way to the comrades. "Stay here, for the children's sake," says the unenlightened wife, "buy them a piece of bread, play with them, help to bring them up, if you have money and time to spare!" "Go away, for your children's sake!" urges the convinced socialist woman. "Fight to guarantee them a better future!" And then in the time he spends with her he will find not only fleeting hours of lovemaking but also lasting friendship.

Hunger and love, they say, are the forces that move the world, and they understand this to mean the love between men and women, which since oldest times has unleashed wars, committed crimes, accomplished deeds of heroism, and created immortal works. But at the very moment in which women entered into public life, yet another sentiment became a force capable of moving the world: maternal love. From the animal instinct to protect the tender infant to that forward-looking love embracing the entire life, which already in the child respects the adults, maternal love has gone through great transformations. Nowhere is it developed more strongly than where the woman is cast deep into the struggle for existence, where she becomes acquainted with misery and grief through her own experiences. No animal defies death with as much courage as the lioness defending her cub, no human being is as unafraid, loyal, and devoted as the mother fighting for her child's happiness. If she is enlightened, if she knows what is required to liberate all humanity from misery, then she will not consider any duty higher than that of assuming her place in the political struggle of the working class and of rearing her children to become her successors. Every glance into her darling's pale face, every wailing request for food, will spur her on to energetic work instead of making her cry tears of fruitless suffering.

Into the hearts and minds of her children a mother plants the seeds of all progress. A generation of slaves with slavish minds grows up where mothers are unfree, fearful, and submissive. Free, strong, independent women are the precondition for free, strong, courageous men. Hence for the sake of their children women must not remain dull and indifferent. Any woman joining the ranks of the freedom fighters is more than one additional force for the struggles of the present time, because her children, on whose youthful shoulders the future will rest, are standing behind her. The name of a good mother no longer goes to the woman who merely washes, dresses, and feeds her children, but to the one who rears them to be fighters and serves them as a model by ceaseless courage, self-sacrifice, enthusiasm, and energy.

Friendship between women is very often a very brittle thing because frequently it is based not on anything they have in common intellectually but on all sorts of externalities. Young girls confidentially share the secrets of their hearts, adult women talk with others about their domestic worries, but only rarely do they seek to elevate, enlighten, or enrich each other morally and intellectually. Here too a special duty will have to be fulfilled: a socialist woman will not rest or relax until she has convinced her friends about the correctness of her views, until she has shaken the lazy into activity, converted the irresponsible to her own seriousness, and mobilized the indolent for her struggle. That will cause many a friendship to go to pieces, but many another friendship will be formed for life. Those who are welded together by their brothers' oppression and by the same hope for a better future, their league turns into blood brotherhood.

But does the party have a right to demand of disenfranchised women that they fulfill duties? It has not only the right but also the obligation to make such a demand, and wretched would be the woman who shirked it. Once she is steeped in socialist ideology she herself will find it impossible not to act in its spirit. Everyone can do this, however poor and insignificant she may be, and the party would never have attained its present size and power had not myriads voluntarily become its agents. And every function in the service of the party is as weighty and as important as all others—distributing leaflets and scholarly work, quiet agitation in the workshop and public oratory at mass rallies. No contribution is held in contempt or remains unutilized; success is assured only if all mesh with each other and work for each other.

The greatest commitment of energy will have to be demanded in periods when the task is to prepare for Reichstag elections. Elections must express the will of the people, and even though women cannot as yet enter the booth themselves with the ballot, they do have sufficient ways and means to make their desires felt. Every public meeting gives them an occasion to speak out, to persuade and to mobilize their listeners. Let none think herself too humble for this. A simple word from the bottom of the heart spoken by a simple working woman often has greater effect than a thousand arguments advanced by trained speakers. Even more important is agitation among neighbors living in the same village or city quarter. Here is a wide field for all kinds of activity; here the task is not to spare physical or mental energies, to be without fear even in the face of jeers or brutality, to knock at every door, leaving a pamphlet or a newspaper everywhere, to talk personally with every individual exploring his or her opinions and interests and then, linking up with this, winning her or him for the cause of the oppressed. Then, on election day itself, what a great variety of tasks await women! They must fetch the slow old voter from his easy chair at home, many an irresponsible young one from the saloon; they must stand in front of workshops and factories to urge everyone coming out to fulfill his duty as a voter. If a woman believes that a man prefers to go home rather than to the polling place, she ought to go with him up to the door so that he learns to be ashamed, he, the citizen put to shame by a disfranchised woman. If each woman in the city and the countryside in this way does her duty, the party's victory on election day will be in part the consequence of her efforts.

The people's well-being is at stake more than ever before. Shame on the female who in cowardice or laziness withdraws! The sobs of starving children, the curses of exploited and oppressed humanity will embitter her life. Whoever bears the scars of battle on his body as symbols of victory will pass by her unmarked body with contempt. That applies not only for just one day of triumph or defeat: every single woman is guilty if the final victory of our cause is delayed but by a short span of time. Of course, our cause demands sacrifice from us; whoever follows the red flag does not do it for the sake of a short pleasant walk followed inevitably by a merry homecoming. Instead, he is undertaking a lifelong trek through unknown dark territory, he himself burns all the bridges behind him, and there can no longer be any return home.

"A sword will pierce your soul," said the angel of the annunciation to Mary, the mother of Jesus, according to Christian legend. And the same thing will be said to all women who become conscious of the great task they face. It is much easier and much more fun for the girl to sit at home after the day's work or to frolic with her friends in woods and meadows than to follow the calling that lures her to life in all its seriousness, to suffering and to struggle. For the gentle feminine character, it is much more comfortable and pleasant to play with the children at home than to be outside in the political stormwinds; and it is much more conducive to the preservation of health and cheerfulness to stay quietly at home than to expose oneself to the enemies' suspicions and insults and to accept all the sacrifices in personal happiness that our cause demands of us.

What despite everything urges us into battle again and again is not only farsighted maternal love, not only the sight of our child, the thought about his or her future that kills all selfishness in us and resurrects our broken spirit, but also our sense of responsibility. We are the outposts in the engagement; our steadfastness, our courage will determine whether the main body of the troops will follow after us. It is up to us to demonstrate that women's strength is not inferior to that of the men but that, on the contrary, it is destined to supplement it, for only the joint effort of both sexes can lead us to the goal that we expect will totally restructure society: *The Defeat of Capitalism.*

. . . I see a legion of women. They stride with firm steps, heads held high, without weapons. They carry their children on their arms and are unafraid of the stones in their path, of the menacing lances of their enemies flanking them, of the threatening thunder clouds in the sky. Like their sisters in France long ago, they venture forth to conquer the future for their needy nation. But they are not just a few thousands: their procession stretches endlessly; far, far on the horizon new legions appear again and again, millions of apparitions wrapped in the cloak of care. And far away, where a ribbon of brightness edges the sky, they disappear . . . Red as blood the sun's orb rises above the earth. Its first rays guild the heads of the victorious women. They went forth to seek bread for their children, they returned with the royal future in their retinue. Many were mowed down by death as they wandered in the gloom; their gaily laughing children testify to their heroism. They wear white garments and hold palm leaves in their hands.

And now day has broken!

MOTHERS' DUTIES IN
THE ELECTION CAMPAIGN

It is impossible not to notice the ruling classes' fear of women, of their growing interest in issues of public life. Attempts are made in every possible way to persuade them against it. They are preached to incessantly about the exclusively domestic duties of the female sex, and if that no longer does the trick, the poor women must listen to unctuous voices talking about their duties as mothers.

What woman is there whose heart will not throb faster when she hears this? She will gladly sacrifice herself for her children, and she will listen eagerly to the warning voices of those who insistently demand that she sacrifice her very own individuality for the sake of her children, voices that tell her: Don't worry about the world out there; your place is by the cradle, by the cooking stove, by the wash tub; renounce all unfeminine ambition, don't stick your nose into things you do not understand and cannot understand—you owe that to your children!

How many who do not know better find these arguments persuasive! But let us see how much is left of them once we go to the bottom of things with the help of examining actual existing circumstances, and then let us ask ourselves what we really owe our children.

According to job statistics of 14 June 1895, the female population of the German Reich was calculated to comprise 26,361,125 persons. Of these, 6,578,362 are wage earners, which means that 24.96 percent, or one-quarter of all German women depend on their earnings. The magnitude of this figure is even more remarkable once we remember that this almost 26.5 million female residents includes the roughly 8.5 million female children under 14 years of age, who generally are not considered to be wage workers. If we subtract this number, that is, the female

"Mutterpflichten im Wahlkampf," *Die Gleichheit*, 7 (no. 13, 1898).

children, from the number of the total female population, and if we then compare it to the number of women wage workers, we find that not one-quarter but more than one-third of all women (except for children) are wage workers. Since the 1882 professional census their number has risen by more than a million, that is, by 1.5 percent, while the number of male wage workers has grown by no more than 0.65 percent. In order to see the root cause behind this displacement of male wage work and the related increase in female labor, all we need to do is to examine a few figures from the professional statistics for 1895. There, for instance, we will find the surprising fact that between 1882 and 1895 female laborers in agriculture increased by 218,245, while male laborers decreased by 162,049. Thus in the line of work where wages are the lowest and the work the hardest, where the workers have no right to unionize and where legal protection hardly exists, there the "weaker sex," the "delicate female," is pushed in in ever growing numbers. This is not the result of any desire for emancipation nor the urge to freedom and autonomy; instead it results from harsh, gray, merciless need.

The oppression and exploitation of the female sex become even clearer when we consider its kind of wage labor in comparison to that of men. It turns out that of all independent wage workers about one-quarter are women, but of wage earners classified as higher service personnel (including technical and commercial administrators and supervisors,) only about one-fourteenth are women. At the same time, females constitute about one-third of lower service personnel such as rural and industrial laborers and family employees. All this shows that women, on whose state of health the future of the human race is largely dependent, are driven by general economic developments into competitive struggle with the men, where in many areas they seem to be the winners but in reality are handicapped and lose out because they are crowded into the poorly paid, subordinate, dead-end work categories as a result of their weakness, their frugality, their modesty, and their altogether lacking or inadequate training. The lowliest slave labor in the service of the rural and industrial barons ruins their bodies already in their early youth.

What is it that has so cruelly etched its grim marks into the pallid, faded, prematurely aged faces of proletarian women? It is not only the misery and torment inflicted upon them in their family life, the children begotten and born under the most unpropitious conditions; on the contrary, the premature loss of their beauty and youthful vigor is to be explained by the lives they have to lead even before marriage. Therefore the woman worker sins not only against her own self but also against her future children if she does not exert every ounce of her energy in the fight, jointly with her sisters, for better work conditions. When the great domestic and foreign policy issues are being discussed, she has no right to stand aside and say those are not my concerns. It is very much her concern whether bread or meat prices rise, wages are cut, work hours are increased, or whether the influence and the power of the workers' party grow sufficiently to bring about improvements in the life of the proletariat instead of deterioration. Once the young woman worker eats an adequate diet, once she no longer needs to overexpend her physical energies, once she has the leisure to enjoy life and to educate her mind, then all that benefits not only her but also is an essential precondition for enabling her someday to be a mother of children who are alert and strong, physically and intellectually healthy.

Therefore do not lead dream lives, girls! Wake up! Look around you with open eyes and participate in your brothers' and sisters' fight for emancipation. You owe that not only to yourselves but also to the coming generation whose mothers you will be.

Once the working woman enters matrimony, the husband, according to the ideals of the good old times, is supposed to be the family's provider, while the wife, to quote Schiller, "wisely administers the concerns of the household." In actual fact things shape up quite differently. Both husband and wife go off to their wage work, both of them contribute their earnings for family maintenance; the German home so celebrated in lyric poetry has often degenerated into a mere sleeping quarter.

Once again the census of professions furnishes evidence. While the number of women wage workers rose by 1.5 percent since 1882, as we have seen, we find that it increased by 3 percent among married women. In Germany 1,057,653 wives must support themselves through the labor of their hands, and here it must be stressed emphatically that this large number includes only those for whom wage work is their principal activity. In other words, all those wives and mothers are not included who engage in work as a side activity, as for instance those who sew, embroider, or wash at home or in some other fashion try to earn some extra money. There must surely be hundreds of thousands of them, and their condition often is by far the worst because it is totally outside all control and is not covered by any legal protection.

As long as the woman is without children, her lot is neither better nor worse than that of her unmarried female colleague at work, because what is generally understood by the term "marital life" exists for her almost only in the physical sense. From the moment, however, that a child is expected, her conditions of work and life do most grievous damage to the budding life. Let us make no bones about the cruelty of the fact that it is precisely the children facing lives of poverty and painful struggle for their daily bread who are born with the very lowest measure of physical energy and mental alertness, whereas common sense tells us that everything ought to be done to render them especially capable for the struggle they will have to wage. While 30.5 percent of proletarian children die in their infancy, only 8.9 percent of their age mates in the upper classes die!

But it is not only the lack of care, rest, and adequate diet for pregnant women that dooms the children of the poor to die even before they are born. Once they are born, the care and nutrition, which strengthens and saves the weakly children of rich people, is so inadequate that as a consequence the proletarian babies die or survive weak and sick for the rest of their lives. The general fate of the little creatures is terrible, but even here we find gradations of misery: those born in wedlock are comparatively better off. Their mothers do not have to go through the torments of shame and despair that unmarried mothers must suffer, who include many hapless victims of irresponsibility and seduction. In 1895 in the German Reich 176,271 illegitimate births were recorded. How much suffering is concealed behind this figure! Under the same circumstances we treat animals better than we treat unwed mothers; and their children, who know nothing of guilt, are treated like criminals.

In the face of all this misery, what have society and government done so far?

The law of trades in the German Reich prescribes a work furlough of six weeks for women who have given birth. Their health insurance supports them during this time in an amount up to 75 percent of the daily wage standard for that locality. However, only the workers in industrial trades are subject to compulsory health insurance, and each local government is free to decide whether or not to include those working in cottage industries or agricultural labor in the insurance scheme. Hence countless poor women in childbed cannot claim support. Hence as soon as they stand on their feet again they have to go back to work and must leave their infant in someone's care which in fact in most cases is totally inadequate. But because the legal benefits for workers who have given birth is inadequate, even those who receive them are in a very sad situation most of the time. What good does it do them that they do not lose all of their personal earnings as long as in their wretched home, possibly surrounded by a whole number of small children, they lack everything that is essential for the health of mother and child: cleanliness, light, fresh air, a nourishing diet, and good care? To be sure, one often hears about the works of private and religious charity—homes for mothers with new babies, institutions for home care, etc. Yet there is no area where the inadequacies of charitable endeavors have been demonstrated as clearly as here. For in all of Germany there are no more than twelve mother-and-baby shelters with a total number of 180 beds! A truly ridiculous number vis-à-vis the enormous misery—puny, just as the governmental support available to the women is puny. Whoever realizes that will no longer be able to tell the women, be modest in your demands, don't worry about political and social issues. On the contrary, he will get up and shake them out of their apathy and indifference, but not so that they might beg the rich people for more active exercise of their much-touted kindheartedness. The nation's mothers have a sacred right to be attended to and cared for at the time when they give life to a future citizen. But wherever there are rights, charity is an insult.

Mothers, learn to recognize your rights, and once you have recognized them, fight for them!

Of course, we women do not have the power to make our convictions speak through the use of the ballot. The government in its paternal solicitude has declared us to be the equals of minors, of the insane, and of criminals. Nonetheless we are able to make our influence felt; with the strength of our convictions and the fire of our enthusiasm we can drive our brothers, our husbands, and especially our sons, forward instead of retaining them through timidity or ignorance. In speech and in print we can support those representatives of our people who are our spokesmen in the legislative assemblies.

It casts a sorry light on a community if misery and poverty in it are so great that an enormous percentage of its female members gives birth to its children amidst worry and wretchedness; but it may be an even more significant indicator of its low level of civilization that it offers the most inadequate intellectual nourishment, and under the most unpropitious conditions, to those of its growing citizens who are least blessed with the means for a good life. It is your children, women of the proletariat, for whom the worst is good enough. Do you want to take that silently? Do you want to persuade yourselves that that is none of your concern?!

Does it not often almost break your hearts, you mothers, when you see the burning eagerness with which your child is studying and learning, and the way he or she devours the contents of every book that becomes available—and then you hear that your rich landlord's son, who with the help of tutors was painfully squeezed through his exams, is now attending the university where he gets drunk and stuffs himself, while your son leads a sad existence, performing mindless labor as apprentice to some harsh master, an unquenched yearning in his heart, and his intellectual potential lying fallow?

Clear the road for our children! That must be our slogan. With this slogan we must join in this year's election campaign. The people have a powerful weapon to assert its will: the people's representatives in parliament. Into that chamber, women, we want to send our spokesmen, too. And with the help of our slogan we want to tell ourselves clearly from the very beginning what demands they have to make on our behalf. We have seen how lack of protection for the expectant mother damages the health even of the unborn child. Therefore we want to have the work furlough for the woman giving birth extended from six to eight weeks, with the provision that all wage work by pregnant women should stop two weeks before delivery. In connection with this we demand that health insurance funds be obliged to pay women on pregnancy furlough support that is equivalent to their full wage.

If we attain this we will have attained a great deal. Yet our children's martyrdom will not be ended by this. The labor statistics for 1895 and an investigation by the German Teachers' Association have lifted the veil that was concealing this martyrdom in all its stations of the cross. As is well known, our worker protection laws have banned children from working in factories. Nonetheless, according to trade inspectors reports, 988 children are still working there. But how tiny appears this figure in the light of the findings of labor statistics, according to which in Germany a total of 214,954 children under 14, among them 32,398 who are not yet 12, are working for wages. Moreover, this figure includes only those for whom wage labor or domestic service is the principal occupation. Among them we find children employed in brick works and mechanics' shops, in the extraction of ore, coal, and lignite, indeed even in stone quarries. Even in federal and local government they are employed. The data gathered by the German Teachers' Association complement the government labor statistics in that they also report about those children for whom wage work is not the principal occupation, that is, they work on the side or temporarily. According to these data, about 10 percent of all school age children, that is 800,000 juveniles, are wage workers!

In this best of all possible world of ours poverty is a crime. Whoever is poor gets pushed around in the world. Whoever is poor, so it is thought, can be insulted in word and deed with impunity. Whoever is poor will be treated with mistrust from the start, as if he had already committed a crime. But among all the consequences of poverty nothing is as sad as the misery of the children. Not only are they being disgracefully cheated out of their youth, but everything good and great in them is systematically nipped in the bud. Even the little intellectual nourishment offered in the elementary school is something that a tired, hungry child is incapable of grasping. Hence the least we can demand is that the child be given an adequate meal before school. In several cities, among them Dresden and Breslau, some charitable organizations have already set themselves this task; and in Dresen it was discovered that 3,400 school children came to school hungry! In Berlin the corresponding figure is no less than 12,000! But we do not want to rely on charity, which always turns out to be insufficient and where religious considerations, pious cant, and toadyism play such great roles. We do not want to see our children deprived of their sense of honor and self-respect and trained to be beggars. We demand that the children's hunger be stilled from the till that the taxpayers so amply fill, and we further demand that a federal law forbid any and all wage work on the part of school age children. Yet such a law would remain without effect unless it were linked to another law that would extend the trades law and the trades inspectorate to cottage industry, work at home, commerce, communications, and agriculture, together with the employment of female trade inspectors.

But the most important reform that women have to demand of the federal lawmakers is that old demand under which workers of all the world have united—the eight-hour day. Or is there anyone among you women who would assert that from the point of view of their children it is unimportant whether she slaves in the factory for eleven or eight hours, whether she has to sit in front of the sewing machine in the sweat shop for twelve, fourteen, or even more hours, or whether she can get up and go home after eight hours? Of the physical and moral ruination of our children one of the chief culprits is the long time the mothers work.

Of course, it is no easy thing for you proletarian women to participate vigorously in the entire vast machinery of political life. Your minds lack early schooling, you have no time, and your energies have been spent prematurely through hard work. In particular you lack citizen's rights! You are permitted to slave and toil like men and even worse than they; you are allowed to pay taxes in vast amounts and work your fingers to the bone in the service of capitalism; with regard to duties you are included in the laws of the land, but with regard to rights you are excluded.

For that reason the struggle we ask you to wage is particularly difficult. But there is one magic charm which makes it easier, which overcomes all obstacles, which makes you strong and invincible: maternal love. Go then and agitate, spread enlightenment, be active within the narrow circle of your family, your friends, your comrades at work. Let no one consider herself too lowly for her energies to be unimportant and unnecessary in the struggle. In this form it is no more than a makeshift expedient for women. But it must also demonstrate that the women of the proletariat are politically mature. In the midst of the hottest battles of class warfare, proletarian women must never forget to demand the most effective means for winning their liberation—the right to vote.

Only one party has recognized women's equality and is fighting without cease for their equal legal and political status. That party is the bitterest enemy of the ruling classes, and from every corner the armed might of church and state is being mobilized against it. There may be some foolish and timid women who tremble in the face of this. But once they have recognized that only the Social-Democratic movement is the party of the oppressed, the unfortunate, and the poor, be they great or small, then their fear will dissipate.

Women, your maternal duties call you to battle. Look at the endless crowds of pale starving children, how they stretch out their arms toward you, how they whimper and weep, how their eyes look with longing toward the redeeming light of a sun that shines for them as well!

Do not listen to the blandishments of false friends. When they pretend to be coming to you in the name of religion, then refer them to the words in that book which they allege is holy to them, and where it is written: Whoever offends one of the least deserves the fires of hell. And when they threaten you with rifles and sabers, be not afraid, for your own sons will not take up arms against you. No pleas nor threats shall cause you to desert the flag that is to flutter in front of your children on their march into the land of their redemption! The inexhaustible source of your energies should be, not selfishness, not ambition, but maternal duty!

INTRODUCTION TO
MOTHERHOOD

The struggle of the female sex for emancipation did not start in identical ways in the different classical countries of the women's movement.

In England, where parliamentarism had very early educated the people politically, among women, too, political interests awakened first and made them demand political rights. The economic struggle of redundant bourgeois daughters for the opening-up of higher professions began only later, when they could no longer without exception be occupied and fed, and when matrimony no longer offered support for all of them.

In North America also, where women were in the minority from the very beginning of European immigration and therefore the competitive struggle against the men not only was absent, but their cooperation in the shaping of political life automatically became a necessity, it was political rights which they claimed at first. And in the exciting battles of the French Revolution, the women of France, if only here and there, chimed in with the demand made by Olympe de Gouges that if they were asked to put their heads under the guillotine for political reasons, they should also have the right to participate in the shaping of the political system.

Things were quite different in Germany and Austria. How could the women have developed political interest when the whole nation was being kept in political dependency? Here it was need alone which engendered the women's movement; struggles for the right to higher education and open access to the higher professions not only constitute its first beginning but also for a long time maintained themselves as its specific contents.

There is only one point in which the historical development of the

"Einführung," in Adele Schreiber, ed., *Mutterschaft* (München: Albert Langen Verlag, 1912).

women's movement in all civilized countries shows one and the same image: The proletarian woman everywhere was the last one to awaken to self-consciousness. Having for a long time fought shoulder to shoulder with the man in the struggle for existence, she had no need to win herself entry into professional work. She did not have to defend her "right to work" theoretically. Her bitter need, on the one side, the capitalists' greed, on the other, confounded all the beautiful tirades about the "protection of femininity" and about "women's one and only calling" with which the philistines used to counter the demands of the bourgeois women's movement. The proletarian woman had long ago climbed up the mountain peak which the others were still trying to reach. But was it the sun of freedom that shone upon her up there?

To be sure, she was allowed to work like a man, no gallant knight of womanhood restrained her; even the coal mines were open to her. She had equality. And with this she was drawn into the men's struggle for better wages and work conditions; her interest for legislation awakened because laws now ruled her life as well like iron fate; she entered the political arena, not as a feminist but as companion of her male comrades at work. That she needed to demand rights and protection as a woman was something of which she became aware only quite late.

This development, almost the opposite of that of the bourgeois women's movement, explains not only the total lack of understanding but also the open hostility with which at first the women workers' movement confronted the emancipation fight of the women's liberation movement.

Only gradually did both movements come close to a stage of joint development, from which the really major problems of the women's question become visible and a new comprehensive women's movement— even if it should remain separate in its organizational forms—will have to emerge.

That the doors to universities and paraliaments can be opened for women has long been demonstrated theoretically. The eventual defini- tive conquest of all academic professions as well as women's right to vote is only a question of time. But while feminists in earlier years believed the political equality of the sexes to be more or less the final goal, from the attainment of which some visionaries expected something like the mil- lennium, all sensible people know today that it is by no means identical with the solution of the women's question.

If, because of changes in economic and social conditions, the task up to now was to achieve women's economic, legal, and political equality with men, then we are now beginning to face the great problem, how to reconcile this equality with the differentiation of the sexes.

Once the woman entered public life, she encountered professional and work conditions that necessarily were attuned to the man's needs and capabilities. However much the increasing demands of his profession may condemn him to the narrowness of specialization and may repress his individuality, his sex life remained unrestrained. It is quite different for the woman: She is able to be successful in the struggle for existence, which in most cases is simultaneously a competitive struggle with the man, only by setting aside her natural sexual needs.

Since the main problem in the bourgeois women's movement for a long time was to provide remunerative work for unmarried daughters without support, we can now understand its one-sidedness and its total lack of comprehension of the real problem.

Within the proletariat, it is the mother who least of all can escape the misery; the more children she bears, hence the more necessary she is to her family, the more she sees herself compelled to go out for a job. In most recent times, the same compulsion has often risen for the woman from the bourgeois middle class. But to this is added another problem which has transformed the original old-maid question into a women's question also for her: The young girl's purely economic need for independence has turned into the woman's intellectual need. She demands activity for her various energies, she demands her own development as an individual; and on the moral high point of her internal growth she wants autonomy, because she is ashamed of the old form of matrimony which, for the woman, degraded the relation between the sexes to a question of support.

Now the monstrous conflict between profession and motherhood begins for her as well. For all the areas of masculine work which she invades, and which demand all her time and all her strength, it seems insoluble. The triple work load—as wage earner, housewife, and mother—to which the proletarian woman sacrifices her best energies early in life, now rests on her shoulders almost as heavily. The natural consequences of this are, first, the physical and psychological neglect of the children and, second, the conscious limitation of the number of children.

And so the problems that have been stirred up by the women's movement become more and more profound and comprehensive: The pros and cons of Malthusianism, racial hygiene, and child rearing broaden the mere women's question into a question concerning all humanity; and just as the liberation of the female sex from being tied to the home—a liberation, it must be emphasized over and over again, that is not arbitrary but is determined by economic and social developments—shakes the very foundations of family life, so it also has a restructuring effect on the relations between men and women. The old form of marriage, its peace and its duration, depended, first, on the support it provided for the woman and, second, on the subordination of the wife to the husband. The modern woman's participation in public life· through her professional work and through her political interest awakened by it has rendered her independent not only externally but also internally. She confronts the man more critically, her sexual needs can no more be reduced to one single simple formula, she has torn the chains of outer and inner dependence which yesteryear's matrimony imposed on her. What now?

The women's movement started so harmlessly; its pioneers never tired to assure us that they would not touch any institution hallowed by tradition and custom, and it turns out to be revolutionary in the profoundest sense of the word. And, instead of arriving at its final goal, once its first demands—the economic, legal, and political equality of the woman—have been fulfilled, it will only then begin to face its greatest task. On its solution will depend not only the future of women but the future of the human race.

In this sense, the present work is a book of the new women's movement. Not that anyone is so arrogant as to claim to have solved any one of the problems touched in it. But it is already a humanitarian deed to help mitigate its temporary hardships and to formulate them clearly. Something that up to now the organized women's movement approached only timidly leads to the road to their solution.

III.

Femininity, Sexuality, Marriage, and Love

In 1901 Lily Braun published a major work of scholarship, *Die Frauenfrage,* that after a sketchy survey of women's history provided a broad and comprehensive overview about women in the world of work. At the time the book came out Braun announced that it was but the first of two volumes; the second volume would deal with cultural and psychological aspects of women's lives. But volume two was never published, indeed never written. Nonetheless Braun in the next (and last) fifteen years of her life wrote voluminously on the subjects that volume two would have treated. All her works of fiction, her fictionalized autobiography, and countless articles deal with the problems of being female. This section offers a sampling of her pronouncements on the theme of femininity and female self-consciousness. Her earliest articles on this subject, not included in this selection, explored German, Scandinavian, and English works of fiction that tried to portray the "new woman" who was at that time being projected by the bourgeois feminist movement; one article of this period explored the ways in which the newly developing feminine self-consciousness expressed itself in women's poetry.

The very long article "The Female Mind," which constitutes the center of this section, is the product of a later decade. Probably written around 1912, it constitutes one of the capstones of Braun's feminist theory and should be regarded as the most important clue to what volume two of *Die Frauenfrage* would have contained. In this article she offers a survey of women's contribution to arts and letters from ancient times to the present. Her aim here is to demonstrate that the creative talents inherent in women are able to come to the fore and flourish only when the entire personality of the woman is given free rein; and since the free and spontaneous exercise of our sexuality is an essential element of our being human, sexual freedom is an indispensable precondition for promoting female creativity. Braun further suggests that the liberation of creative potentials in women is essential for the survival of the human species, since women have special and vital contributions to make. She ends her article with a vision of a feminized world in which feminine sensibility inseminates and humanizes a world sick with the macho spirit.

Some years earlier she had examined the alienation of sexuality, especially women's sexuality, in a series of articles dealing with Christian morality and the institution of marriage. Here too, although with reservations, she had advocated sexual emancipation. Christian morality she denounced as a sin against nature, the bourgeois family as an intolerable and irremediable institution. She recognized productive work as a liberating and revolutionary force and identified the combination of meaningful careers with love relationships and motherhood as the deepest problem facing us, a problem not solvable either within the present family structure or within capitalist society. What I have included here is but a small sampling of several passionate articles she wrote on the subjects of love and marriage.

Among the most controversial opinions Braun voiced were those regarding prostitution. In her youth she repeatedly expressed a certain envy of prostitutes: They were at least exercising their sexuality, while a woman living in conformity with prevailing conventions was condemned to celibacy until at last she became the mate of a man chosen by her parents for reasons unrelated to love, affection, or sexual attraction. More than once in late years she expressed the opinion that it was sexual much more than economic need that drove women into prostitution, although she was not, of course, unaware of the economic pressures that often led women to choose this wretched and perilous profession.

In "The Female Mind" and in lectures series she used to give as well as in some of her works of fiction (the opera libretto, *Madeleine Guimard,* and the novel *Die Liebesbriefe der Marquise*) she added to this that the really creative periods in history have been those in which sexuality was liberated and great courtesans played major roles in public life. Nonetheless she was aware that in her own society the prostitute was one of the most deplorable victims, an object of contempt and self-contempt. Prostitution was a recognized and licenced profession in Wilhelmine Germany, while unlicenced work of that kind was outlawed. Under such a system the sexual worker was subject to gross exploitation, degradation, harassment by the authorities, and dangers to her health.

From the beginning of her activities as a publicist, Braun expressed concern for the women practicing this profession. She agitated for the abolition of official licencing and for the decriminalization of sexual work; she urged prostitutes to organize and demanded that the Marxist movement support them in this.

The article included here is a response to an antipornography campaign launched by a group of conservative women. It denounces the campaign as an attempt to censor art and literature, suggests that prostitution and venereal disease are the result of an unhealthy repressive attitude toward sex, and asserts that a positive attitude toward sexuality and early sex education are needed to combat the twin menaces of prostitution and venereal disease.

THE DETHRONING OF LOVE

The history of love is still waiting for its historian. We have to destill it out of economic and cultural history, out of the history of marriage and prostitution, literature and religion. In doing so, we must not confuse its outer forms, essentially conditioned by purely economic causes—as proven by the diverse forms of matrimony and prostitution—with its inner evaluation and its significance for our sexual and emotional life, which are subject to the influence of moral and religious conceptions. That becomes most clear when we get to know the Heathen and Christian periods of its development: the one as an era of the cult of love—when the temples of Isis, Myrrha, Astarte, and Venus would gather the priests and the faithful, when Nature was the diety who revealed to humans love as the fountain and the principle of all life—and the other as the era of its banishment—when churches reared their domes over the temple ruins, when the condemnation of the "pleasures of the flesh" branded love as something sinful and satanic, and when asceticism created saints. The religion of love has pushed Love from her throne and has thereby sinned against the laws of nature. Whatever contributions Christianity made to humanity in such virtues as self-denial, neighborly love, compassion, and mercy, they cannot compensate for what it took away. Into a "vessel of sin" the female turned, for, says Saint Paul, the woman, not the man, was tempted and "hath introduced transgression." Tertullian condemned matrimony as a vice and the woman for "providing entry to the devil," while canon law declares that the woman entices the man to sin and therefore, as punishment, must be his servant. In logical consequence of this chain of thought, virtue became synonymous with chastity. Sexual intercourse between male and female became sinful and was cleansed of sin only when the blessings of the church hallowed the couple. The madonna cult, too, is closely connected with all the life-

"Die Entthronung der Liebe," *Neue Gesellschaft*, 1 (no. 22, 1905).

denying and nature-despising content of Christianity: for it is no mother cult pure and simple, but a cult of the *virginal* mother. The sin of human conception was not supposed to stick to the birth of the world's redeemer.

Crimes avoid the light of day; vice is ashamed of itself and flees into the dark, pulling the cloak of hypocrisy over itself. So it happened to Love when Christianity drove her from her heathen marble temple, sun-warmed and bright, and branded her as sin; so also was done to Beauty, who sires Love. The glistening images of the Gods disappeared before the ascetic's body of the crucified one covered with wounds; down to the Lex Heinze* morality of our days they are covered with fig leaves, persecuted, and damned. None of the believers' souls here is aware of the blasphemy implied in the condemnation of the human body as it issued from the hand of the creator. Naked the Greek boys and girls grew up together in the time when Athens flourished; Sparta's youth practiced running and tossing games in common. The segregation of the sexes, the anxious veiling of bodies from early youth, are consequences of Christian notions of education: sex, being sinful, must hide; love, being sinful, must not be aroused. The classical art of education aimed for the development of bodily strength and the cultivation of beauty. The large mass of good Christians, whose ancestors whipped and maimed themselves for the greater glory of God, still today scorn the joy in our body, and the cultivation of beauty is, in the eyes of the great majority, fit only for the priestesses of purchasable love. A characteristic instance is that legend about a Catholic saint which tells about the pious girls whose "sinful and seductive" beauty was mercifully taken from them after earnest prayer!

We call ours the era of natural science; but even it has been defeated by the Christian denial of nature: The learning child receives explanations and plastic demonstrations of the human body in all its parts—but as a totally sexless one. Only that child is considered innocent and pure whose mother either told lies continually, from the fairy tale about the stork to the mystification of the greatest and holiest laws of nature, or at least taught the child to lie and to pretend with the warning that "these" are matters one does not discuss and must not know anything about. And so it happens that even the love between father and mother, to which the child owes its existence, appears, at the moment of recognition, as something filthy and disgusting; and so those children are reared who lewdly seek to glimpse the secret and the hidden, lasciviously inflame

*Lex Heinze was an antipornography law passed in the mid-1890s.

their fantasies, and tell cynical jokes in the dark corners of the class-room. Moreover, in this rotten air of hypocrisy grow those lonely, bashful souls who are ashamed of their bodies and their mysterious, in-comprehensible appetites, whom their supposed sinfulness oppresses, robbing them of all joy.

What follows the education received in school and at home is a life dominated by hunger and love. The young man who never learned to venerate Love as a goddess no longer is hurt when he encounters her in the prisoner's garb of the street hooker; the puritanical Christian religion was forced to tolerate the fact that the safety valve of prostitution remained open for the muck which it helped to stir up. Let no one argue that the church is innocent because prostitution was known long before this in the heathen world and because it is nourished by economic conditions—financial need on one side, the impossibility of early mar-riage, on the other; for we know that heathendom did not know the *contempt* we have for the whore and that in fact there was prostitution sanctioned by religion. It was only the Christian religion, which taught us to regard sexual activity as contemptuous, that placed the courtesan among criminals and created that entire system of persecution which chains the "fallen women" to her "profession" for the rest of her life. In this it has rendered faithful yeoman service to the capitalist economic order with its degradation of the poor. It is not always the best young men, it is often only the cautious ones who, instead of availing them-selves of prostitution, tie some poor trusting girl to themselves for a shorter or longer time, only to make her one more statistic in the official roster of streetwalkers once their position and income make it necessary and possible for them to "rearrange" their lives by marriage to a woman of their own class. For note carefully: Our Christian morality judges the woman's surrender not by the absence or presence of love, but by the absence or presence of governmental and ecclesiastical certification; in the one case, the female is the fallen woman and is expelled from "good" society; in the other, she is a reputable spouse!

The sanctimoniousness of our morality, which makes judgments on the basis of the crudest external indicators, becomes fully apparent only when we realize that, indeed, it demands premarital celibacy also of the man but in fact closes its eyes against his disobedience, which is easily hidden, and condemns only the female whose child bears living witness to her violation of the command for abstinence. It is that same rotten morality that tolerates prostitution and indeed makes it into a profession licenced by the government, even while persecuting the prostitute as if she were a criminal.

From all this we see that when a woman acts in accordance with her natural sexuality, it can turn into a tragic disaster for her, while the man emerges from the adventures of his sex life an untouched citizen worthy of all dignities. But the life of the young woman, as regards her need for love and its fulfillment, has an even more tragic side, much more disastrous in its consequences, compared to which the man's life offers nothing similar: the enforced self-denial. They have always preached to women about the sinfulness of the natural urge, have always asserted that lack of desire in this matter was something inborn, so that every emergence of sexual desire appeared abnormal and immoral. The decent young woman is allowed to know love only in the form of matrimony; hundreds of thousands therefore are forced to kill their sexuality. Today, when the women's movement has loosened the tongues of the female sex, we notice more and more the reaction to this artificial repression. Countless statements by women in prose and poetry testify that the sexual needs of the female are in no wise weaker by nature than those of the male, and that the contrary is nothing else than a phenomenon of degeneration caused by emotional and physical crippling. The good bourgeois male accuses of shamelessness those women who dare talk about this most gruesome slavery oppressing their sex, and he shelves their books among his pornographic literature, to be read in private for exquisite sensual arousal. Meanwhile the large mass of love-starved, unhappy women, who often do not even know themselves what the cause of their suffering is, are not yet being reached by their call to rebellion. But it will and must get to them. The right to work, the right to (participation in) public activity mean little for the liberation of woman and for the full flourishing of her personality as long as she has not fought for, and won, the right to love. For the healthy woman needs love no less than the man. After all, for her, her sex life is of far more trenchant importance, for, as the precondition of motherhood, it constitutes not only the most important physical but also the chief emotional contents of her life.

All too often today we see respectable bourgeois daughters in full consciousness envy the poor servant girl or seamstress who at least has experienced a bit of love in an hour's ecstasy. Some of them, idle at home, wait in vain for a man; others seek to smother their yearning in professional work. All of them are branded with the stigma of the crime against nature: hysteria, melancholy, neuroses, masturbation, and finally that sorry surrogate of lesbian love which is spreading so terribly among the lonely and which in the vast majority of cases is not likely to have sprung from an innate contrary sexuality. Countless women have had to repress their young strong love because they lack a dowry for a household fit for their social class, or else a lengthy engagement with all its secret excitement and its much-admired celibate faithfulness eats at her strength and cheats her and her man of the best in life.

Without doubt there is profound meaning in that ridicule-cum-contempt to which popular wisdom subjects the "old maids": the instinctive recognition that a woman who cannot follow her sexual destiny must become crippled in an important part of her being is expressed in this. People here are as unjust as kids who jeer at a hunchback. They should bemoan a tragic fate instead of mocking it. Let us not forget the following: when we compare the respective accomplishments of the two sexes, the comparison almost always is unfavorable to women. The cause of this is to be sought not merely in poor education and intellectual neglect, but specifically in the area of their repressed sexual life. Love gives wings to the man's intellect. It awakens his powers and spurs him on to higher achievements. How little heroism and artistic mastery there would be in the world without it! But the woman must do without it either entirely or much too long, unless some sorry remnant of love offered to her in marriage makes her thirst even more burning.

Oh, incalculable are the victims of lovelessness; clad in bright mourning cloaks, the victims of love face their dark and somber crowd.

We have accustomed ourselves to regard economic need as the root cause of prostitution, and there is no doubt we are right in this, even though Lombroso and other scholars have recently tried to explain it, on the basis of rather inadequate data, more as the result of inborn drives or irresponsibility. But even though we will have to go on regarding social conditions as the root cause of purchasable love, we will nonetheless have to revise our theory in one specific direction. For surely it is only in exceptional cases that the young woman, from the very beginning, sells her body to the first comer as commercially as she sells her labor power out of economic need. The first "fall"—this nice word for the fulfillment of a woman's sexual destiny, which in reality is *ascent* to the dignity of motherhood, we also owe to the church—is almost everywhere submission out of love or forcible seduction. Economic need leads to prostitution only because of our social morality slams the doors to all other professions in the faces of girls who became women without going through church and City Hall and, moreover, robs them of their children, those firmest moral supports of female life. They are not sinners because they loved, but we who condemn them to immorality are.

Between these two female worlds there are those who have landed in the port of marriage. Here we take a deep breath; here Love has not been dethroned, here we find her again in all her purity. Here Christian morality has had only a hallowing, not a desanctifying, effect! Or has it? Let us take a closer look: history teaches us that marriage in its different forms was a union of man and woman for economic ends. If a man desired to create a homestead, he needed the housewife; if he wanted natural heirs for his possessions, faithful comrades in arms for their defense, he needed a legitimate spouse. This economic aim of marriage is quite clearly expressed in the observation of class differences in the contracting of marriages; the difference between a highborn and a lowborn woman is known still today in princely houses. And how little love and marriage were connected among the heathens is demonstrated by the nonchalance with which the Greek man sought satisfaction of his erotic needs with the courtesan. Christianity, which had to adjust to economic conditions, has not succeeded in changing much of this, not even by elevating matrimony to a sacrament.

Every animal mates on the basis of mutual attraction and reproduces itself on the basis of instinctual selective breeding. The human animal, however, looks for a "good match," and it is not primarily moral corruption that compels him to do this but economic necessity. To maintain a family costs money, and more money the higher the rung of the bourgeois ladder to heaven on which the individual is standing. For this reason the poor girl with a magnificent body and longing eyes becomes a wall flower, while the degenerate daughter of the tycoon will be the mother of the next generation. And how many women have been prostituted to the husband by relations and friends, by mutual calculation or by a newspaper ad for the female commodity! No social class is exempt from this, for even in the proletariat, where marriage out of affection generally is most frequent, the man looking for a bride often prefers the aging cook with the fat savings account to the poor young working woman, and the girl, in turn, looks out for the man with the highest and most secure position.

But what often is the fate of those who marry out of love? It almost seems as if they are punished for thus violating the general rule! In only too many married couples who believed they could build their happiness on love alone, the difficult struggle for daily bread, the breathless wrestling with that gray ogress, worry, extinguish everything in them that was pure, great, and strong. Concern for the family makes them into climbers, cowards, and ass kissers; it constricts their horizon, smothers their free speech, and hinders their participation as citizens in public affairs, no matter whether as workers they are dependent on the entrepreneurs, as writers on the public and the publisher, or as public officials on the government. Marriage flaws their character as it flaws their lives.

And how many of the little boats of love that ventured out with swelling sails founder on the rocks of marriage instead of dropping anchor in its port! With all her unquenched thirst for life and love, the young woman sinks against the heart of the man for whom marriage is no more than the finishing touch of his life, who expects out of it only peace and quiet—what disappointment, what daily torment for the hungry senses of the woman! Or else in tender love the man draws to his heart a pure girl flower only to encounter frigidity, or even disgust, as a result of the antinatural upbringing that condemns our sexual life. How often in such cases does love turn into hatred and contempt or turns to another object. The variations of the way in which marriage smothers love are numberless, for love is a sensitive plant demanding continual care if it is to thrive. But married people think that once they have the marriage certificate in hand, they are also holding on to love, and then more and more they show themselves to each other in their dressing gowns and slippers. Wherever the wish arises for divorce of a marriage, which deep down ended long ago and in the best case is kept together only by the purely physical routine of everyday life, the wish is suppressed by concern for the children, for economic dependence, for the opinion of the world. This is true particularly in the case of the woman, by law and custom the most disadvantaged marriage partner. And at the grave of these martyrs of matrimony, the priest of the religion of love will say words of praise for the "faithful" wife, the "faithful" husband!

We are at a turning point in the history of Love. The best of our contemporaries are beginning to see that the image of their goddess lies in the dust, and strong arms are stirring to reerect it. Are we strong enough already? Could we already draw blueprints according to which a new generation will be able to build it a new temple?

THE MARRIAGE PROBLEM

When Luther nailed his ninety-five theses on the Wittenberg Castle church, he thought he was propping up the cyclopean walls of the Catholic church, which had begun to crumble in places; he did not know that he was driving a wedge right into it. When Montesquieu wrote his *Esprit des Lois* and Rousseau his *Emile,* they thought they were using the light of their intellects to brighten some dark areas of state and society: They did not know that they were tossing a torch into the entire ramshackle structure. The first carriers of some new developments have only in the rarest cases also been the prophets of its ultimate consequences.

The pioneers of the women's movement, too, at first envisaged no more than reforms on behalf of the female sex: Legal, economic, social, and moral ones. Only their antagonists, their enemy instincts sharpened by fear of danger to their ancient and treasured privileges, soon became aware that in this area too any reform carried out consistently inevitably turns into revolution. Maintenance of marriage and the family! That is the slogan with which they confront the women's movement, even though the other side keeps assuring them that they themselves only wish to defend and strengthen marriage and the family, that they are far from preaching "subversion," that conservation and construction are their only concerns.

What precisely is it that is to be defended and that supposedly is endangered? Austrian law defines matrimony as the legal union of two people of opposite sex for the purpose of procreation and mutual support; the union of man, woman, and child in the common home, that is the family—the primary cell of society, according to ancient natural law. For the German mind, there is no better description of the two than that in Schiller's *Ode on the Bell:* The man as the provider, as fighter in "hostile

"Das Problem der Ehe," *Neue Gesellschaft,* 1 (no. 10, 1905).

life," the woman as maintainer and keeper of the domestic hearth—a clear division of labor, necessarily given in its time, whose ideological consequence was the division of interests and the total subordination of the woman to the man. Whatever material or intellectual concerns went beyond the four walls of the home belonged to the man, was ruled and understood by him. The woman, whose experiences and activities filled the house completely, bowed to his judgment as a matter of course, while he left her in complete control over her world. On this rested the happiness and especially the peace of the marriage: There was no possibility for friction, no occasion for clashes of interests. The man would return to his home as into a haven of calm; being with his life partner was for him also an intellectual resting.

But the external frame of marriage gradually has shifted, the woman's circle of activities within the house has shrunk; economic need, on the one hand, inner emptiness, on the other, drive her, too, into "hostile life." She too must "work and strive and plant and create." With the widening of the field of work the intellectual horizon widens as well. The foes of the women's movement are entirely right: Every time a new women's secondary school is founded, new professions open up for women, and public rights are extended to the female sex, the old-style marriage is threatened dangerously, a marriage that its defenders regard as marriage pure and simple, that is, the only morally defensible form of the relation between the sexes.

Whatever strengthens our thinking power and our will leads to the development of autonomous personalities. But, once the female has turned into a human being, that is, an individual personality, with views, judgments and life goals of her own, then she has been spoiled for the average marriage. And the conflict between the traditional economic dependence on the man and her new intellectual independence is inevitable. Even if often it can be covered by the rosy veils of love, or prevented from erupting by her capacity for endurance, life together can separate people more sharply than any physical separation can. Many friendships have been wrecked by it, when they involved two autonomous personalities. The same thing is true when marriage, according to its blind reformers (who often desperately try to be blind), will have attained its ideal form—that of a friendship.

Nothing in the world is covered so carefully as matrimony's abysses of suffering; faithlessness and adultery are not always the greatest disasters— often they can have a liberating effect. Our crime statistics report nothing about the victimizations, the moral and intellectual suicides, of countless women; and our divorce procedures, which on the basis of our crude laws have to be conducted in terms of entirely external and brutal arguments, only rarely touch the deep psychological problems. The few who once in a while tell about them are poets with prophetic vision—Ibsen!—women to whom the god of unhappiness gave the voice to tell their sufferings, and women's faces, into whose features life has deeply etched itself. How many girls passed by us intelligent, cheerful, proud, and free, offering the guarantee of brightest development; we see them again as women, tired, resigned, bored, joyless—they have sacrificed their own lives to the dead idol of matrimony and now bear and rear children! They have learned quite well that matrimonial peace—and within a marriage peace is a blessing even if it has nothing at all to do with genuine happiness—depends on the subordination of one partner to the other, hence, according to tradition, of the woman to the man. But they have not realized that this subordination must be totally natural and self-evident if it is to make both partners happy.

The marriage reformers have cooked up their own marvelous theory. They argue: Precisely the union of two equal, intellectually and morally mature people is the happiest, nicest, and most enduring. The man will see in the woman no longer merely his lover and the mother of his children but a comrade, a friend, who shares and furthers his interests. Family life will thus renew itself. For the man no longer needs to pursue intellectual stimulation and interchange outside the house. And yet, all these beautiful arguments rest on false premises: As if sensual instinct were identical with intellectual understanding! There is no guarantee that two intellectually gifted individuals who want each other in ardent love will harmonize in all the fine stirrings of their emotional and intellectual lives—stirrings which are the more differentiated the higher the development of each individual. A normal, healthy human being, however, who is in love will not make the union with the lover dependent on an examination in philosophy, politics, and ethics. If nonetheless there happens to be harmonious agreement, who will guarantee, especially in the case of the best people, that it will always remain that way without one of the partners doing violence to her/himself? And who can tell that, despite intellectual agreement, their love will not cool or direct itself toward another object? For amorous emotions and amorous desires, too, have become less uniform, more differentiated and refined: They are no longer satisfied so easily and unconditionally.

The marriage reformers who take for granted that all sexual intercourse between two people, whether within or outside matrimony, is immoral if it is not done on the basis of love—of course, we are in full agreement with them on this—therefore demand the maximal easing of divorce procedures. Their antagonists counter with the assertion that giving in to this demand would make marriage itself illusory.

Are they not right? Can we hide from the realization that, given the heightened possibilities for friction in modern marriages, their long duration would become more and more exceptional? For all the love and all the agreement will not take away the fact that autonomous individuals can feel tormented by being chained to each other day and night through legal compulsion; that the yearning for solitude, for self-absorption, can, at times, totally wipe out the yearning for the partner. In olden times marriage was for the man a safe haven of comfort near a woman who was untouched by the internal and external conflicts of the time and lived only to care for her loved ones. What he finds at home today is a wife who is intellectually his match and who is practicing a profession. He also finds the same nervousness, the same intellectual tensions as outside. For the woman of bygone days, the man coming home was the sole symbol of all external life, the only one from whom she faithfully received the message of the outside world, views and judgments about it. Today his interpretation is no longer gospel for her; she knows life from her own experience, thinks independently, and often overlooks him. To her he is no more the creator of her inner life than she is for him the source of rest and well-being. Since she became a personality in her own right, she can no longer merge with him completely.

Something else still must be added: The more deeply the woman feels, the more autonomously she develops, the higher her conception about the sanctity of the love relationship, the more painfully will the economic chains burden her that keep marriages together more firmly than do city hall and church. She therefore will seek professional work that makes her economically independent from the man; and we know economic developments in general and also the tendencies of the women's movement are promoting this trend.

But with the woman's economic independence the main pillar of marriage collapses, for marriage was primarily an economic union for the purpose of producing legitimate heirs of the father's property: The man acquired, the woman administered; he was the lord, she, the caretaker of the house. For this reason, the enemies of the women's movement instinctively hit the target when they direct their furious hatred against household communes and similar proposals. True, these schemes do no more than dissolve the private household, but they are symptoms of more profound processes of dissolution and are one more stimulus for woman to go into professional work and to make herself independent.

All in all, they promote reforms—economic, legal, moral—and become carriers of the revolution.

The forms of cohabitation of the sexes are subject to laws of development like all other forms of social life, and it would be submitting to gross self-deception if we were to deny the process of dissolution now affecting the institution of marriage. Doubtless the solution of the grave conflicts to which people are exposed particularly in this period of transition would be easier if the courage were there to look things straight in the face. Hundreds of questions then arise: How will life shape itself? What will we sacrifice, what will we gain? And foremost, what happens to the children? There is no prophet who could figure out future developments with mathematical precision, all we can do is to derive possibilities from present developments. That shall be left for later essays.

A MANIFESTO TO
GERMANY'S WOMEN

The mothers of the present have become knowing. Even today, wide circles may still regard the girl's naive ignorance in sexual matters as a necessary precondition of virginal chastity. But even with the best of intentions, the mature woman could no more be kept in blindness and deafness: she knows that the greater percentage of all men has, or has had, venereal disease; she knows that most female illnesses have their origin in this fact. Hence she trembles with fear as she watches her well-protected boy leave his childhood, with fearful anxiety she sees her blooming daughter sink into the arms of the man of her choice. And she would like to continue being their protectress as in olden time, when with loving care she protected the darling's little feet from rocky roads, the tender body from wind and weather; and fighting against a whole world does not seem too difficult for her great love.

Down in Silesia, not far from the borders of that country in which the policeman's nightstick is the symbol of all educational knowledge, the women seem to have had bad experiences too. Fresh and healthy, the son went out to the great university, to return tired, pale, with faded cheeks; gaily laughing, the daughter left the parental home at the side of the man of her choice, to return sick and crying. The pain and the indignation let the mothers forget all their shyness and reticence; they resolved to join forces against the veil that threatened to destroy their children. And so, that manifesto of the Patriotic Women's Association came into being, which today the conservative press has printed, commented upon, and interpreted and exploited in the interests of reactionary politics.

How, ask these women, does one counter "life's increasingly more blatant temptations appearing in words and in pictures"? And they answered:

"Ein Aufruf an Deutschlands Frauen," *Neue Gesellschaft,* 4 (no. 7, 1908).

Here only the strong arm of the government, infused with moral seriousness, can interfere in order to come to the aid of that popular
consciousness which at last is beginning to rebel against all this immorality allegedly serving the purposes of art and against prostitution of all
kind. We do not want to touch the great blessing of civil liberty nor the
unlimited practice of genuine and noble art; but we want to have the
purity of our young people protected against unbridled powers of seduction and temptation aimed only at the ruthless acquisition of money.

The pedagogy of the nursery: Forbid the child those dishes that might
spoil its stomach as long as it is not reasonable enough to be persuaded by
arguments of their harmfulness; we put bars against the windows as long
as the child cannot realize that its bones will break if it were to fall out.
And then they scream for the "strong arm of the government" because
the sons and daughters emerged from the mother's hands so weak that
they are not able to protect themselves.

The mothers' declaration of bankruptcy—that is this manifesto, an
attestation of poverty for the women. Even though they have become
knowing, yet their knowledge has not made them free. Just as in olden
times, when princes' mistresses and ministers' courtesans directed the
public activity of their lords and masters from their salons by pulling
invisible threads, so their politics is nothing but backstairs politics. For
they have turned, not to the nation which lives in a constitutional
monarchy, not to its representatives in parliament who—at least so we
are told—make the laws, but to the Empress, the "mother of the country". What they imagine in their petty and oh-so-clever female logic is
that the wife should influence the husband, the husband his ministers,
the ministers the Reichstag, until the suppression of art, literature, and
science, draping itself in the moralistic white cloak of innocence, is
revealed to be their real aim. Will they then be saved, your sons and
daughters, you German women?

A different manifesto, directed to a different address by different
women, is just now being sent to the press with the request to give it
widest possible publicity. It reads as follows:

> German women: We turn to you in the name of your
> children, in the name of those yet to come. You must
> join together in a mighty league for protection and
> resistance—a league without bylaws, because its
> bylaws are what you learn from life; and without members'
> dues, because your energy be your dues.

An insidious poison threatens to destroy the body of our nation and menaces our children's flourishing bodies and pure souls. Born in misery, often without knowing the father, surrounded by distress, spoiled by bad example, neglected at home and in school, paid starvation wages for heavy labor, young and yet excluded from the happiness of youth, hungry for life and yet cheated by life—in this fashion thousands and many more thousands of our sex turn into whores. Whenever an investigation has been made it turned out that the overwhelming proportion of prostitutes originated in the proletariat, so that it was poverty that compelled them to sell their bodies. Nor has the force of this coercive whip abated. Just in Berlin in the last twenty years the number of prostitutes has increased at twice the rate of the total population. The confines of our Reich capital contain from 50,000 to 60,000 "joy girls," as lewd cynicism is wont to call them, and in all large industrial centers the proportion is similar. Sticking to the heels of these unfortunate women are parasites of the basest and most exploitative kind: procurers and procuresses, pimps, landlords, innkeepers and—to round up more "consumers"—the makers and peddlers of pictorial and literary filth.

As soldiers and students, as workers, businessmen, and public officials, young males come into the city. Their sex draws them to the woman, just as it draws the woman to the man, and nature tells us that new blooming life is to grow out of the love of young men and women bursting with strength. But misery has defeated even Mother Nature and has contorted her noble face into a grimace. They are not allowed to choose the woman they love for the mother of their children, because maintaining a family costs money; to live with her "in style" costs many people a fortune, and they will have that only when their youth begins to wane. But those who have the money are taught by custom and are often admonished by their own fathers: enjoy your freedom, don't tie yourself down. They get to know the mystery of love in the filth of the street. The goddess thus desecrated takes fearful vengeance on them: venereal disease takes hold of their bodies. The daily number of incidents of venereal disease in Prussia is estimated to be 100,000. At least 80 percent of men in big cities have been ill with gonorrhea at one time or other in their lives, at least 20 percent with syphilis. The prematurely broken strength, the intellectual and physical feebleness of their sons, for the cause of which so many mothers search in vain—it is to be found right here. And here too is the cause of the life of suffering of countless of their daughters. They enter marriage, the hoped-for child does not come—almost half of all cases of barrenness are to be explained by venereal disease transferred from the man to the woman. The host of female ailments that destroy zest, energy, and family happiness is its consequence. With dreadful force, Jehovah's monstrous curse, which promises vengence for the fathers' sins into the third and fourth generation, is fulfilled: idiotic, blind, crippled, with a body that willingly grants entry to all sorts of disease

germs—thus countless children of such marriages come into the world;
those incapable of survival are still the luckiest among them.

In the face of this misery, it seems to us to be all women's most sacred
duty as mothers to declare once again a crusade to liberate our children
from it. But let us not act in the manner of lazy and short-sighted people
who cover the filth and then tell themselves it is no longer there—no, we
want to hunt it into its most hidden sources, even when in the end they
lead us where the discovery hurts the most: to our own selves. Our
children are well bred, well behaved, and obedient we tell ourselves for
our own excuse. Was it not our upbringing which broke their will, so that
it submit to ours, instead of steeling it so that it remain stronger in the
fight with evil? We have kept everything that is unclean from them, we
argue once again. But would it not have been better to show it to them as
it is, so that it might not later overwhelm them dressed up in the
deceptive garb of enjoyment? And is it not our fault if our sons look for
love in the gutter? Have we, after all, ever proclaimed to them the
greatness and magnificence of love? Have we not ourselves desecrated the
wondrous growth of new life by offering our children lies and old wives'
tales instead of the pure truth? But our guilt grows to even more menacing proportions when not only our own children's misery accuses us but
also we become conscious of our responsibility in the face of all earthly
wretchedness.

It is us they accuse, the outlaws of our sex. Why do we not fight for their
right to life? Why do we not see to it that full wages for honest work be
guaranteed to women as to men without abridgement? It is us they
accuse, the "fallen" men. Why do we not, all of us, come to their side?
Why do we all too frequently hinder them in that great struggle for better
work conditions, which would make it possible for them to create and
maintain the children of their love? It is us they accuse, the children
marked by disease and death, and the vast number of those unborn.
It is us they accuse, the outlaws of our sex. Why do we not fight for their
right to life? Why do we not see to it that full wages for honest work be
guaranteed to women as to men without abridgement? It is us they
accuse, the "fallen" men. Why do we not, all of us, come to their side?
Why do we all too frequently hinder them in that great struggle for better
work conditions, which would make it possible for them to create and
maintain the children of their love? It is us they accuse, the children
marked by disease and death, and the vast number of those unborn.

Not from the palaces of the princes, not from the green tables of the
cabinet ministers do we expect and beg for help: from ourselves, and from
you, mothers of the nation, we demand it. If you are united and if you are
without fear—and when was a mother ever fearful where the life of her
child was at stake?—then the words of princes and the wisdom of
ministers will be blown away before your power as chaff before the wind.
Come, the time is ripe, humanity is waiting for you.

FEMININITY

In the last few months the police have arrested two representatives of the bourgeois women's movement because their outer appearance seemed to give rise to all possible kinds of assumptions. The entire left-wing press voiced its indignation over this—the more tamely and tepidly, the more it leaned toward the right—but in the columns of our conservative papers one could hear a more or less gleeful derisive laughter when their cases were mentioned. Indeed, the *Deutsche Tageszeitung* seemed all set to deliver a stern sermon against the "lack of femininity," and its editor, Representative Dr. Oertel, spoke in the same vein on the floor of the Reichstag. To him, the police seems to be the defender of good old morality, and he is therefore willing to concede "extenuating circumstances" whenever they feel called upon to come out as the most competent guardians of femininity. And so once again as a result of these events the controversy over "feminity" threatens to become a matter of current concern.

Words that evoke old, traditional reverence among the great mass of people, because an obscure notion of something especially precious is attached to them, such words have forever been the most potent weapons in the fight against progress. Manliness and courage are made to march in, with jingling spurs and rattling saber, against the friends of peace and those who oppose dueling; with appeals to meekness and contentment, the attempt is made to silence the starving and the disfranchised; and femininity is to be the giant who will smash the women's movement to pieces. To be sure, an intelligent grade school pupil—male or female—is likely to develop some second thoughts about our notions of virtue: for the heroic virtues of heathen antiquity, when measured against Christian standards, frequently turn into vices. But academically trained people react with horror against the idea of the evolution of morality; once they

"Weiblichkeit," *Die Zukunft* (1902).

were recognized, the ground beneath our feet would be shaking. And in fact it is shaking everywhere. The main beams supporting the floor have rotted, the soil has been undermined; hollow space exists where one used to assume an abundance of the richest spiritual treasures.

What is femininity, this femininity which they all, on both sides, feminists and antifeminists, mention so frequently? Is the connotation of this word as fixed as a mathematical concept? Has it not rather changed many times in the course of history, depending always on the woman's social and economic position?

To the Greeks and Romans, the slavishly servile woman who never left the female quarters of the house appeared as the model of femininity, while the ancient German demanded that she follow him into battle and even fight with him if necessary. In certain primitive tribes even today it is one of the principal female duties that the wife or the daughter give herself to the stranger who enters the house; the Mohammedan regards that woman as unfeminine who reveals to a stranger anything more than her face. Differences of this kind could easily be complemented by a whole number of additional examples. But the sharp conflict between the conceptions of femininity reigning today cuts much deeper yet. One of these conceptions is the result of a period of development that began with Christianity and came to an end about a hundred years ago; the other has begun to come to the fore since then.

From old times on, the woman was by nature tied much more firmly than the man to the house; motherhood forced her to stay put and to withdraw: through it she turned housewife and became the inventress of all primitive technology comprising the house, clothing, and nutrition. The orbit of her activities gradually became so wide that it required a high degree of conscientiousness to do it justice. But it remained confined to the home. Hence the domestic virtues came more and more to constitute the contents of the notion of femininity. To this was added one other very important feature of femininity, the roots of which go deep down into the darkest beginnings of civilization: subordination to the man. It was the man, less tied down than the female, who brought prey and booty home from the hunt and from war, who created possessions and defended them. The more he possessed, the more the status of the female declined to that of a mere stewardess and manageress, who also gave birth to rightful heirs of the possessions. She became a piece of the man's property. That is clearly shown by the fact that the man not only could steal or buy the bride but also until well into the Christian era could indeed give away, sell, or bequeathe his wife. And here too the moral concept obediently followed the social and economic position: mute subordination, blind obedience, unresisting humility were considered the virtues of genuine femininity. Christianity fashioned into dogma the experience of the time. It became quite specifically the religion of women; and devoutness was considered primarily a female virtue. "She was devout and spun," "faithful servant to her wedded master": those old grave inscriptions rendered the quintessence of all femininity. Not the era of troubadours, with its worship of women, nor later centuries with their frivolousness were able to shake this loose; for all this affected only a very few women of the topmost strata of society; for the millions at the bottom a real turnabout was preparing only very slowly. Its pioneers were not the lovely ladies of the knightly bards, nor the erudite women of the eighteenth century skilled in all the amorous arts. Instead, it was poor spinning and weaving women, who, as early as the fourteenth and fifteenth centuries, stepped out of the domestic sphere as independent wage earners. And the new concept of femininity was not born in the thunderstorms of the revolution, nor heralded by the trumpet blasts of the Declaration of the Rights of Man; neither Olympe de Gouges nor Mary Wollstonecraft were its midwives. Rather it arose in the hellish noise and the thick smoke of the machine, and it was the countless thousands of hapless women first entering through the gates of England's factories who helped create it.

The more numerous the housewife's tasks that industry took over, the more the range of feminine duties contracted; spinning and weaving no longer are part of the necessary inventory of femininity nowadays. The more the woman is compelled to go after wages outside the home, in rank and file with her male work colleagues, the less will the honor of femininity be bestowed only on those who take care of house and home. And the more autonomous and independent the woman with regard both to her economic position and her intellectual development in confronting the man, the more surely servility, subordination, and a lack of any will of her own will gradually cease being the identifying marks of femininity. But we are only at the beginning of this great transformation; the vast majority of women is not yet active in professional life and is neither materially nor intellectually independent. For that reason, the old notion of femininity will continue for a long time to spook around in people's heads; the full awareness of its untruthfulness will come only wherever it collides more sharply with reality.

Some examples: in trend-setting bourgeois circles it is regarded as gravely damaging to femininity if men and women study medicine together; but yet it is considered feminine to the highest degree if women, as nurses, take care of the sick of both sexes and constantly deal with male physicians. What is feared is the joint education of the sexes as a threat to female morals; but yet no misgivings are voiced against joint work of proletarian men and women. A woman will be called unfeminine as soon as she enters a profession which is regarded as a male preserve—say, that of a lawyer, architect, preacher, or even physician—but the reproach is not repeated in the case of a woman who hews rocks, hauls loads, tiles roofs, sweeps chimneys, or paves roads. All the protective spirits of femininity are summoned against those "grandstand females" who have the presumption to defend their political convictions before the public. Whereas the backstairs politicking of princely mistresses and of influential ladies from "good society" has never been stigmatized as unfeminine. Feminine is that weepy sentimentality which gives alms to the poor, and unfeminine is the stubborn struggle against conditions that produce poverty.

From all this we can see that for the large mass of people, femininity denotes not a sum of living character traits but a number of virtues fossilized into tradition. Their judgment concerning femininity depends on the maintenance of this external appearance of tradition, not on the moral value of the personality. But this tradition, as the result of good breeding, is regarded as the almost exclusive attribute of "educated" society. This view is unintended and automatic, but just because of this it is all the more deeply rooted. It is strengthened by the well-known fact that even people with liberal minds are rarely able to see beyond their own social circle.

There is one integral part of the concept of femininity, the psychological significance of which has been neglected far too much; and its development supports my arguments. I mean female clothing. Greek women, bound to the home, wore long, draped trailing gowns, but their natural sense of beauty did not anxiously conceal the forms of their bodies. For the German woman, more mobile, ready for battle and for play, a short, loosely belted shift was sufficient. A loin cloth—or not even that—was the clothing of the African Negro woman who had not yet been spoiled by European civilization and was used to doing the same work as the man. It was only after the beginning of the reign of Christianity, for which sin and sensual joy are one and the same thing, that women started to cover themselves tightly up to the neck. The rich and noble women of the middle ages wore one skirt over the other, and the nobler and richer they were, the less they were compelled to set foot in the street, the longer the trains that they dragged on the floor. But the skirts of the bourgeois girl, the peasant woman, of all those who had to work, were short. Once morals loosened up, once religion turned more and more into an external showpiece, once women, especially those of the elite, saw themselves increasingly forced, as a consequence of the growth in luxury, to angle for a rich husband or a rich lover, they began to display their female charms with growing openness, emphasizing and highlighting them with all the means of cosmetics, especially the hooped skirt and the corset. This has nothing at all in common with the ancients' unveiling of the female body: on the one side, there is consummate artfulness and perversity; on the other, naturalness and an appreciation of beauty which had learned from early childhood to admire perfection in the naked human being. It took the thunderstorm of the French Revolution to destroy the phony hothouse culture: in the gowns of the period, which continued to be worn until the end of the reign of Napoleon I, not only a reawakened natural taste finds expression but also a new type of femininity: corset and crinoline, wig and powder all disappear, the countless skirts fall; in soft folds, the dresses cling to unrestrained limbs. But the storm had not troubled the waters deeply enough. Just as the Revolution was followed, first by the empire, and then by reaction, so a new constrictive fashion followed the loose dress, the stiff wide bell skirt succeeding the natural drape of the cloth. The nineteenth century offers the most variegated picture of dress fashions: as confused, as styleless as its total social and political life. Only one thing seemed to have become an inalienable attribute of female clothing—the armor that with its tight laces lifted the bosom and extended the hips. Its demise was not going to be threatened by the Revolution, nor by the moral sermons of a Rousseau, nor even by the imperial command of a Napoleon: instead, it was to be prepared by woman herself. She was being compelled to work for wages. And the constant pressure on her vital organs destroyed her labor power; in the struggle for existence, her self-consciousness grows in step with her abilities, she wants to climb mountains, ride the bicycle, do fencing and gymnastics: the armor hinders her. Once she steps out from her narrow four walls, her intellectual horizon widens also: she learns to see, to understand beauty, and to condemn prudishness. To the autonomous woman, matrimony seems less and less the only institution providing material support; using every means to catch a man becomes less and less necessary. Growing knowledge about the origins of life and the preconditions of creation tears the veil off the body that has been mysteriously hidden by deceitful tradition: the adult female of our time is aware that by squeezing vital organs into tight laces she harms the unborn life in her womb, and that by doing so she cuts off the infant's motherly foundation of life. A result of this development is the movement for clothing reform. To the applause of the overwhelming majority, Deputy Oertel on the floor of the Reichstag called it "masculine-feminine" clothing. Here, too, therefore fossilized tradition is considered feminine; unfeminine is anything that strives to adapt outer forms to new conditions of life.

But do we have new ideals that we can advocate against the dead ones, with which at times their defenders still manage to frighten us as if with ghosts? Is not the new type of female much too young to demonstrate anything definite about its eventual blossoming to maturity? I do not think so. Instead, it seems to me that the confusion about how to evaluate specific feminine traits is so great that we have the duty to delineate the increasingly firm strokes. The material for this is presented to us by life as well as fiction.

From Ibsen down to the artistically worthless products of women writers posing as supermodern, it is a red-hot ego drive that courses through all the fictional female figures. Life's experiences agree with this. The wish to become something, the urge to freedom, the fear of all constraints—those emotions rule the daughter of a "good" family who wants to get herself a higher education; they also dominate the worker's child who, despite the horror of unemployment, prefers the relative freedom of factory work over the shelter, the sure meal, and the dependence of the domestic servant's life. Conflicts between daughters and parents, about which past ages knew very little, today are everyday occurrences. The ties of matrimony loosen, and the number of unhappy women grows—of course, there are no statistics about this. All of this expresses the growing rebellion against authorities, the stripping off of servantdom. Independence in the widest sense thereof seems to me to be the goal that will have to be the base chord of the new concept of femininity. Since dependence was the quintessence of the old concept, these sharp opposites must clash.

Fermenting new wine easily bubbles over, and young movements with their excess energy all too often shoot beyond their target; and so it is inevitable that this drive for independence, too, will often disregard aesthetic and ethical boundaries. That became apparent in the way the first female university students, quite justifiably ridiculed a lot, totally neglected their outer appearance; it still shows today in the mock-masculine cut of clothing that the English women have introduced into fashion; in the removal of the most beautiful natural ornament women have—their long hair; in the imitation of bad male habits such as smoking, drinking, and dueling. And an offense against moral bounds—which, curiously, often merge with the aesthetic ones—can be encountered wherever the drive for independence manifests itself, not as a natural drive, but is intensified artificially. There are plenty of girls and women who believe they must "live it up", that is, mock at all limits of propriety. Nowadays they "are into" the wildest sexuality—cf. Marie Madeleine, Dolorora, and others—which wears its inner mendaciousness on its brow. They are joined by a growing number of girls and women of the bourgeosie, most of them not working, who in the hothouse atmosphere of their inner and outer existence devote their lives to the cultivation of artificial, overrefined, insincere feelings. We may count among them also those by no means rare individuals who interpret freedom and independence as the renunciation of all and any kind of self-discipline. It is all these excrescences of modern women's life that first strike the eye of the observer, especially the hostile one, and he then believes himself entitled to condemn the women's movement in its totality.

In fact, however, independence is the restorative of femininity. We have learned no longer to regard slavish traits as virtues, and we are beginning to learn this also with regard to the female. Toleration of intellectual and moral coercion, subordination even to those morally inferior, suppression of one's own individuality: those virtues of the woman of yesterday have almost turned into vices today. The duty to be a human being before one is a woman or man, master or servant, is more and more becoming the most important of all duties. But since our entire social order, the conditions of our life and our work, continue to impede the fulfillment of this duty, the growing power of the female urge to independence must lead to ever sharper collisions and conflicts. The armor that constricts our free heartbeat and our free breathing is a symbol of the armor with which law and tradition constrict the feminine psyche. Woman wants to be free, free in her love: not only do legal and economic considerations force her to tolerate life even with a man she does not love, but need even compels her to sell her love itself. Freedom is what she wants to gain through her work: but, because of deplorable work conditions, she becomes a slave of the free enterprise system. Mother is what she wants to be, in the fullest sense of the word: But she is less and less able to attain this goal. Almost from year to year it becomes more difficult to feed the children and to secure them a future; and the woman finds it increasingly difficult to combine her motherly duties with the duty to work. The unchangeable bases of feminine nature are kindness and compassion. The more the immediate observation of misery brings out this character trait, the stronger will be the urge to help: but with every thrust forward they run against the fortress walls of our society, and the law that still regards the female as a dependent servant ties her hand and foot. It is only a few individual women who today are able to come close to the ideal of the future, and among those ought to be those who visibly stick out from the large mass. A good part of the responsibility for the psychological development of their sex falls on them. Already for them, to be feminine ought to mean the development and effective use of all the best traits of the woman, internal and external. It should also imply the resolve neither to disregard their bodies nor to distort them into caricatures. Being feminine ought to signify being free but not unreined. To win freedom through struggle, to transform it from the privilege of a few to the possession of all, is a goal worth fighting for. Then the new femininity will be in much higher measure what the old femininity was at the time of its first flourishing: the softening and invigorating, elevating and happiness—bringing element, effective not only in the narrow confines of the home, but beyond it in the entire realm of societal life.

THE FEMALE MIND

There was a time, and it was not all that long ago, when the pioneers of the women's movement established as a main principle the primeval equality of the sexes with regard to intellectual and emotional predispositions. All actually existing differences were declared to be consequences of different upbringing and life conditions. The driving force behind the women's movement at first was essentially economic necessity, which drove women into seeking gainful employment, forcing them into a competitive struggle with men. It was therefore natural that women would regard complete equality as the highest aim. Only gradually, as women learned to confront their own endeavors more objectively, as they grew in experience and knowledge and began to analyze their own intellectual and emotional lives, did they realize increasingly that gender differences are not limited to the purely physiological aspects but that they also exert a most profound influence on women's emotional life and intellectual development.

The history of the development of the female sex provides proof of this in every way. It was neither different upbringing nor forcible oppression by men that rendered the female in primitive tribes dependent and etched the mark of slavery into her daily life. If we trace women's lives down to gray prehistoric times, we will always find that their personsl existence is narrow and confined. Motherhood limited her mobility and made her need protection. While the man was not hindered by sexual fetters in freely following his desires and devoting all his energies to the realization of his personal wishes, it seems that the first law of nature that came into the consciousness of human beings was that which tied the mother to the child and forced her to subordinate her own wishes and

"Das geistige Leben des Weibes," in Robby A. Kossman, ed., *Mann und Weib, ihre Beziehungen zueinander und zum Kulturleben der Gegenwart,* Vol. I. Second edition. (Stuttgart, Union Verlag, n.d.).

inclinations to those of the child. This compulsion to dissolve one's own being into that of another, weaker, being, the compulsion to protect, foster, and care for another determined not only the intellectual and psychological development of the female. It also meant that self-sacrifice, devotion, compassion, and love became the basic traits of her emotional life; the dark side of which, however, spelled submissiveness, timidity, and lack of independence. And her intellectual life found its guide in the care for children; it taught her to create the first warming garment, the first protective lean-to, to till the soil and to provide animal milk as supplement to her own. In a time when warfare and hunting were the only pursuits worthy of a free man, the woman became a worker; to be sure, she was given a status almost as low as the slaves, but she became the promoter of civilization and the champion of peace.

Once the division of labor had been perfected, the intellectual distance between men and women was bound to increase steadily. Her children and her household were her world—a world that demanded all her energies. The upbringing given to girls intensified the once necessary one-sidedness of the female gender. Only really extraordinary circumstances would have been able to break these limitations. But another circumstance was added that was bound to influence particularly the artistic side of women's intellectual life. According to the customs and laws of almost all nations in ancient time, only the woman was obliged to keep marital fidelity. Only she was punished by death for breaking this vow. She lived isolated in the house, almost as if in a jail, and since she was married young, most of the time without ever having met her future husband whom her parents picked for her, she was denied any erotic life in its fullest flourishing; and it is on this soil alone that the great dreams of artists come to fruition. Love, which made the man into a poet and a hero, which poured fire into his veins, was known to her at best as only a little hearth flame, good enough only to warm the home.

How much this interpretation is verified by historic evidence can be seen already in the fact that in the period of Greece's highest flourishing, the only women who personally participated in the intellectual culture of their country were hetaeras, and they became important and influential not only because of their beauty but also because of their intellect. To be sure, we do not know much about the legendary *Sappho*; only one thing seems certain: she was neither a wife nor mother. And other historic female figures of antiquity, for example *Semiramis* and *Cleopatra*, should essentially be classified among the hetaeras rather than among mothers and housewives of the old style.

Intellectual development presupposes freedom. The stunting of wide areas of emotional life must necessarily lead to the stunting of intellectual creativity.

In this direction, Christianity has done women much more harm than heathendom by stigmatizing sexuality itself as sinful. Saint Paul aimed his sermon about the greater holiness of the celibate life at both sexes; moreover, he expressly prefaced it by saying that he was merely stating his own opinion, not a commandment of the Lord. But nonetheless, ascetic zealots clung to sentences such as "It is a good thing for man not to touch a woman," and "Adam was not seduced; but the woman was seduced and has introduced transgression." Then they condemned matrimony as an evil, and the woman as the agent who allowed the devil to enter. Canon law gave the Church Fathers' interpretation of these doctrines the force of law by decreeing, among other things:

> Woman was not created in God's image. Adam was seduced by Eve, not Eve by Adam. Therefore it is proper that the man be lord and master over the woman, who has enticed him into sin, so that he may not fall again. The law commands that the woman be subject to the man and be his servant.

The "mortification of the flesh" came to mean flight from the woman. At the Council of Macon, the majority decided to recommend that the clergy flee from women. The Council of Metz sharpened this command by forbidding priests to have anything to do even with their mothers and sisters. While in the first period of Christianity only monks had submitted to the vow of chastity, it now became obligatory for all the clergy. The consequences of celibacy being imposed on a large number of men, usually the most intellectually outstanding men, were profound. To be sure, in them the Church created itself an army of devoted militants who were not distracted from their duties by any family concerns. But if the Church believed it acted in the service of a higher morality by glorifying chastity and destroying sexual drives, then it reckoned only with abstract theory, not with living nature. Not only did it accomplish the very opposite of what it had intended, but in addition to extramarital intercourse and the rapid spread of prostitution, various unnatural vices flourished, particularly in monasteries and convents. It also inflicted damage on the entire moral life of the nation, damage that it still suffers today, and which afflicts the female sex with the greatest severity. It demeaned the most natural relations of the sexes toward each other and sought to veil them as something of which the human being ought to be ashamed. For the Church, marriage was primarily a "union of souls"; even in marriage, sexual love was considered sinful or at best a tribute that the human being had to pay to his moral weakness, to his alienation from God. The formal sanctification of matrimony (by raising it to a sacrament and declaring it indissoluble) has not prevented the inner destruction of this most intimate relation of human beings to each other. The consequences of this are hypocrisy, prudishness, and repression of the noblest sentiments by a false morality. And a large portion of the psychological and moral sides of the women's question is based on the thoughts about love and marriage that the Roman Catholic church has inculcated into the consciousness of the people.

It is often argued that by elevating the Lord's mother to the throne of heaven the Church has demonstrably accomplished the general elevation of the female sex. But in fact, the cult of Mary has not been able to change anything in the actual situation of women. After all, it was not the *female* that was venerated in the madonna, not the personification of erotic love or of motherliness as in many heathen cults; it was rather the immaculate virgin who became a mother not through surrender to love but through a miracle.

Sexual love was branded as sin and reserved as a privilege for the most despised among women. In the most extreme development of this, which the Church has promoted, it has caused severe and lasting damage to the intellectual and emotional life of the female. It has caused nothing else than the violent dismemberment of her very self, whereas only the intimate union of her erotic life and her motherliness could have brought her personality to its maturity and freed her intellectual potential.

At the same time the activity of the Church in another area— monastic life—seems to have furthered women's intellectual develop- ment. The number of single women grew, all the more because of the mass of men who were drawn away from married life by a clerical career. The uncertainties of life made women look around for some safe protec- tion. At that time the convents served as havens for thousands. In large masses women flocked into their protective walls. The only choice they had was between the convent and the women's house; and even though many of them entered only in search of food and shelter, nonetheless the number of those grew who were yearning for a place where they might work in peace and deepen their intellect. In convents, women received scholarly training on a level that was quite high compared with the general educational level of their sex. They studied classical languages and various other branches of learning, and many a wise convent woman became the adviser of popes and kings. Such a woman was *Hildegard von Bockelheim,* abbess of the convent in Rupprechtshausen, who in the eleventh century wrote not only about the lives of saints but also a number of treatises on physics and zoology. Standing on the same high level of learning was the much admired "seer of the North," *Brigitta of Sweden,* and also *Hroswitha,* the Latin-language poetess of the time of Emperor Otto. Many learned nuns spent their time copying old works or painting initials and miniatures, while others were active as teachers in the girls' schools of their convents, as nurses, embroiderers, weavers, or launderers. In this fashion the convents provided a partial solution to the medieval women's question not only by providing shelter for a large number of women but also by raising them to a higher intellectual level and opening independent careers for them.

Yet really great works representing feminine intellectuality could not be created by the learned nuns of the Christian Middle Ages any more than by the educated prostitutes of heathen antiquity; both of them were hybrid creatures, incapable of independent creativity and, in the best cases, imitators of male role models.

II.

When on the basis of the Classics, the arts and sciences of ancient Greece and Rome awakened to new life in the Renaissance, women, to the extent that they belonged to the more affluent classes, participated in the intellectual treasures that were being dug up in virtually inexhaustible plenty. Their time and energy were no longer claimed exclusively by the extensive household activity of previous centuries, since handicraft and industry had taken over the making of a large number of articles of use, and the grubby daily chores could be left for the servant maids to do. Thus the propertied segment of the female sex was liberated from monotonous and burdensome labor, in consequence of which these women took an active interest in the art that surrounded them and the science they heard being discussed. Some individual women of outstanding talent entered scientific careers or became active as artists. In the houses of commercial lords and in princely palaces, children of both sexes received one and the same course of instruction from humanistically trained educators. Outstanding pedagogues devoted all their energies to the rearing of their young charges so that, for instance, *Cecilia Gonzaga,* a pupil of Vittorio de Feltre, had acquired full mastery of the classical languages at the age of ten, and *Olympia Fulva Morata* gave learned lectures at the age of sixteen.

One-sided book learning, however, was not the goal of their education; instead, the goal was the harmonic perfection of the entire personality, the individualization of the human being. Hence for the female sex the great achievement of the Renaissance was not that universities were opened up to women and that the fame of some individual female scholars filled the world at the time; it was the recognition of the woman as an autonomous human being. Proof of this already is the higher form of relations between the sexes about which the Italian storytellers and biographers report. Social life no longer consisted merely in culinary and erotic enjoyment, and the woman no longer was a mere housekeeper or lover; she now participated in scholarly discourse; before her, Dante, Petrarca, and Boccaccio, recited their works of fiction; her mature judgment was respected as much as that of the man, indeed, it often outweighed the latter. Women like *Catarina Cornaro* in Venice, *Isotta Malatesta* in Rimini, *Emilia Pia* in Urbino, *Isabella d'Este* in Mantua, or *Veronica Gambarra* in Bologna, were centers of intellectually alive circles on whose opinions the fame of many a writer and artist depended. The greater freedom enjoyed by the women of the Renaissance, the independence with which they let themselves be guided by their own convictions and feelings, has caused religious and moral zealots to depict them as altogether immoral creatures; and many people still today adduce them as exemplifying the rule that the woman is spoiled as soon as she seeks to place herself on equal footing with the man. Yet when we compare the women of France in the fifteenth century or the women of England in the sixteenth with the highly educated women of Italy in the same period, such a comparison must without doubt be decided in favor of the latter. They were neither silent, apathetic sufferers nor scheming intriguers, hence they often tore the bonds of demeaning marriages and followed the voices of their hearts.

For centuries, however, marital fidelity has been considered a specifically feminine virtue that the man has a right to demand of the woman, because from the moment of her entry into matrimony she becomes his property. Therefore the guardians of virtue in old times and the present have always regarded a woman's infidelity as a crime, while the man's infidelity earns tolerant smiles. These people are unwilling to acknowledge that the erotic needs of many women are often just as much subject to change as those of men, though the history of the female sex offers examples enough. In all periods or social classes in which women have enjoyed freedom of development, not only has their intellectual level been raised, but their emotional life, too, has become more versatile. One glance at the painted and sculptured portraits of Renaissance women suffices to suggest this: Titian's *Elenore de Gonzaga* ("La Bella") with her deep eyes; his *Catarina Cornaro*, with a face in which energy and melancholy contend with each other; Leonardo da Vinci's *Mona Lisa* with the strange ambiguous smile of the knowing one; Laurano's bust of the *Princess of Naples*, whose lowered lids veil ardent glances; Settignano's *Princess Urbino* with her lips pursed in contempt—they all portray individual personalities strong from a full life, and they provide a really astounding contrast to the conventional madonna faces of the thirteenth and fourteenth centuries.

And yet what art represented was but a faint reflection of female life at that time. One person above all has managed to give it consummate expression in all its ardor and greatness, its virtues and its vices: *Lucrezia Borgia,* daughter of a pope and a whore, the woman under whose twenty-year reign Ferrara became a center of artistic culture and humanist education. As her erotic feelings were passionate, so was her motherliness profound, and whoever traces the real sources of her being, which roars and rushes past us like a mighty river, will discover that its source was the richness of her emotions. Indeed, the feminine intellect is genuine only when it is fertilized by emotion.

The age of the Renaissance offers the most convincing proof that cultural peaks always coincide with a conscious rejection of asceticism, with a decidedly positive attitude toward life and its joys; and its women, too, demonstrate that for women freedom is the basic precondition for the full development of the individual personality. In periods of history such as this something we observed in the period of Greece's flourishing repeats itself: the intellectual elevation of the hetaera. Women like *Imperia, Tulia d'Aragona,* and *Veronica Franco,* should be considered the equals of Diotima and Aspasia. If Lucrezia Borgia's personality is typical for her time and her social class, then that of *Diane de Poitiers* can be regarded as the personification of the same period's highly intellectualized hetaerism. To this lovely mistress of two French kings, France owes the most beautiful flower of its own artistic Renaissance. Her knowledge, her intellect, her taste undoubtedly had a more lasting influence on her period than the learned works of her contemporaries who were only vying for the laurel of personal fame.

For whenever women's general education degenerates into one-sided book learning, and where women appeared in public as artists, writers, or orators, one character trait usually stood out: their scholarship and their art would carry an altogether masculine stamp, and the highest praise they would be given would be that they had a masculine intellect. As early as the thirteenth century, the theologian *Boulonnois*, who preached in Bologna and became a professor, was famous for the "masculine power" of her oratory. *Novella d'Andrea*, the lovely teacher of canon law, and *Magdalena Buonsignori*, the highly praised author of *De legibus connubialibus*, were legal scholars with "sharp minds like those of men." *Isotta Nogarola* lectured before popes and emperors; *Cassandra Fedele* taught at the University of Padua; *Ippolita Sforza*, at the Congress of Mantua, gave the address to welcome the Pope; *Isicratea Monti* and *Emilia Brembati* attracted hundreds of listeners with their oratory—they all regarded it their highest ambition to make people forget their gender; and this view was so widespread that important women swore vows of chastity to themselves because they could not find any harmonic link between service to scholarship or art and the biological life of the wife and mother. One of those women was *Vittoria Colonna*, the celebrated writer and friend of Michelangelo. Despite the intellectual heights she had reached, despite the power of her mind, she too was unable to bridge the gap between the woman as a sexual being and the woman as artist and scholar. And at this point even the women of the Renaissance were bound to fail in the final analysis because the roles they played as active forces in intellectual life—not just as inspirers and arbiters—were not the result of a movement growing out of the inner development of the entire female sex but were only the spontaneous emancipation of individuals from intellectual limitations. For that reason this phenomenon left no lasting and significant results; it was not even sufficient proof of women's equal intellectual potential because they were too anxious to follow in men's footsteps instead of demonstrating that they were capable of going their own way.

A superficial survey of the countless works of that time on women, their fame, and their capabilities might lead one to infer the existence of a broad women's movement. More detailed knowledge, however, shows that many writers, aping the custom of the ancient civilizations, indulged in a veritable cult of heroes. Everyone thought himself a Plutarch for writing biographies of famous men; and then biographies of famous women were bound to appear, because everywhere they were in the forefront of intellectual life. Boccaccio took the lead, and in a treatise written in Latin he depicted a number of outstanding women from the Greeks to his own time. How little this made him a pioneer of the women's question is demonstrated by a vicious satire on the female sex that he wrote—*Il Corbaccio*. He had numerous imitators; they sought to best each other not only in cleverness and wit but also in the mass of women they celebrated, until at last Peter Paul Ribera outdid them all with his work about the immortal triumphs and heroic adventures of 845 women. It was only one step further on the same road if with great display of ringing words they now praised the higher worth of the female sex against the male, and this question then became a topic of society conversation on which oratorical art and clever repartee could be exercized. In the long run, this whole literature did not make a lasting impact in Italy because it was too far removed from real needs and could be of interest only to those few women who because they were favored by a privileged position could contest the men armed with equal intellectual weaponry. Ribera's 845 famous women notwithstanding, their number remained small measured against the large mass of women and the length of the period. The same can be said about Spain. Its women at that time, more than all others, took pride in their masculine intellect; but the country produced only few truly outstanding scholars. Among them the theologian *Isabela de Cordoba* and the orator *Juliana Morelli* of Barcelona, who was equally well at home in fourteen languages, were particularly distinguished.

While in Italy and Spain women participated in giving as well as receiving intellectual attainments almost as a matter of course, their situation in France and England, but especially in Germany, was entirely different. They were oppressed by economic misery, and scholarship and art reached them only second- and thirdhand. Hence there were only a few women in whom the example of the Italian women generated the wish to develop their minds and to attain intellectual equality. And, typical of the conditions in Central Europe, this wish arose frequently in conjunction with the women's need to earn a living.

The French writer, *Christiane de Pisan,* is a classic example. Widowed early, she was compelled to feed and rear her children. She had received an education that, according to the standards of the time, was quite good, and with iron energy she educated herself further and managed to earn enough by writing to survive with her children. Her novel of the Rose and her history of Charles V made her a name far beyond the frontiers of her country. But for an understanding of the women's question at that time her pamphlet, *La cité des dames,* is of particular interest. In it she portrays the life and work of the Italian jurist *Novella d'Andrea* and in this connection speaks out on behalf of scholarly education of women, asserting at the end that men oppose this only because they fear that women might become more intelligent than they. Christiane de Pisan has earned the glory of being the first one to have made a contribution, in this work, to the issue of women's emancipation; she was destined to do this in consequence of her own struggle for survival. The fertile soil on which the women's question and the women's movement could grow turned out to be the countries of Central and Northern Europe, where the struggle for existence involved everyone including women, not the South, which poured such an abundance of wealth and beauty out over its children that even women could not remain standing aside. Those who first became conscious of the misery and oppression of their sex and dared express this in words could not, of course, be the ones suffering the most abuse; they had to find themselves on a certain minimal level of education and understanding; for the most abject misery stifles the mind and destroys all strength, it does not even allow the feeling of discontent with one's own misery to arise.

Hence the first successor of Christiane in France was a woman from the same social class as she, *Mademoiselle de Gournay,* Montaigne's adopted daughter. She proclaimed the equal rights of the sexes, except for the duty to bear arms. Of course, her endeavors did not have any immediate practical results but, in conjunction with the influence of Humanism, with the flourishing of art and literature, and the growing wealth of the upper classes based on the intensified exploitation of the people, they did contribute to the rise in the education of women. As far as intellect and learning are concerned, one queen who has become an almost legendary figure stands out from among a large number of learned women: *Marguerite de Navarra,* the sister of Francis I. Her stories, her poems, but especially her correspondence, vividly render the spirit of the sixteenth century with all its frivolousness and grace, but also reveal everywhere traces of the imitation of Italian models. Her equally intelligent but, in contrast to her, amoral namesake, *Marguerite de Valois*, Henry IV's spouse, wrote in a much more independent style fifty years later. Full of contempt for the weak-kneed, mean world of men surrounding her, defiantly trusting in her own energetic mind, she was the author of a work on the superiority of female reasoning power.

Nonetheless, the women of France have not left any important achievements in scholarship. Only one of them stands out from the mass: Anna, the daughter of the learned philologist Tanneguy Lefèbre, and wife of his insignificant student, André Dacier. The first French translations of Plautus and Aristophanes, Terence and especially Homer, came from her pen, and her polemical phamphlet, *Traité des causes de la corruption du goût*, has retained lasting value; in it she forcefully repudiates Lamotte's attacks on the *Iliad* and the *Odyssey*. It is easy to understand why Anna Dacier remained such an exceptional figure; for scholarship, instead of turning into a means for intellectual liberation, for fashioning a more profound and refined style of life for all, became a modish fad for "high society" and finally ended up as a ridiculous caricature. As in Italy, women did not succeed in finding the required harmony between their feminine nature and their scholarly education. They too often renounced erotic love and motherhood in order to pursue their studies undisturbed. For instance, the *précieuses* of the Hotel Rambouillet gave learned women a deservedly bad reputation, and when Molière in his comedies, *Précieuses ridicules* and *Femmes savantes*, administers lethal blows to their degeneracy, he revealed himself as being, not the enemy, but a friend of the female sex.

The revival of classic antiquity had a much more lasting effect on the intellectual development of Germany than on that of France. But times were too hard, the masses of the people too poor, the women much too deeply caught up in the narrow confines of domestic cares to be able to participate in this to any significant degree. It was only very slowly that the spirit of the new time emanating from the scholars' studies and the lecture halls of universities began to reach them. While in Italy, in Spain, and in part also in France, the fifteenth and sixteenth centuries were the high period of feminine scholarship, in Germany it began only in the early seventeenth century. Long before that, however, the Humanists engaged in theoretical discussions of the women's question, which the Italian Renaissance had posited by not closing the gates to classical education for women. While in Italy this had happened without struggle under the immediate impact of the great intellectual achievements, the brooding German first had to devise long-winded theories; and the sluggish, artifically repressed intellect of the German woman could take the strange new nourishment only in homeopathic dosage.

Despite all the theoretical discussions, however, women's education remained limited to the most elementary knowledge; and woman like *Charitas Pirkheimer* belonged to the very isolated exceptions. In her brother's house she found the shining lights of German art and scholarship assembled, and, similar to the princesses at the courts of Italian Maecenases, she lived among them. By and large the nobility was a crude lot, the burghers were limited and jejune, the princely courts impoverished and small. A change began to set in only in the seventeenth century. But precisely at that point, when the scholarship of the men had a rather tired, unproductive, epigonic character, women's need for higher learning, which at last began to manifest itself, could not be satisfied in life-giving fashion. To be sure, there were princesses and scholars' daughters who studied the classical languages, and prodigies like *Anna Marie Kramer* astonished everyone by defeating old professors in a disputation at the age of twelve; some individual women attained such high degrees of learning that their works did not at once die with them; rivers of ink were spilled to write their praises; and yet not a single personality can be found among them who was genuinely learned, intellectually mature, and at the same time really feminine. Their learning merely stuck to the surface, it was not more than that baggage of useless knowledge denounced by Faust, which strong natures shook off like motley rags in order to become their own selves from inside. An attempt of this kind may have been made by *Elizabeth of the Palatinate,* daughter of the hapless Winter King,* who through great suffering attained a profound world view. She started out as a diligent student of Descartes, with whom she corresponded actively, but in the end threw all her learned books away—they left her emotions unsatisfied. Her hunger for a full meaning for her life was not to be stilled by all the scholarly wisdom hammered into her mind. So she turned to the mystical sect of the Labadists and finally to the Quakers because she too did not find that unity of life and knowledge. One of her friends was a woman from the Netherlands, admired far beyond her merits: *Anna Maria Schurmann.* She was praised as the

*Frederick V of the Palatinate was elected king of Bohemia in late 1619, but he lost his kingdom in the following year at the battle of White Mountain.

wonder of the century and as the tenth Muse; and yet she too floundered in her belief in herself and her wisdom, and she also followed the new prophet Jean Labadie as a simple penitent. The fate of the learned Queen *Christina of Sweden* was scarcely different. Her learning, too, did not become the contents and the enrichment of her being, and she in the end sought, by converting to Catholicism, what up till then she had not been able to find: something to satisfy her neglected emotional life.

III.

Our image of women's intellectual lives up to the threshold of the nineteenth century would remain incomplete and lacking its essential character if in addition to ordinary women we would not consider the female ruler and the salon lady of the seventeenth and eighteenth centuries. *Maria Theresia* and *Catherine II* of Russia through their lives and works have provided interesting inferences about female psychology. Both were not only quite adequately prepared for their calling as sovereigns but in fact surpassed dozens of male crowned heads in forcefulness, effectiveness, and intelligence. Burning ambition characterized both of them, but while Maria Theresia subordinated all her personal needs and inclinations totally to it, Catherine's ambition was not an iron ring constricting her but merely one of the many passions through which her total nature expressed itself. Maria Theresia was the "born empress"; everything human, everything feminine, everything individual in her was increasingly smothered under the pressure of the one task she set herself. Catherine, in contrast, utilized the freedom of development given to women only in such high positions for the purpose of fully living out her potentials. And the result? Had she been a man, it would not have had to be anything else; those amorous affairs that helped her favorites gain influence and rank were the same that lent historic significance to the mistresses of male rulers. But what is more important: Catherine, as a ruler at least as outstanding as Maria Theresia, differed from her also by her literary achievements, among them not only her dramas, but also her memoirs and her correspondence with the leading men of her time. With this she manifested a wealth of intellectual life that was not given to the Austrian ruler. To be sure, only a large number of fully valid examples could provide proof of the intimate connection between the satisfaction of women's erotic needs and their individual intellectual development and creative potential. But in connection with other knowledge we have of female psychology, one single example like that of Catherine is quite weighty.

When women's intellectual achievements are discussed people mean, in analogy with men's achievements, only positive attainments in scholarship and art, to which at most they may add works in the art of government, with regard to important female rulers. What is forgotten here is an area of women's intellectual influence on their times and on its male representatives that cannot be measured in books and canvases. And yet the female mind expressed here has often been more significant for the progress of humanity than many a sophisticated treatise written by a woman scholar.

Seen from this point of view, the salon lady of the seventeenth and eighteenth centuries does not in general deserve the contempt she is being shown today. To be sure, in comparison with the Renaissance woman she looks like a pretty toy next to a classic work of art. Just as fashion repressed all nature, forcibly constricted the waist, grotesquely magnified the hips with hoop skirts, robbed the hair of its natural color with powder, and with the help of rouge and beauty spots made the face into a mask, so all natural feelings often were smothered and distorted. Like a contagious disease, a kind of moral corruption spread, according to which love was not the supreme driving force of life but merely a source of pleasure. And yet even in this period the female psyche spread her wings. There was the *Marquise de Pompadour*, whose vivid personality helped the arts of her time flourish wonderfully and whose seminal influence could be felt in the most varied areas of public life. Or consider women like *Mademoiselle de Lespinasse* or *Ninon de l'Enclos*, in whose salons the leading minds of their time received their inspiration. We ought not to judge these people with the arrogance of moral judges just because their erotic lives were not to be cramped into conventional forms. In reality, the memoirs and correspondence of that time reveal a wealth of intellectual life and a warmth of feeling that could never have grown on the swampy soil of vice; instead, they demonstrate that an environment of freedom is a vital precondition for the development of the female psyche. Coercion and oppression have always generated slaves' virtues at best but much more often slaves' vices and a slave's frame of mind. Hence all those character traits that have heretofore been condemned or praised as specific to the female heart or the female mind can be called natural gender traits only after the external oppression and the obstacles to development have been removed.

The influence of the Renaissance can be traced down to Ninon de l'Enclos—that woman whose everlasting glory it will be to have revived the ancient civilizations' enjoyment of the beautiful body and to have shown once more that physical beauty can intensify the good life just as much as the mind. And if the Renaissance loosened the bonds under which women's hearts had not been able to throb naturally, then the educational project of the eighteenth century doubtless was to sharpen women's minds, even if frequently at the expense of the heart. Their critical judgment developed to a hitherto unknown degree. Women came to dominate not only in social life, fashion, and the fine arts but also in politics. Kings, ministers, and diplomats came to be guided by them in their decisions and influenced in their sympathies and antipathies. The threads of domestic and foreign policies came together in the salons of *Countess Boufflers*, of *Estrades*, the *Duchess of Gramont*, of *Prin* and *Langeac*. As Montesquieu put it, the women's world was a state within the state.

> Whoever sees the ministers make decisions but does not know the women who dominate them is like someone who watches a machine at work but does not know the forces that move it.

Because they were deprived of public rights, women has to resort to engaging in backstairs politics, which was bound to have a deleterious effect on their character, because the more they used cunning and intrigue, the greater their success. But at the same time this activity awakened their interest in public life and taught them to look at it through their own eyes; and thus the salon ladies of the *ancien régime* helped pave the way for the heroines of the revolution.

Yet if we take an overall view of this entire period and the position of women in it, one fact immediately leaps to the eye. Despite the influence women wielded, despite the great roles they played, despite the development of their critical judgment, there is an almost total lack of independent creative accomplishment either in scholarship or in art. If works of the shoddiest kind written by women could get recognition or even reap enthusiastic praise, that may perhaps be the clearest indication of the manifest inability of women to do really creative work. Under the influence of Gottsched, women like *Frau von Ziegler* or *Zäunemann* were declared poet "laureates" when in fact they were nothing more than vain rhymesters of the most miserable kind, or their works, like those of *Mrs. Gottsched*, bore all the earmarks of the tortured attempt to become a celebrity. Just as in some circles of the French nobility young girls were trained for the desirable "career" of King's mistress, so especially in German scholarly circles daughters were artificially drilled to become writers or scholars. *Dorothea Erxleben,* who in 1755 obtained her doctorate at Halle with the express permission of the young King of Prussia, may have been one of the best of them. Even the once world-famous *Anna Luise Karschin* can appear only as a tragic-comic figure to us because her admirers twisted her natural talent into a formal kind of verse making in which slick gimmickry was the chief standard of evaluation. There is only one woman in German intellectual life of that period who looks to us like a real human being: *Friederike Karoline Neuber,* a traveling comedienne. The German stage owes her its liberation from the Punch-and-Judy show that until then had kept it vegetating on a very low vaudeville level. Neuber got her education from life, not from Latin grammar.

For those who have studied this period, the reasons for the general intellectual barrenness of women, confirmed by the exceptions of isolated but altogether inadequate achievements, are obvious: The sophisticated ladies dominating in the salons and the great lovers (grandes amoureuses) despised motherhood and denied the child. As soon as a baby was born, the mother sent it off into the village to a wet nurse; she refused to nurse the baby herself so as not to ruin her figure. Once the child was back, it was handed over to a chamberlain or governess who tried as quickly as possible to transform the child into a young adult. Meanwhile the mother would pursue her pleasures without being aware she was seeking that which only her abandoned child could have given her: a rich emotional life. Since she herself remained but a crippled human being, how could she have created anything great and whole? But once the effort was made to make the woman into a scholar or writer instead of a salon lady, the only aim was to make her accomplishments equal to those of men. Thus here too the same thing: the artificial repression of specifically feminine nature.

It was Rousseau, who, with the acuity of genius, diagnosed the ailment that gnawed at the woman's vital nerve, who traced its causes and exposed them unmercifully. Granted that with his prescription for healing the ailment he overshot the mark by demanding that in opposition to everything he observed the woman should be trained only in the home and for the home; yet this exaggeration weighed little in comparison to the service he rendered women. He reclaimed childhood for children, and for women, feminity; and his redeeming word for the tightly laced-up souls of women was, "Become a mother!" Like all great pioneers of progress, he perceived the mute sighing and yearning of his fellow human beings and found the first words to express them. Countless people hailed him like a savior; for he merely said what they themselves had sensed dimly, and he showed them a way that, haltingly groping like blind people, they had been seeking for a long time. *Madame d'Epinay* in her memoirs expressed the impact he made most beautifully.

"And if I were to speak with human or angels' tongues and did not have love, I would be sounding brass and a tinkling bell"—that applies especially to women. No equal right, no freedom, can be useful to them and make creative human beings out of them, nor can they benefit from freely living out their sexual urges, if they allow themselves to be robbed of the one good that nature has bestowed on them alone: maternal love. It is this emotion that is the source of women's deepest social instincts: compassion and the courage to make self-sacrifices.

IV.

All great revolutionary movements have had their female militants and martyrs. Compassionate, self-sacrificing love of humanity has led women to the cross and to the scaffold, whereas freedom and justice were the guiding stars of the men who fought and suffered with them. If the best women of their time understood, encouraged, and participated in the emancipatory struggles of the eighteenth century, this is due to the intellectual revolution that preceded them. The most important pioneer of this revolution for the female sex was Rousseau. The memoirs and correspondences of the time demonstrate how his ideas won over women in particular. At the age of nine, *Manon Philipon*, later *Mme. Rolande*, read Plutarch and became enthusiastic about the heroes of antiquity. At the age of fourteen, while in a convent school, she read Diderot and d'Alembert, lost her faith, and became an ardent adherent of Rousseau. A similar development was that of her charming rival for influence over the heroes of the beginning of the revolution, Sophie de Grouchy, *Marquise de Condorcet*, whose first devotional reading was the *Meditations* of Marcus Aurelius. By the time she was barely twenty, she had already absorbed the spirit of Voltaire and Rousseau and was to remain faithful to them to her very end. Other women, who were not destined to play a role in the history of the Revolution, nourished their minds from the same sources and, having been inspired by Rousseau to devote themselves to their children, gave them the best they had. It is no accident that the time of the first enthusiasm for *Emile* coincides with the time of the birth and childhood of the heroes of the revolution, Robespierre, Danton, Desmoulins, and others; for in their mothers' hands was the *Contrat Social;* with their mothers' milk they drank in the ideals of liberty and equality. The thinkers' theories, the philosophers' dreams, appealed to sentiment as never before and therefore made women into their most ardent advocates. The leading minds gathered in their salons and respected their judgment as equivalent to that of men. All social life was replete with that electifying aura that envelops everyone who comes under its influence and stimulates all slumbering intellectual energies into vivid activity. While some of the women were satisfied to sing the praises of Nature, Liberty, or Equality, others were alert to the practical implications of the new truth and participated in the workings of domestic politics not only by expressing their opinions but also by assuming leadership roles.

In considering French women's participation in politics, one circumstance must not be overlooked: the influence of America. Just as it can be seen affecting the Declaration of the Rights of Man in the National Assembly, just as the emancipatory wind originating in the War of Independence swept much medieval baggage out of Europe, so too the women's movement of the revolutionary period can be explained by it in many of its features.

From the very beginning the women of America stirred up their country's resistance against British rule.

Mercy Otis Warren, the sister of the fiery freedom fighter James Otis, gathered the leaders of the movement in her drawing room; long before even Washington wanted to discuss the definitive separation of the colonies from the motherland, she demanded America's independence. She conducted an active correspondence with Jefferson, and the Declaration of Independence shows traces of her mind. Moreover, she and her friend *Abigail Smith Adams,* wife of the first President of the United States [*sic*], were the first to advocate equal rights for the female sex. When in 1776 the Continental Congress was to discuss the Constitution, Abigail Adams wrote to her husband: "If the coming constitution does not pay thorough attention to women, we are resolved to rebel and will not consider ourselves obliged to submit to laws that do not secure us a voice or the representation of our interests." At the same time she demanded the admission of the female sex to public schools and justified this claim by declaring that a state that wished to produce heroes, statesmen, and philosophers, would first need truly educated mothers. As a result, schools were opened to women, whereas the wish for equal political rights for the whole population of the United States remained unfulfilled. Only New Jersey and Virginia, as the first states in the world, granted their female citizens the right to vote, a legislative accomplishment that caused a major sensation far beyond the borders of America.

All those facts together caused the enthusiasm for the women's movement to flame high in France. Since the soil had been prepared, the movement could not remain without fruit. What first became manifest was the desire for higher education, to allow women to participate more effectively in the conflicts of the period. Salon conversation and private reading no longer sufficed, and so, in 1786, under the management of Montesquieu, La Harpe, and Condorcet, a *lycée* was created. It soon became the gathering place for the most outstanding women, who were joined by a small circle of men—a total of about seven hundred people. There the last of the Encyclopedists and their successors lectured on mathematics, chemistry, physics, history, literature, and philosophy; but, once touched by the fiery breath of the Revolution, their scholarly lectures soon turned into heated agitational oratory. La Harpe appeared on the lecture platform wearing a Phrygian cap, and the students, among them *Mme. Rolande, Marquise de Condorcet,* and *Mme. Tallien,* turned from listeners into actresses in the drama developing outside.

From now on, however, the intellectual emancipation of women and their participation in public life were no longer restricted to the educated and the wealthy. No scholarly learning was needed to understand the misery of the masses, only an open eye and a warm heart. The poor women's march to Versailles, that dramatic prelude to the Revolution, was dictated not only by personal misery but also expressed the strong feminine sentiment that in every natural female engenders maternal love and maternal concern toward all who suffer and are oppressed; it is this sentiment that makes the poorest and the most despised into protagonists of world-historical turning points.

In this period so rich in genuine women, two personalities can be regarded as typical: the French woman *Olympe de Gouges* and the Englishwoman *Mary Wollstonecraft.* Olympe's real name was *Marie Gouze.* Her parents were simple bourgeois in Montauban; but it is possible that she owed her existence to an affair of her mother Olympe—whose name she later took—with the poet LeFranc de Pompignan. Still very young, the strikingly beautiful lass with the Bourbon face (which led to rumors that her father was Louis XV) got married, but only a few years later threw off the chains of her deeply unhappy wedlock. Olympe went to Paris, where despite her very inadequate education she became the center of a merry social life on account of her sparkling mind and her great beauty. It is not astonishing that this inexperienced creature was not able to protect her heart against strong passions. She got to know the depths and the heights of life in every possible way before she became the militant leader of her sex. At first she sought an outlet for herself in literary productions for the stage but, of course, with little success, given her lack of formal education. Soon, however, under the impact of the ongoing Revolution, she turned her back on this activity and on her entire previous life. "I am burning," she wrote, "to throw myself unreservedly into work for the public good." She did it with all the forcefulness of her character. Her brilliance easily overcame all the difficulties she encountered. The misery of the people and the oppression of her sex gave her unusual energy. According to the judgment of her contemporaries, she surprised them again and again by the wealth of her ideas and the power of her language. Even the National Assembly listened to her brilliant oratory with amazement and often followed her suggestions. But in everything she wrote and said, feminine nature in its most beautiful traits expressed itself. Reacting to the famine, she published a manifesto that caused many women to follow her example and to vie with each other in the self-sacrifice of donating their jewelry to the state. In moving terms she described the squalor prevailing in the Saint Denis poorhouse, and she dealt with the burning question of the increase in the numbers of beggars. At first she demanded the institution of public welfare funds to combat this evil, but then she became aware of how humiliating it is to receive alms and then agitated in speeches and in print for the creation of public model workshops for the unemployed, an idea that partly was put into practice.

Compared to what she did on behalf of her own sex, however, all these endeavors were of only transitory significance. In the area of women's emancipation her activities were epoch making. Already in her address to women she had exclaimed, "Isn't it time that a revolution begin among us women as well? Shall we always be disunited? Will we never take an active part in the shaping of society?" And when the *Declaration of the Rights of Man* appeared, filling everyone with enthusiasm, she published a

manifesto, a *Declaration of the Rights of Woman,* which in a few bold
strokes contains the program of the women's movement. It begins with
some introductory words in which she demonstrates that ignorance of the
rights of women, or forgetting about them or dismissing them, was the
cause of national disaster and moral corruption. Then she continued:

> Woman is born free and by rights is equal to the man. The aim of
> every law-making community is to protect the inalienable rights of both
> sexes, which are freedom, progress, safety, and resistance to oppres-
> sion. . . . But the exercise of the rights that by nature are due to women
> has so far been kept within narrow limits. The nation on which the state
> is founded consists of the community of men and women, and law
> making must express the will of this community. Female citizens just like
> male citizens must participate in its shaping personally or through their
> elected representatives. The laws must be equal for all. Hence all female
> and male citizens must be admitted equally to all public positions,
> distinctions, and professions, in accordance with their abilities; the only
> criterion for their selection ought to be differences in their virtues and
> talents. Women have the right to mount the scaffold; they should have
> the same right to mount the speaker's platform. Women's rights, how-
> ever, should serve the welfare of all, not the advantage of their sex only.
> Women like men contribute to the material wealth of the state, hence
> they have the same right as men to demand an accounting concerning
> the way it is being administered. A constitution is invalid unless the
> majority of all individuals constituting the nation has participated in
> shaping it. . . . Awake, ye women! . . . The torch of truth has dispelled
> the clouds of foolishness and tyranny; when will you open your eyes?
> Unite; against the forces of raw power posit the forces of reason and
> justice. Then you will soon see how men will no longer lie at your feet as
> languishing worshippers but will stride hand in hand with you, proud to
> share the eternal rights of humanity with you.

Her declaration did not remain without consequences. Numerous
pamphlets for and against the women's demands appeared. The insignificant fashion journal, *Journal des femmes,* was turned into the first
periodical for the women's movement, renamed *l'Observateur féminin.*
The National Assembly was showered with a flood of petitions demanding political and social equality. "You have just abolished privileges," said
one of them, "now abolish that of the male sex." "The people are given
possession of their rights, the Negroes are freed, why not free the women
also?" it said in another one.

Olympe de Gouges correctly saw that the moment had come for
uniting the scattered militants for women's rights so as to lend greater
force to their endeavor. She founded the first political women's associa-

tion and became its leader and its most brilliant agitator. Alas, her activity was to be cut short much too soon. Her feelings rebelled against all cruelty that she saw being meted out in the name of freedom, and she was not one of those who know how to silence the voice of conscience for the sake of prudence. "The blood even of the guilty that is spilled cruelly dishonors the revolution," she exclaimed. To be sure, she was an enthusiastic republican; as early as 1789 in a letter to the National Assembly she had demanded that the king be deposed, and in view of the famine she had cried out to him in an address, "It is high time that you begin to tremble for your fate and that of your people. Do you wish to rule over pyramids of corpses and mountains of ashes?" But her compassionate heart was revolted by the manner in which the king's trial was conducted. "If you fell the tree of monarchy with crude hands," she wrote, "watch out that it does not fall on you." Already this statement aroused suspicion. She was accused of having been bought by the Royalists; against this she sought to defend herself by pointing at her poverty—she had given all her possessions to the poor. There was no willingness, however, to trust this uncomfortable admonisher, who with her oratory knew how to capture the masses, and in the Jacobin Club she was accused of heading a royalist conspiracy, for which, as a natural daughter of Louis XV, they said she felt especially predestined. At that point, instead of becoming more cautious in her attacks on the leaders of the Revolution, she became more reckless, because the death sentence against the king aggravated her extremely. She not only regarded it as cruelty but also dreaded the consequences for the further development of the Revolution. "Blood transforms minds and hearts; one tyrannical form of government will merely be replaced by another," she wrote. She felt the need to try everything to avert the impending catastrophe, and with that urge, shared by all people of deeply passionate disposition, to stand up for her convictions regardless of consequences, she offered to defend the king before the Convention. After his execution, mindless of the danger she conjured up, she wrote the sharpest pamphlets in which she vehemently attacked Robespierre in particular, and called out prophetically, "Your throne too one day will be the scaffold." She also tried to influence the women's associations toward her own views and frequently succeeded in making them assume a threatening stance and openly side with the victims of the guillotine. But Olympe de Gouges herself could not escape this fate. In the summer of 1793, at the age of 45, she was arrested, and on 3 November, her head fell under the guillotine.

Mary Wollstonecraft worked more through her pen than with oratory. A life filled with inner and outer struggles and deprivations had acquainted her with the sufferings of her sex. In her profession as teacher she had been keenly interested in problems of child rearing and education, and her first published work was a small treatise on the education of young girls. There followed quite a number of translations from the German and a few independent works that secured her a living and at the same time brought her into personal contact with her publisher, Johnson, in whose house she found intellectually stimulating company. He himself, like all his guests, followed the events of the French Revolution with burning enthusiasm; after all, it was Thomas Paine, whose brow bore the laurel of the American War of Independence as well as that of the storming of the Bastille, who set the tone in this company and proclaimed the rights of men in Johnson's drawing room. Thus Mary Wollstonecraft was drawn into the maelstrom of the revolutionary movement, and Burke's attack on her provided the fiery woman with an occasion to proclaim her ideas publicly. *The Justification of the Rights of Men* was the title of the book that made the author's name famous beyond the circle of her friends. But this was only the prelude and preface for her major work, the *Vindication of the Rights of Women*, which she dedicated to Talleyrand in the hope of exerting an influence on the restructuring of the French school system.

In a rush of passion she wrote this voluminous work in just a few weeks without taking time to reflect calmly. Indeed it shows the traces of its origins and consists of rather unsystematic thoughts that often shift suddenly, but all without exception testify to Mary Wollstonecraft's originality and sharpness. She laid the greatest stress on education, in the neglect of which she sees the cause of the faults and weakness of the female sex. She explains the behavior of women by an unhealthy spirit and compares it to a plant rooted in over-rich soil that brings forth beautiful blossoms but no fruit. Education produces "ladies" but no women; they are taught manners but not morality; their ambitions are directed toward vanities and meaningless trifles but not toward serious goals. They are accustomed to waste their time with idle games and to divert themselves with empty entertainment instead of getting used to work and to spending their leisure in pursuit of the joys of art, nature, and scholarship. In this fashion, those weak and thoughtless beings are reared systematically, and then their own educators, the men, blame them unmercifully for being weak and thoughtless. But whoever examines their education in detail will not be astonished that they are victims of prejudice and prone toward a lack of independence in their judgment and toward a blind faith in authority. The conditions surrounding them have in fact made them into inferior beings. But since they have been reduced to this low level artificially, wrote Wollstonecraft, it would be unfair to judge the entire female sex on the basis of its present status. Women would have to be given space for their own self-development and for the exercise of their potential, and then one might determine the place they should occupy on the intellectual and moral scale. And once they have been educated into rational people, they should no longer be treated as slaves but should enjoy the same rights as men.

With regard to one point Mary Wollstonecraft turned out to be more cautious and reticent than Condorcet, whose ideas in general she shared. He assumes universally applicable equal rights of men and therefore attributes equal political rights to women; nor does he make women's lack of education a pretext for inequality, arguing that men, too, are not subject to an intelligence test before being recognized as fully qualified citizens. She, however, makes reforms in education the precondition for reforms in the law. Yet in all other parts of her work she is the genuine pupil of the Revolution. Not only that in many of her asides she vehemently attacks the ideas of royalty, standing armies, and aristocracy, but she also discusses the problem of poverty and declares it to be one of the most basic causes of vice and crime. For women she deduces from this the need to be economically independent from men. She is the first to have expressed this demand that even today is still radical; and that places her into the ranks of the most enlightened and farsighted pioneers of the women's movement. But she was ahead of her time in other respects as well. In the name of chastity, which ought to be the same for both sexes, she demanded that boys and girls be educated together in public schools. Love between men and women, she wrote, would be purer and deeper, and marriages would be happier, only where innocent comradely intercourse and intellectual competition between the sexes from the earliest years on could be found. And physical education should complement intellectual training, so that a stronger and more handsome generation could be reared and the nation might have mothers who could produce and rear healthy children.

With this the fundamental note of the book has been struck: For the sake of their sacred natural calling, for the sake of the coming generation growing in their wombs and receiving from their bodies and their minds the first nourishment that determines its later development, for the sake of all that, women should stand beside men fully as equals and be free citizens also.

Armed for the struggle facing them—the struggle for the liberation of their own sex from the bonds of economic, intellectual, and moral slavery—women stood at the entrance gates of the nineteenth century. For the time being their work could not yet speak for them, but the marble was waiting for them to hew it, the silent language for them to give it life, the tones for women to awake them into melodies, and humanity in particular, boundlessly suffering humanity, was waiting for liberated women to help liberate it.

V.

Economic progress turned out to be the greatest emancipator of women: On the one hand, it destroyed their old world that had filled their thoughts and claimed their energies—the world of the home; on the other hand, it drove them with the whip of necessity into the struggle for existence, into wage work outside the home. Although women had always worked, their work, even when it was work for wages, had always been done within the four walls of the household. But the road into the factory, into the physician's operating room, onto the lectern or the judges' bench, led them at the same time into public life, into the conflict of interests between classes and parties. In previous centuries, isolated individual women, favored by privileged circumstances or driven by strong personal talents, had stepped out of the narrow sphere of their sex to be creative, active, or to teach; others, prescient of things to come, had shown the way toward the coming emancipation of their sex. But a women's movement could arise only when masses of women had to face the necessity to earn their living in the same lines of work as the men.

To the wives and daughters of the laboring people factories and workshops opened wide. No pretense of tender concern over potential threats to their femininity prevented entrepreneurs from using their cheap labor power to raise profits and to depress men's wages. Meanwhile the daughters of the bourgeois middle class, who were increasingly forced to fend for themselves because the prospects of marriage as the only secure source of support became more and more uncertain, faced closed doors. The women of the bourgeoisie had to fight for what the proletarian already had—access to male professions. For that reason the women's movement in its beginnings was a purely bourgeois movement. But it was also primarily an old maids' movement, and that gave it its peculiar character for a long time and often steered it into false directions. Single women sought work in order to keep alive and fought for access to higher professions in order to give some content to their lives. They were able to compete with men in their own areas because the duties of motherhood did not claim their time or energy. For that reason they could also establish that mechanical principle concerning the equality of men and women that assumed not only the equal abilities of both sexes but also equal possibilities to develop them and to utilize them professionally. The man's sexual function does not in any way hinder him in the exercise of his labor power; but the manner and form of labor in all lines of work is tailored to suit the men; hence where the woman competes with him she either is compelled to renounce the fulfillment of her sexual functions or to do physical and mental damage to herself and her children. In both cases—save for a few outstanding exceptional personalities—she remains handicapped; in the one case, she cannot attain the full development of her personality and the peak of her efficiency, for only a woman who has traveled the entire cycle of female life can represent the wealth and the greatness of her sex; in the other case, however, the conflict between motherhood and career can become the tragedy of her life and restrict her energy and efficiency. Hence the proletarian women's movement which represents not only the mere struggle for the right to work but also the struggle against the mode of work, signifies not only a new stage in time but also substantial progress and a deepening of the original women's movement. Its main principle is the adaptation of work conditions to the nature of women, not the adaptation of women to given work conditions. This has become more and more prevalent in the contemporary women's movement, because from demanding that work conditions be adapted to the nature of women to demanding that they be adapted to the nature of human beings in general, and hence to the condemnation of an economic system that has as its highest aim not the enrichment of all people's lives but the accumulation of capital, is only a step.

The question now is how the women's movement thus summarized in its basic principles has affected women and whether it has released intellectual values of lasting significance. What is essential here is not to find out that so and so many capable female physicians, lawyers, teachers, factory inspectors, and so on have shown themselves just as capable as their male colleagues. Instead, we must determine whether the mighty current of the women's movement, swelling to ever greater strength since the beginning of the nineteenth century and watering the fertile soil of the entire world of women—whether or not women themselves are conscious of that—has helped female personalities to flourish who can be placed next to leading men, not as equals in kind, but as equals in worth.

A glance into the gallery of female character portraits from the last hundred years leads to strange realizations. Although sharp boundary lines between the discrete manifestations of the female psyche cannot be drawn because in many cases there is a good deal of overlap, it is nonetheless necessary, for the sake of clarity, to establish certain categories, viz., the female scholar, the writer and artist, the woman as a source of inspiration, and the woman as political agitator.

Up to the nineteenth century women were never barred on principle from scholarly learning. In the Middle Ages, during the Renaissance, and in the seventeenth and eighteenth centuries there were always a few of them who attained the doctorate and held professorships. To be sure, the female sex in these periods did not produce a Galileo or a Newton, but, to the extent that this can be ascertained by historians, they performed respectably, mostly above the male average. That testifies to women's natural intelligence all the more since as a rule they did not receive specialized education equal to that given to men. *Caroline Herschel* acquired the necessary knowledge only by working as her brother's assistant, and yet her scientific achievements are not all that much inferior to his. *Mary Somerville* studied almost entirely on her own and yet attained heights of learning that the British Astronomical Society ungrudgingly recognized by making her an honorary Member. But it is always only exceptional people whose talents are so great that they overcome all obstacles, especially the limitations placed on women. For this reason their achievements cannot be credited to the female sex in general. Comparisons between male and female potential for scholarly work can be made only after a larger number of women have entered the learned professions, only after it is not just the irresistible compulsion of an inner calling that attracts select women to the universities, but when the need to earn a living has led even average women to advanced studies. That has been happening increasingly under the pressure of the same economic progress that drove the women of the proletariat into factories and workshops. Hence it was only in the beginning of the nineteenth century that we saw the struggle for admitting women into higher professions erupt, a struggle that is being waged by both sexes in all civilized countries with a bitterness corresponding to one gender's fear of competition by the other, while the other gender is haunted by the scourge of economic heed. Step by step women are conquering the field; in most countries universities have opened up for them, yet they are still being kept out of a number of higher professions, particularly in Europe. Hence when there is the need to make a living, women, unlike men, are not yet able to choose their professions in line with their inclinations or aptitudes. That implies not only an intellectual compulsion that frustrates the mind but also makes it impossible, for the time being, to make meaningful comparisons between female and male aptitudes.

A comprehensive view of this entire matter yields the following findings: To the extent that women are given a choice at all, they generally choose a field of study leading to a profession that permits the exercise of women's quintessential character traits, i.e., motherliness. *Women are unconsciously guided by compassion and the wish to care for others.* For centuries the teaching and nursing professions have represented the two main aspects of motherliness—the educational and the caring ones. But there are other contemporary women's professions in which we find them being acted out. Biographies and statements of American women lawyers reveal that it was not so much an interest in the abstract study of the law that made them into what they are today but rather the wish to help the poor and to remedy injustice. And it was not a penchant for theological subtleties that led many American women to the pulpit, but having their hearts filled with sermons about Christian neighborly love. Similarly we see the great and, fortunately, growing number of female physicians perform best as practitioners, not as researchers. But the most striking confirmation of this view comes from our experience in another field. Besides medicine, the field most often chosen by women today is the study of economics, and within this study, problems of social reform interest them the most. In previous times women's unschooled social consciousness could express itself only in the practice of charity; today this same emotion is guided and dominated by much better developed knowledge and places itself at the service of social reform. Here the achievements made by women are quantitatively and qualitatively on a par with those of the best of men.

For instance, female factory inspectors are just as expert and thorough in their reports and special investigations as they are self-sacrificing in their professional work. Female social workers in the field of poor relief and female health inspectors are usually preferred over their male colleagues because of their effectiveness. Moreover, in the field of research, too, women have shown a maturity of judgment, a depth of penetration into the material, a freshness of ideas, and a degree of productivity that give rise to the most optimistic expectations for the future. The authority of *Florence Kelley* with regard to cottage industries is indisputable; the first women's settlement created in the most squalid of Chicago slums by *Jane Addams* has become a model of its kind; *Charlotte Perkins Gilman's* works are pioneering achievements for the future of the women's movement because they proclaim and defend the principle of women's economic emancipation with full clarity; the scholarly investigations of *Elisabeth Gnauck-Kühne* and *Gertrud Dyrenfurth* about the conditions of women workers have shown their successors the way. All of these women attest to the outstanding aptitude of the female mind for the important area of social policy and economics. Towering above them is that woman whose genius has placed her into the ranks of the classics of political economy for all time to come: *Beatrice Sydney Webb* [sic]. To be sure, she collaborates with her husband, and their works are published under their joint names; but everyone knows that the greater importance must be attributed to her. This is suggested already by her maiden work, the epochal history of the English cooperative movement. Her history of British trade unionism and her history and practice of English trade associations are standard works in the best sense of the word. And since we are contemporaries of her works, we can state at the same time that she has nothing, but absolutely nothing, in common with the caricature of the "scholarly female" developed in the time of Gottsched. She has remained entirely a woman and has developed her natural beauty into a kind of feminine beauty that will one day be typical of the female sex. For one thing seems certain and jumps into our eyes as we contemplate ancient and contemporary women's portraits: Changes in the external appearance of the woman take place in step with changes in the intellectual contents of her life; the charming, infantile roundness of the face, the softness of the lines, gives way to more sharply lined features; the astonished, clear Madonna's eyes turn darker and more expressive, and greater varieties of beauty develop—for the mind is the greatest sculptor of all.

I have argued that the urge to ease the pains and worries of humanity tends to guide women even in their scholarly activities and has the potential of sparking the most significant achievements. That view can be supported by additional evidence.

In natural science and philosophy the achievements of women are quantitatively the lowest; that can mean only that they do not in general feel drawn to these branches of knowledge. But when, in the exceptions to this rule, they devote themselves to an abstract field like physics, chemistry, or mathematics, their achievements are above the male average, because it is always exceptional talent that has led them to this kind of study. I have already mentioned Anne Dacier, Caroline Herschel, and Mary Somerville. But the first place here belongs to the mathematician *Sonia Kovalevska*, whose theory of partial differential equations made her famous throughout Europe at a very young age; despite her early death, her life's work will retain its honorable place in the history of science. But while she has demonstrated with this that talent for theoretical science is not an absolute privilege of the male sex, her life, which on the basis of her friends' reports we know as well as that of few other women, gives us much more interesting revelations about the feminine psyche.

In her intensive devotion to the intellectual work that dominated her, her sexual urges had for a long time been dormant. For ten years she was able to live in a pretended marriage, and even when this turned into a real sexual partnership, this was occasioned only by a moment of profound emotional crisis. Her husband was not congenial to her. Even her child did not become a deep emotional experience for her. Only later, at the peak of her fame, her strong passionate nature broke through. It was as if the rich fullness of feminine erotic life had silently accumulated inside her and was now erupting like a volcano. Her scholarship had been able to fill and develop only the intellectual side of her being; her sexuality now loudly demanded its due. But the man whom she encountered at this stage in her life was not one who could have satisfied someone like Sonia Kovalevska; she had already progressed too far to the lonely height of really great minds. This tragic conflict destroyed her; in spite of all her glamor and fame, she was famished emotionally. Her life seems to me to be teaching one lesson: Devotion to theoretical science—rare enough among women—in the final analysis has a destructive effect on a woman if, in addition to her purely intellectual activity, her sexual needs and her emotional life are not fully satisfied. *Madame Curie*, the famous codiscoverer of radium, an authority in science who has succeeded her husband in holding the chair in physics at the University of

Paris, does not gainsay this hypothesis. To be sure, we know little about her inner life, and her closed, somewhat dour features do not betray any of it; yet decades of collaboration between two spouses are conceivable only if a happy marriage is the precondition, so that the woman, as a female, is not left empty-handed.

Education, medicine, social policy, theology, indeed even the law, all enlist the emotive side of female nature; even if her sexual urge is to remain unsatisfied, at least the energy of her maternal instincts can become active in caring for others. Hence even if we were to find no women who attain to the fullest their potentials for growth, we will certainly find strong and satisfied personalities among those women who have taken up any one of these fields of knowledge, even if they never had a chance to give themselves in love or call a child their own.

In conclusion, a general survey of women's scholarly achievements will cause us to concede that, indeed, they often rise above the male average, and once in a while are on a par with the very best male accomplishments; but not a single learned woman can measure up against a Newton or Galileo, a Spinoza or Kant. The limitations placed on their internal and external lives, the one-sided education, the inadequate opportunities for training, the almost insuperable prejudices women face are doubtless among the chief reasons for choking off many a talent even before it could have begun to develop; yet for the time being it has remained unexplained why there has been no single genius, as there are among men, who was able to overcome all these obstacles. Even among the educators, whose field probably has the most affinity with women's nature, the pioneers—Rousseau, Pestalozzi, Fröbel—were men. And philosophy, for one, has not produced a single woman of any stature whatever. These clear facts notwithstanding, we ought to be cautious in what we may deduce from them. Infallible conclusions will be possible only on the basis of experiences based on centuries of unlimited educational and training opportunities equal to those of men.

VI.

Scholarly work presupposes a certain level of learning, and diligence and thoroughness can in fact substitute for natural talent, at least to make the achievements of average accomplishments possible. But in *art*, especially poetry, drama, and music, talent is the sole precondition for success. In order to create works of enduring value here, an individual personality must be the carrier of the talent. But women have only in exceptional cases been given a chance to develop their individual personalities. They have almost always been but a herd, never individualities. A woman like *Vittoria Colonna* could be brought forth only by the Renaissance, a culture that secured freedom of development for a few lucky and privileged individuals.

Then came the great global change that began with the age of the Encyclopedists and found its resounding expression in the French Revolution; and with it came an era that, often forcibly, tore women into the maelstrom of life from out of their narrow circle of experience. Gradually the chains fell from the woman's soul, she discovered her own ego just as she discovered the world around her, and this discovery loosened her tongue. In his work, the writer presents himself and the wealth he has within him; how could the woman have presented herself at a time when *she* did not own herself?

One of the most outstanding women of all times was the first to open the gates of the new life with vigorous hand: *Louise Germaine de Staël.* Like other persons of genius, she cannot be categorized; she was everything at one and the same time: writer, politician, agitator. The spirit of the time lived in her with all its fire, its revolutionary spirit, its abundance of seeds for the future. She was not only the first woman who with inspiring poetic élan fought for the social emancipation of her sex. That even a man like Napoleon could not subdue her, that she was the only enemy whom he never defeated, testifies to the extraordinary character of this woman. But the fact that her *Corinne* and her *Delphine* can still provide intellectual guidance in our time raises their author to the ranks of humanity's great pioneers. Next to her, the German novelist, *Sophie La Roche,* seems like a tiny little star next to the shining moon. And yet even her *Geschichte des Fräuleins von Sternheim* is of importance for an assessment of women's fiction. What is expressed here for the first time is the personal life experience of the unsatisfied upper-class girl. She found numerous imitators; novel-writing women no longer were a rarity, especially in Germany; it is a good thing to leave them to their well-deserved oblivion. It was only Staël's country that once again produced a world-conquering personality: *George Sand.* When her *Indiana* appeared, it created an extraordinary sensation. In impeccable form it renders all the misery, all the inner conflicts of the time, and the deep emotional conflicts of women. In her other works the basic note remained the same: sharp criticism of the rotten society, the unmerciful unveiling of all the abysses of life—but the view of the future changed. If at first she fought for women's emotional rights vis-à-vis conventional marriage, for truth-fulness and morality as against the hypocrisies of conventional morality, later her ideal of liberating the female sex turned into one of liberating all the oppressed. She became the greatest promoter of the revolutionary ideas of 1848. Hatred pursued her; slander stuck to her heels. But just as in her early years when gnawing worry had not made her collapse but had generated new creative energy and allowed a work like *Indiana* to be written, so hatred and smears did not now deter her from her path and did not break her spirit. Her significance for an assessment of the nature of the female, however, just as in the case of Staël, far transcends the value of her written work. As different as Staël and Sand were in their ideologies and achievements, there is one thing they had in common as human beings: they were alive! Storms of passions raged through their hearts and shook up their lives; their erotic energy seemed inexhaustible; but all was dominated and outlasted by their touching maternal love. One of them was a more solid and consistent character, the other more unpredictable and mercurial in her love relations. But both had smashed the chains of conventionality and emptied the cup of life down to the last dregs. Let us join to them their famous English colleague *George Eliot;* her life, too, was extraordinary. In her prudish country, she dared to live in a common-law marriage and, already an aging woman but with an eternally youthful heart, to enter a new love partnership. Are we rash in asserting that the wealth and variety of personal life are deeply and intrinsically related to the wealth and fullness of the expressions of the mind—in women as well as in men? Or that—to put it differently—the nature of the female artist is just as much in need of this rich and full life as that of the male?

Do not tell me about those countless women "novelists" in all lan-guages who for the last hundred years have showered us with the children of their Muse and whose lives ran in smooth and gentle grooves. Their achievements usually are on a par with the much maligned knitted pair of socks, which is the best that those good old aunties behind the stove ever produce. *Luise Mühlbach* is a typical representative, and there are lots of them like her today. Female gabbiness, intensified by boredom and the need to make a living, has simply taken command over their pen and ink and gladly satisfies the reading public of the family weeklies who measure the worth of a novel by the needs of spoiled upper-class daughters reared in hothouses.

In Mme. de Staël and in George Sand we admire that strong individual note. We find it again only in most recent times in a growing number of women writers. Of course, the two great ones could be no more than precursors and exceptional individuals. It required progress in the emancipation of women from the limitations of their internal and external lives to produce genuine individuals. Today what gets them recognition is no longer the "masculinity" of their achievements but the fact that they are *their own* achievements. It is not my task here to define the difference between men and women in the writing of fiction. But do get acquainted with some of the best that we know today: *Marie von Ebner-Eschenbach's Gemeindekind, Selma Lagerlöf's Jerusalem, Clara Viebig's Das tägliche Brod,* or *Ricarda Huch's Aus der Triumphgasse,* and you will have to sense the specifically feminine in these works, the depth and warmth of feeling, the empathy and compassion, in short, everything that comprises the term "motherliness." Then there is another thing to be considered in the fiction of female authors: Their subject not only is very often one of the great problems of the women's question—free love, marriage, maternity—but also quite frequently has the character of a personal confession. It is as if in the books of these women the sex that for centuries has been condemned to suffer and be silent wanted to vent all the pent-up ache and pain, the despair and the struggles. Beginning with *Gabriele Reuter's Aus guter Familie,* from which the misery of a lonely girl cries out painfully, to works such as *Sybille Dalmar* (by *Hedwig Dohm*), *Ellen Olestjerne* (by *Countess Reventlow*), *Halbtier* (by *Helene Böhlau*), and *Ich bekenne,* as well as *Tagebuch einer Verlorenen* (by *Klara Müller-Jahnke*), these are books of self-revelation and at times even self-laceration. Similar books written by women confront us again and again. Often the cloak of fiction has been thrown over it only very thinly. Very often the pen was moved by a yearning to speak up and speak out so as to roll the pressing burden off the soul. That is then proven by later works: the first book has exhausted the energies, the entire ego is deposited in it; what follows is no more than feeble repetitions, torturously produced. The talent for fiction is lacking that can create new figures again and again.

This predominance of the purely personal in very many female writers gives them a special talent for poetry. What made *Annette von Droste-Hülshoff* a good poet was the depth and warm intimacy of her feeling for nature, her love and understanding of the area in which she grew up—emotions so strong that they often lend dramatic power to her poetry. But despite her great talent everything she created is tuned to this one tone only because her hermitlike life allowed no other strings of her soul to be touched. Hence it is wrong to put her on a par with *Elizabeth Barrett Browning,* as Georg Brandes has suggested, because the latter stands more than a head higher than she. If she had written nothing else than those forty-four sonnets in which the pain and the longing and the ecstasy of her love sob and jubilate, she would have to be placed side by side with the greatest poets. No woman has written erotic poetry like hers in which depth of feeling is combined with such beauty of expression and perfection of form. To be sure, no woman has had a fate like hers: a protected childhood, a youth undisturbed by painful physical and emotional suffering, complete and undisturbed happiness in love that was at the same time a harmonious meeting of minds on the intellectual level and a friendship without barriers, the fullness of maternal joy in a child that nature had endowed with an exceptional mind and body, unfettered freedom in developing and applying a creative mind—is that not a rich woman's life? Her work *Aurora Leigh* most magnificently reflects the wealth of her ideas and sentiments, her versatility, her forcefulness, and her courage. In it she also summarizes what she regards as the first task of her sex: the liberation of the individual personality; and as its highest aptitude she regards the creative power of the emotions. Surely we must rate the judgment based on a rich life made by a woman of genius more highly than the theorizing of speculative intellectuals, especially when the greatest women of their time—women like Staël, George Sand, and Elizabeth Barrett Browning—find themselves in agreement, despite the differences in their experiences and accomplishments.

In the same abundance as wildflowers after the spring rains, so the more we approach the present time and the more the icy bonds of winter in the hearts of women were defeated by budding life, women have stepped forth as poets. Apart from their literary value or nonvalue, many of their poems are valuable as self-revelations. As long as women are bound in a thousand painful chains, no god can make them speak out about their suffering, because it takes courage to affirm one's own special identity. But courage is the virtue of the free. As long as prudishness and conventionality sealed women's mouths, it was possible for people to regard Chamisso's *Frauenliebe und Leben* as a typical representation of how women pretended to love and how the world understood their love. In most recent times, in contrast, a mania for confession with regard to erotic life has got hold of women. Its results both in the form of poetry and in novels have a character of their own. They express that vain preoccuptaion with physical beauty that has been fostered in women in that the degree of their attractiveness for men was virtually the only measure of their worth and signified the only insurance for their future. In many of their love songs and ego-centered novels they describe their own beauty, their irresistibility, the numbers of their pining lovers, and their cruelty toward those lovers. At the same time we encounter that poetry of the "liberated woman" who confuses unreined lust with freedom, makes no distinction between sexual licence ranging into the perverse and sensual joy. This has many representatives, since for many women it is easier to liberate the tongue than the soul, and many contemporary girls are eager for the reputation of "living it up." Typical representatives are *Marie-Madeleine Dolorosa,* in whose poems sexual lust and religious devotion mingle, who wallows in incense, the confessional, and crowns of thorn, and whose hysterical imagination rises to intoxication with blood and pain.

Abnormities of this kind are natural consequences of liberation from centuries of emotional bondage, of a kind of liberty that was grafted onto the dried-up old trunk of girls' education as a foreign sapling and thus was bound to degenerate. Women lack not only the intellectual training but also the firm base of moral autonomy that alone would make them capable of handling freedom. But there is something else that this poetry teaches us: it destroys the widespread myth about the basic stunting of sexuality in women and demonstrates the aberrations into which female sexuality must go and has always gone as long as it is repressed and hindered in its natural practice; the only thing lacking until now was the courage to talk about these things. A similar observation can be made in another direction. There is a generally accepted view that with the onset of physical maturity sexual needs that are so powerful become manifest in the man that their nonsatisfaction results in physical and emotional damage, but that the same is not true of women. Wherever women manifest similar tendencies, the tolerant will consider them pathological, while the moralists will consider them sinful; nobody dares suggest that there is a need to satisfy these urges, even though everyone could point to women from among his or her own circle of acquaintances whose good health dates from the day of their marriage. Our female poets reveal the secret of women's sexual yearning, which is most deeply hidden because it is the most severely tabooed.

Recognizing and emphasizing the erotic aspects of women's love, which we find again and again in contemporary women's poetry, is not, however, merely their reaction against its previous moral condemnation, but it is also one of the strongest demonstrations of the liberation of the female sex from intellectual and emotional bondage. She no longer wants to seem but wants to be, not only to be loved but to do her own loving; her surrender no longer is a sacrifice but a free gift.

How firmly tied down the woman of the past was, how even her literary achievements followed narrowly male models, is shown not only by the fact, still encountered today at times, that as soon as she began to sing songs of love she imagined herself into the soul of the man; it is shown even more clearly by the extraordinarily interesting fact that the one emotional experience she shares with no one else, which is centered on motherhood, has not found artistic expression despite its width and depth. I think there is hardly anything that testifies more weightily about the degree of inner bondage in which women lived for centuries, about the way they were socialized to veil their own selves, about the judgment that sentenced them to keep silent about the most exalted and the most profound emotions stirring in them. Only today is the female psyche beginning to awaken in this area as well. *Mia Holm's* tender mother songs, *Anna Ritter's* poems that talk about the thousand blessings of being a mother, *Agnes Miegel's* songs in which the longing for a child begs to find lyrical form, *Ada Negri's* splendid poetry in particular, in joy and bliss—they all allow us glimpses into women's emotional life that even the best male poet would not be able to give, were he even a genius with the eyes of a seer.

There is yet another area of female poetry into which *Ada Negri* leads us: the social one. In her *Cry of the Children*, Elizabeth Barrett Browning was one of the first to launch a passionate attack on the existing social order that converts even children into machinery in the service of capital; but Ada Negri was the first one to become the poet of class struggle. She had grown up in a hovel of most abject poverty; her mother was a tired, spent factory worker who already as a child had been compelled to work for a living; for a long time she taught in a miserable little primary school for children of the rural proletariat and had experienced the dreary cycle of working-class life on her own body. Hence like nobody else she was able to become the songstress of poverty and an intellectual pioneer of the worker's movement. It seems to me that she shows the way into the future of feminine poetry, which will be filled not only with love's pains and love's ecstasies but is destined, in accordance with the essence of feminity, to find the most stirring and moving tones also for the great suffering of all humanity.

With this we have exhausted women's activities in literature so far. In writing for the stage, women's talents have found a limit that until now has been insurmountable. Whatever attempts have been made here, they are all of little worth. If some individual works, such as *Elsa Bernstein's Königskinder*, stick out from the mass they do not do so in consequence of any dramatic power they might have but because of their deep poetic contents. The deeply engrained subjectivism of women seems to be unsuitable for creating genuine, well-rounded personalities and putting them on the stage. Here the writer's individuality ought to take a step back so that the individual character of the people his or her imagination has created can come to the fore; but about the literary achievements of women in general one can say that they are the more valuable the more deeply their creator's personality has been imprinted on them. Hence in narrative prose and in poetry women can make outstanding contributions often on a par with those of men, whereas the playwright's laurels are attainable to them, if at all, only in exceptional cases.

VII.

What applies to drama writing also applies to sculpture. In both cases the problem is to create figures, to breathe life into dead material. And here too the female talent turns out to be inadequate. There is not a single woman sculptor of genius, only a number of handsome little talents and able workers for the kind of minature sculpture that contemporary craftsmanship has placed into the foreground. And even for the art of interior decorating—which one would think should be the proper field for women—only men have been pathbreakers. Women turn out to be clever imitators, but none of them has been able to create new viable forms. Once a new form is given, however, only women usually know what to do with it; that ineffable charm of a cozy home is their work; the genuine character of a room is determined by them, not by the style of the furniture. What a difference between the room of a male student and the girlish chamber of a woman who is his equal in age and education, or between the bachelor's apartment and the home managed by a genuine woman. From this we must deduce: In the construction of a chair or a table, calculating reason, i.e., the man, comes more into play; the feminine element, the *feeling* for harmony and beauty, becomes important only in the manner in which they are used, the way they join in the harmony of the living space, and in the value of the effects thus created. That often is much more important then many of those supermodern products from female hands which are called art crafts.

For painting and the graphic arts the female sex seems to have pronounced aptitude. The history of art tells us of medieval nuns who made important achievements in miniature painting. In the Renaissance and in the seventeenth and eighteenth centuries a number of women painters appeared who became celebrities in their own time. But most of them share two traits: They were painters' daughters and thus were able to absorb the craft skills of their art from earliest childhood almost in playful fashion, and they almost exclusively limited themselves to portraiture and to the painting of flowers and miniatures. That is true also for the two greatest representatives, *Mme. Vigée-Lebrun* and *Angelika Kauffmann*. Both belong to that revolutionary era in history to which so many important women owe their intellectual life and their individual identity. Yet, despite their incontrovertible artistic importance, they cannot be placed on a par with their greatest male colleagues. Their human figures lack strength and character. I also find it characteristic that they succeeded best in their self-portraits. The beautiful Mme. Vigée-Lebrun did no less than sixteen, and of them the portrait showing her in tender embrace with her child takes first place from the artistic point of view. Goethe said about one of these pictures that it had been painted "with obvious intention to please." His judgment applies not only to all the others but also to those of Angelika Kauffmann, about whose style of painting Goethe said that "serenity, lightness of touch, and pleasantness are the only predominant features of our artist's numerous works."

Once we are in the nineteenth century we encounter women artists who have transcended the conventionally feminine in their works and have managed to give artistic expression increasingly to the naturally feminine. One of the classic examples of this is a women like *Rosa Bonheur*, who has steeped herself in the life and character of the animal world with a love of which a man would be incapable; another would be *Marie Bashkirtsev*, whose group of Paris street urchins, entitled "Meeting", must be regarded as one of the most brilliant achievements of feminine art in general. Her diaries have given us an opportunity to gain deep insight into the emotional life of this artist; by nature she had been richly endowed with talent, but the unsatisfied female in her threatened to destroy all germs of greatness; but then her last, and only genuine, painful love for Bastien-Lapage had the effect of stimulating hothouse air and caused the fruits of her talents to ripen. Technically she worked with means that he provided, but through her love she grew beyond him as an artist.

Almost as numerous as the women who supply novels to the family weeklies we find today women painters. But even though most of them may be on a low level artistically, most of them do manifest a more vigorous personal note. Some of them excel the mass of male painters, especially in women's and children's portraiture, and artists like *Sabine Lepsius, Dora Hitz,* and *Julia Wolfthorn*—each one totally different from the others, each one with her own interesting individual character—are quite on a par with the best of their time. Yet what is typical once again is the limitedness of their subject matter: wherever they go beyond portraiture, i.e., beyond immersing themselves into, or showing understanding for, other people, their works usually cease to have an artistically individual character. Only a single artist of the present time offers proof that one-sidedness in women's art is not necessarily related to the nature of the female in general: *Käthe Kollwitz.* Her subject is the life of the people, but not the idyllic one. She leads us into the depths of their squalor and despair, onto the heights of their enthusiasm and fanaticism. She does not even require color to intensify impressions; by switching from the paint brush to the etching needle she renounced color altogether and precisely through that means achieved the greatest artistic effects. The bloody orgy of her dance around the guillotine, the stark hunger and misery of her weavers' cycle, the riotous peasants, crazy with fanaticism, in her pictures from the Peasant War—nobody who has ever seen them will forget them. And that poor emaciated proletarian woman with an infant on her flabby breasts is more moving and more provocative in its effect than all mass oratory or pages and pages of description of misery could ever be.

In the fine arts we see the female sex going the same way it did in scholarship and in literature. From copying the men to conquering and asserting her own personality; from expressions of the purely individual to an understanding of the world around her; from the mother whose only world was her own infant that she was nursing to the female who feels herself a mother to all those on earth in need of care, and whose world-embracing maternalism is the motive force of all her actions, the Muse of her artistic genius. If indeed women are dominated and guided by the depth of their feeling, by their subjectivism, why is it then that the most subjective of all art forms, *music*, has remained closed to their creative potential? Women have never been prevented from practicing music; it has always been an essential part of women's upbringing; as performing artists women have attained perfect mastery in all areas. And yet the history of music does now know a single woman composer of significance worth mentioning. Is that not a direct refutation of our attempt to demonstrate that feelings are the strongest determinant of female creative potential?

Now first of all we do not know to what extent women participated in creating the most primeval music, i.e., folk song. How many an age-old lullaby or children's song may have been sung first by a mother! Further, it seems to me that music has been inaccessible to women so far precisely because it is the most subjective of all the arts. The development of music into what it is today began relatively late even for men. To think in terms of tones, to construct a world out of tones—that requires an intensification of one's inner life, a degree of refinement of sensibilities, a personality so forceful and well rounded that it is a kind of personality that women will be able to attain only after a long period of gradual humanization. In music, women are still at a stage that in other areas of intellectual life they left behind some time ago: they reproduce, they adapt to the thinking and feeling of the men, they are the instruments on which he plays.

Women's masterly standing as actresses, undeniably acknowledged for the last century and a half, confirms this view. But let us here too note the facts, first, that for a very long time custom and convention barred women from the stage, and, second, that their artistic importance dates only from that turning point at which women's emancipation as individual personalities begins. Women like *Rachel* or *Corona Schröter* are personalities whom the prerevolutionary period could not have produced; and the peak of acting artistry reached by such women as *Agnes Sorma* or *Eleonore Duse* could not have been scaled even by artists of genius without the direct and indirect effects of women's struggle for emancipation. Even such outstanding individuals apart, if actresses in general not only rival their male colleagues in talent and potential but often outdo them, we will have to find reasons other than the argument that reproduction must come easier to those who have difficulty producing. I myself believe I have found the principal reason for their truly outstanding accomplishment in the fact that actresses, in comparison to other women, enjoy greater personal freedom. Not only is their public life richer and less isolated from the world, but also their intimate lives are not as constrained by false shame and societal conventions. The fact that once they were reckoned among vagrants and were assigned a place outside bourgeois morality has in the course of developments benefited them. They are quicker to follow their instinctual drives, their sex life has not dried up; the fire of erotic love that inspires men, especially artists, and enables them to do great and beautiful things helps women too to light the flaming torch of their minds. For them, as for most people of their sex, it has not been turned into a flickering little hearth fire just good enough to warm their fingers that are numb with cold. Duse's female roles are not mere reproductions but new creations out of the fullness of her rich emotional life. Can we imagine a Duse whose own heart has not been moved profoundly by all the pains and ecstasies of love? But this precondition of greatness in art, it seems to me, is a precondition for greatness in any creative endeavor. And for women, who possess this precondition only rarely, this is true to a much higher degree than for men, who have always possessed it. Nature does not arrange things senselessly. Sexuality with all its implications plays an incomparably greater role, physiologically, for women than for men; naturally therefore, it is bound to have a deeper and more determining impact on women's mental state than on that of men; and the elimination of sexuality in women is bound to bring with it the destruction of great psychic values. If only the experts were to do some thorough research on the relations between sexual life and intellectual creativity, they would surely contribute more toward the solution of the deeper puzzles of the women's question than all those investigations into the differences between the female and male brains with which so many a scholar tries to make a name for himself.

VIII.

With the description of their scholarly and artistic creative potential, the intellectual aptitudes of women have not yet been exhausted; indeed, we may have been treating only that part which is least appropriate to the nature of the female. I have expressed my conviction that the value and the height of women's intellectual creativity depends not only on the degree of freedom they enjoy in developing their own individuality, i.e., on the equality of rights in education as well as public life, but even more on their opportunity to act out fully their sexuality. But at the same time I believe that our great teacher, Mother Nature, teaches us about yet other links between mind and sex.

From ancient times two facts have become part of the inalienable basic store of truths founded on centuries of experience: that outstanding men always had *important mothers*—important by virtue of their personalities more than because of their own independent intellectual accomplishments; and that in the life of almost every great man, a woman played the role of *Egeria*. * "The eternally feminine lifts us upward." To have inspired a Dante or given birth to a Goethe will secure a higher place in the memory of humanity to the woman who accomplished that than to many a woman who created a great intellectual work.

Both roles identify the importance of women as *sources of inspiration*. What made *Mme. Councillor Goethe* immortal was not only the gifts her motherly nature gave to her child as seeds of coming greatness, but much more her art in promoting the growth of these seeds, her maternal instinct which is the basis for the understanding of the child's emotional needs. For this reason the bonds between mother and son most of the time are much more intimate than those between son and father. And it is the same maternal instinct that is mirrored in those women who filled the lives of humanity's leaders with happiness and lent élan to their activities. This maternal instinct can also be called devotion—a way of giving oneself that has the strength to separate the best from the own self only to give it away as a gift. These were often courtesans, despised by the world of "proper" manners, especially when they were the only ones who enjoyed a life of freedom and access to higher education. But even when they were not, bourgeois morality has almost always taken offense at them. It took later generations to build them altars. Among these women we must list *Julie Récamier*, whose home at the beginning of the eighteenth century was the social center of the Paris intelligensia. *Charlotte von Stein* must also be named in this connection. Goethe's letters to her are leaves in the most beautiful wreath of immortality that any woman has ever worn, and the fact that the most wonderful gifts of his genius were given us in the period of his intimate intercourse with her is the best proof of women's power to inspire.

This power emanates from the mother and from the lover, and has its impact on one man. But the maternal instinct can also be aimed at the

---

*Egeria is a figure from Roman myth; a nymph who served as the advisor to the legendary second king of Rome.

circle of friends and apply its life-bringing encouraging powers here also. Two women of the nineteenth century represent this type: *Rahel Varnhagen* and *Malvida von Meysenburg*. One has left us letters and diaries, the other, memoirs. Although their personalities continue to make an impact in this way, their real life's work, which cannot be weighed or measured, towers high above the literary works they have left us. Drawn as if by a magnet, the greatest minds of their times established contact with these women and through them established connections with each other. In their quiet chambers they found empathy, friendship, help, and vital energy; here their hearts were filled with great feelings; mean and common urges were suppressed; ideas about humanitarianism and justice, truth and peace, were awakened and promoted. Women such as they—often even their names are not known to us—are like fountains of youth for the soul, they possess the rod of Moses that by its magic lets life-giving water rush from dead rock. And these inspiring women then turn into agitators for the great ideals of humanity, women whose maternal love spills over into love for all human beings and who from this derive the strength to serve a good cause even if it means sacrificing their own lives.

Bettina von Arnim is one of these agitators, in view of her work, *Dies Buch gohört dem König*, in which the passionate social consciousness of this woman speaks out with such lack of restraint; even more *Harriet Beecher Stowe*, whose book *Uncle Tom's Cabin*, is artistically totally inadequate, yet so overflowing with the sense of justice that in the struggle for the emancipation of the slaves it could be carried ahead like a sacred banner. It deserves to be emphasized as particularly characteristic of women that in almost every case they employed their power of agitation first on behalf of oppressed strata of the population; thus in North America, for the slaves, in France 1789–1793 and again in 1848, for the underprivileged classes, especially the workers. Even in Germany, where women's public activity was considered altogether improper, the pioneer of the women's movement, *Louise Otto-Peters*, at first fought under the banner of the revolution of 1848. And the courageous American women led by *Lucretia Mott* and *Elizabeth Cady Stanton*, fully conscious of the just cause they were advocating, braved sneers and derision and hatred of all kind in making the equality of political rights for women their first demand, because during their participation in the slave emancipation movement they had recognized that the possession of this equality was a necessary precondition for success. The women's movement in England developed in similar fashion. At first it was women like *Elizabeth Fry* and *Florence Nightingale* who developed their strength in the struggle against misery and squalor by organizing women to care for the poor and sick and then transformed this care into institutions of local or central government. Is it not once again specifically feminine emotions that are expressed here in the fact that devotion to others outweighs self-interest and the interests of their own sex? And just as women develop all their inner resources only as mothers for the sake of their child, so it is only as helpers to the poor and the disinherited that women have perfected those talents that today enable them to play leading roles in the great social clash of cultures that is shaking the world, taking the form of two parallel movements—that of the women and that of the workers.

While at first it was almost exclusively men who began to theorize about the women's question—Condorcet, Hippel, Thompson, Mill, Bebel, to name but a few—it was primarily women who due to their great talent for agitation drew the practical conclusions from these doctrines and carried them into the masses. "Equal rights" at first was their only slogan, and frequently it led to a forcible repression of sexual differences and to those caricatures that have quite rightly been dubbed the "third sex." The natural energy of women has managed to overcome this aberration very quickly. "A child and employment" is perhaps the slogan that best characterizes the thrust of the contemporary women's movement, because it summarizes its aim: to combine a career with motherhood, the full development [of woman] as a well-rounded member of human society and as a sexual being. In order to come close to this goal, all those struggles today being waged by women have proven to be necessary: the struggle for the right to an education, for political rights, for social reform, and for economic independence. In all civilized countries armies of women are engaged in identical struggles, and it is difficult to single out a few of them as particularly representative. *Susan B. Anthony*, the leader of the American suffrage movement until her recent death, was able still at the age of eighty to move audiences with the fire of her oratory. *Josephine Butler* with incomparable heroic courage began a crusade for the most unfortunate of her sex, the prostitutes. *Louise Otto-Peters* devoted her whole life's work to the slogan "I am recruiting women to be citizens in the realm of freedom." *Ellen Key* is a pioneer of the contemporary women's movement who has elevated the mother and the child onto the throne of the earth and regards equality in educational opportunities and legal status only as the bases on which the woman's individual personality can develop freely. They all have been active with all the triumphant energy of that genuine gift for inspiring others, they have promoted life, warmth, and progress, and have demonstrated that genuine femininity was never a hindrance but a precondition of their successes. And just as misery, squalor, and injustice made women into abolitionists and suffragists, just as knowledge developed out of their feelings, so the torments of suffering humanity have driven them on to other areas of struggle. There is the temperance movement, today a worldwide organization of millions of women. From a ridiculous moral campaign against drinkers, it has increasingly turned into a reform movement against those social and economic conditions that cause alcoholism. It was created and led by a woman, *Frances Willard,* whose great personality America appreciated so highly that the country put up a monument in her honor. However skeptical we may be with regard to the practical results of the peace movement so far, yet for the time being it undoubtedly mobilizes hearts and minds against the madness of war. It owes its existence primarily to the enthusiastic leader of the Theosophic movement, *Annie Besant,* whose overwhelming gift for oratory has attracted increasing numbers of adherents to her cause.

This, however, does not exhaust the range of effects emanating from woman's world-embracing motherliness: Empathy, compassion, understanding, and joining in the struggle—these have always been the stages in her course, but the circle defined by her feelings, her knowledge, and, finally, her active energy can be small or large.

For the most advanced women this circle has widened so as to create room for the suffering of all humanity. What good, they argue, is the right to work to us if it means no more than the right of the few privileged to exploit the labor power of the many poor? What good is the right to love as long as we are unable to carry out our maternal duties, as long as the fruits of our loving are condemned to the same misery as we? What good is a struggle by women only for women as long as we are cast into the same chains of wage labor as the men?

That argument is the road that leads women into the ranks of the workers' movement and makes them into socialists, whether from observing the misery of others or from suffering themselves. These socialists include the women of the Russian revolution of 1905, who not only knew how to die for the cause of the people but also lived for it, and lived for it even after the gates of the most terrible prisons closed after them. Even as prisoners they functioned as nurses and consolers of their male comrades-in-suffering; voluntarily, they followed them into exile in order to help them bear their sad lot. These revolutionary women are women of deep feeling and loving care. The more their hearts were filled with love for the oppressed, the deeper also their hatred of the oppressors, and their hearts drove them into struggle. No woman's history can testify to this as brilliantly as that of *Louise Michel*, the heroine of the French Commune. Her entire life in freedom and in prison was one unlimited act of devotion. She was poor, but always happened to have enough to help others; she was persecuted and cast out and yet always managed to be a helpmate and a refuge for the persecuted. Again and again she filled those who had lost their courage with new enthusiasm. This woman has not erected herself any important monument with some major work, and yet surely she has done more for the cause of humanity than many women scholars or novelists: In our hearts she has planted seedlings of strength, self-sacrificing courage, and love of humanity, that cannot wither.

Our great teacher, Mother Nature, I said at the beginning of this chapter, shows us additional connections between mind and sexuality. When we consider the importance of the woman as source of inspiration and as agitator, we get an explanation of this; for here her mind and her heart express themselves most strongly; these roles have not been artificially grafted onto her but pour out of her innermost essence. Might it not be that the determining influence of gender is reversed in the area of the human mind? The woman brings forth into the world living children from the man's seed. A recipient, inseminated by the man, she is responsible for the reproduction of the human species. Is there not perhaps a process in which the *man is inseminated* by the soul of the woman? And is she not thereby helping create a way of life that is the richer, the more perfectly she develops her personality to its fullest potential? If that is so, then any repression of women's opportunities would be not only injustice against the female sex but also a crime against humanity. If that is so, we will have to provide a free course to the feminine genius, to the highest creative power of women in this area. If that is so, we will have to let women develop totally without hindrance, obedient to the inner urges that inspire them. To be sure, our antagonists believe that intensifying the influence of women would mean to feminize civilization. If that means nothing else than greater security of peace among the nations, the gradual victory of social justice, the realization of the command to love our neighbor—preached for millenia but never followed—then this feminization is the *penetration of the spirit of motherliness into hitherto purely masculine culture,* hence the *marriage of the male and the female principles,* through which alone anything genuinely viable develops both in the world of nature and in that of the mind.

IV.

Heroism, Individualism, and Joy

Steeped in the Romantic tradition, Braun deplored the gray bleakness, the dirt, the noise, the joylessness of life in the modern city and often returned to this theme. She saw joy alienated not only by Christianity and capitalism, but also in the Marxist movement, which she regarded as Puritan, humorless, single-minded, and dour. Moreover, in its cold rationality it seemed insensitive to people's need for festivals, rites, rituals, and celebration.

There is a story about Emma Goldman being at a gathering of fellow anarchists and dancing with one of them. Her lover, Alexander Berkman, growled disapproval: "We should not be dancing," he said, "as long as the revolution has not been won and the downtrodden freed," to which Goldman is said to have replied, "If I can't dance to it, it isn't my revolution." Braun would have been in agreement.

When she first began to rebel against the conventions of her aristocratic class, she expressed this rebellion in tones of wild hedonism possibly inspired by Nietzsche or by the incipient Décadence movement. The poem from her unpublished papers in the Leo Baeck Institute is written in this mood. By reading it aloud at a party in 1886 she greatly shocked her peers. Once she had joined the Marxist movement, her cult of joy concentrated on the de-alienation of labor, as shown by her sketch, "The Sermon about Joy."

Some of her most important formative years were spent in Münster, where her father was commandant of the garrison. She was then in her early twenties, living the giddy life of an upper-class debutante, a life that disgusted her with its emptiness. The city was solidly Catholic, and the pre-Lenten period of carnival was a time of continual partying; it was the high social season. The carnival season of 1889 brought to the fore all her bitterness in the face of the wild frolicking in the four-line verses printed here, and several articles in later years deal again with carnival in a more socialist framework of ideas. What remains the same is the emphasis on the emptiness of fleeting carnival joys that are now contrasted with an altogether de-alienated life in which we no longer have to don masks. In "Two Festivities" she contrasts the degenerate pleasures of the rich with the more genuine but still much too fleeting and inadequate joys tasted by the working class.

"How We Nonbelievers Celebrate Christmas" is addressed to the fanatic purists in her party. Every Christmas season, Clara Zetkin published an editorial in her journal denouncing Christmas as a pious fraud and urging class-conscious workers not to celebrate it—which did not prevent her from celebrating it in her own home with her sons. Braun wrote many responses to these editorials in which she urged the workers not to boycott Christmas but to convert it into a revolutionary holiday. Our emotions, she argued, need nourishment just as much as our rational minds. To be sure, we do not believe in religious dogmas, but we do have a faith of our own—a faith in the coming deliverance through the exercise of our own human talents and energies. The article roundly denounces the zealots in the Marxist movement who by denouncing Christmas celebration rob the workers of joy and hope.

Marxism around 1900 was a deterministic dogma based on a simplified and mechanical understanding of writings by Engels, Marx, and Darwin and on a primitive faith in science. Braun's revolutionary ideas, in contrast, were derived from Goethean notions of human autonomy and Nietzsche's critique of modern civilization. While she shared the movement's belief in inevitable progress, she stressed the need for heroic defiance of things as they are. Her strong collectivism was tempered by concern for the autonomous individual; and her hope for a radically different social order was based on reverence for great women and men of the past and the cultural treasures in art, ideas, and inspiring practice that they had created.

In the Social Democratic party (SPD) Braun's views were considered unorthodox, her motives were suspect, and the entire style of her personality fitted poorly with the masculine working-class culture fostered by the movement. But one of her attributes was always greatly appreciated by her party comrades—her fiery style as an orator and agitator. Her essay "Agitating" gives a glimpse of her in this role; it is also an obvious attempt to demonstrate to her readers that she had no difficulty whatever getting along with rank-and-file proletarians.

The upbeat confidence of the campaign described in that piece was followed by disappointment, as the election brought heavy losses to the SPD. "May" is a defiant response to that disappointment. Here Braun argues that it is human beings, not bland dialectical mechanisms, who make history; and the greatest force of all is the human spirit, its most potent ingredient is discontent with things as they are. Hence nothing gives the movement greater strength than its setbacks.

UNTITLED POEM, 1886

The ocean roars, my ship rolls up and down;
    Hooraying loud, the foaming waves I greet;
    The storm sings the most beautiful of rounds,
    And to a wild dream rocks me to my sleep.
    What is the end when surging waves are landing?
        Stranding.
My horse rears high and carries restlessly
    Me on its light back across field and plain;
    To tear me from this terrible tranquility
    I gladly trust myself this steed untamed.
    As long as fields grow lush and green under the sun
        Have fun!
A toast! And fill the glasses up once more!
    The champagne bubbles, it foams life's own mirth.
    A light mood suits this godly store,
    With joy the heart beats all it's worth.
    And so that all our cares may sink,
        Let's drink!
The night is mild, the roses sweet above,
    My mouth is pressing yours in conflagration
    There's time still for caresses and for love;
    Each instant be a celebration.
    It's written in the stars, in buds so tender—
        Surrender!
The time that ends all blossoms soon is due,
    The brief span of our youth is meant for pleasure;
    She is the goddess who bestows such bliss on you;
    Of life's worth it alone can be a measure.
    You also will, when all the flowers fade away,
        Decay!

Original in the Lily Braun Collection, Leo Baeck Institute, New York City. Translated by Charlotte Melin and Alfred G. Meyer.

OCCASIONAL VERSES,
CARNIVAL 1889

When carnival comes, what blooms in profusion?
  Lies, arrogance, envy, and vain illusion;
  And what fades most quickly, leaving no trace?
  Youthfulness, beauty, and a cheerful face.

Start with a few poems, clever and sweet,
  Then some stupid jokes in the mixture you beat,
  Add lots of flattery, ogling, and sighs,
  And you'll always rate highly in women's eyes.

You dream of the light of love—
  Poets have sung of its bliss,
  But it's mostly a will-o-the-wisp today,
  Which lures you to an abyss.

My sharp thorns and your sharp tongue,
  Woe to who by them is pricked.
  If we were to fight with weapons like these,
  I wonder which one would be licked

Trust in no one whomsoever,
  Mistrust doubly him who drops the mask.
  Second masks stay on their faces forever,
  Telling truth from fooling is a hopeless task.

"In Münster reigns darkness."
  What else is new tonight?
  But tell me, sir, where on earth
  Is it light?

Original in the Lily Braun Collection, Leo Baeck Institute, New York City.

Of Bismarck's last speech an admirer
  At a party I recently met.
  "Where did you read it?" I asked him,
  And he: "O, I haven't read it yet!"

High riding boots and close-cropped hair,
  Trash in your heart, a brain that's full of air—
  Thus you are well equipped without disgrace
  Bravely the problems of the world to face.

You want to resemble the moon
  Which spreads her gentle light;
  Remember: the curs bark madly
  At her throughout the night.

What makes these masked people so bashful?
  Why are they so deeply embarrassed at heart?
  All their lives they have been playing comedy
  And are not clever enough to play more than one part.

Why are you scared that the prick of my thorn
  Will quickly make you bleed?
  And don't you think that letting some blood
  Is just what heroes need?

THE SERMON ABOUT JOY

It was evening. I lay in the forest on the soft moss and glanced out through beech and spruce trunks to the brilliant sky. The sun was setting. In his red fire the little white clouds were glowing, while the big grey ones, which could not glow, merely surrounded themselves with a fine silvery lining. Nothing was dark any longer. And suddenly I saw a man stepping from out of the shining splendor: clad in white like the priests of the heathens long ago, with two stars below his forehead, and a smile that seemed like a reflection of the sun. He was walking at the head of a crowd that was emerging, endlessly, out of the valley. None of those who followed him looked like him. The men wore dark clothing, the women were clad in threadbare garments, and the little children wore patched-up rags from men and women. Nor did their eyes shine. They gloomily looked down to the ground and were red from tears.

Under the beech trees, still glowing from the red rays of the sun, the leader halted. He surveyed the crowd that gathered around him. Who was he? Was he the prophet from Nazareth who used to like preaching in the mountains? No: his bearing was too cheerful and proud! Was he a serene philosopher of the Greeks, who knew how to shake off life's toil and trouble? No: his eyes showed too much loving warmth and compassion as they rested on all those miserable people around him. And as I was still pondering, he began to speak. His voice was sonorous and gentle, and the eyes of all turned toward him. And he spoke thus:

They have preached to you about the right to work; you have heard people speak of the duty to work. The liberating power of work has been preached to you, and in solid faith you have held on to this doctrine; in firm hope you are waiting for the bliss you have been promised. You are all working, that right has been granted to all of you, even to the tenderest

"Die Predigt über die Freude," *Die Gleichheit,* 7 (no. 21, 1897).

194

among you, the children. Do you now feel the blessing?! Or is it not true that you are collapsing under the burden? Have you been liberated? Or is it not true that the chains of slavery oppress you even more than before?! For know ye: those who hold power have transformed the pure, joyful goddess of work into a miserable whore. Hence in their mouths it is nothing but hypocrisy and blasphemy if they preach of her to you. Do not believe unto those who speak thus, and do not let yourselves be seduced by them.

There are many among you, I know, whose minds have been dimmed by anger, and who curse work and would fight against it with speech and the sword. But I say unto you: whoever turneth his back to it will perish. Therefore collect yourselves, therefore be alert and ready to serve the goddess of work as faithful divine servants. It is she who will liberate you, if you liberate her.

Regard the beasts of the forest around you: the little birds are servants of labor, for they build their nests; the bees serve her, for they search for honey; all living creatures seek nourishment in her service and as her subjects build their shelter. But, hand in hand with the goddess of labor, perceive another heavenly image who seems to be inseparable from her: that is Joy. The little bird builds his nest, and when it is done he serves the goddess of Joy; he trills gaily into the laughing morning, he sings his ardent love song, he teaches his little ones to sing the song of joy. And the deer of the forest frolic with delight, gnats and dragonflies float on the sun's rays. Wherever human feet have not yet trod, the altar of joy still stands intact within the temple of labor.

But those who wield power on earth have torn asunder the bond. They have chased Joy away so that she fled far into the mountains; they took Labor's splendid garment from her and clad her in the hair shirt of slaves. You, my brothers and sisters, are called upon to liberate the goddess and lead her comrade back into her arms. Or has she not yet vanished to you altogether? Do you still retain a dim dream of her? You, serious man standing before me, do you know her?"

The man he had addressed looked up:

"I left work tired. I was hungry and thirsty. Then I saw brightly lit windows and open doors, and I entered. I drank, and forgot I was tired; I sang and laughed with the others and thought that joy reigned here."

"But when you went home, your tiredness was even greater, and in the morning, want stared into your face, more horrible than before, is it not so?"

And the man lowered his head and knew that he did not know Joy.

"But you, young woman, can you tell me about her?"

With eyes full of tears she looked up.

"I was young and beautiful. Into the glittering ballroom it drew me, for I knew only the grey walls of my narrow chamber and the dark factory with its roaring machines. I was looking for Joy. In the arms of a lover, in melodies, I found her."

The woman fell silent.

"But when you went home you were alone! And your lot became more miserable, your chamber narrower, your sufferings greater. For no longer was it yours alone, but now also that of your child!—and it is Joy who is said to be the children's goddess. Tell me, little boy, what do you know of her?"

The pale little lad answered softly:

"I saw a Christmas tree once in the home of rich people. They gave me apples and nuts and old toys and old clothing. I was satiated and warm and felt good."

"But when you returned home to your hard cot, you cried in despair. And the next morning when you had to drag your tired limbs from door to door for the sake of a few miserable copper coins, you saw the rich people's children play with new toys in warm rooms, and your torments grew great and inextinguishable."

Quiet reigned all around. Only gentle sobbing sounded from the rows of human beings. The sun had disappeared behind the clouds. Once again the speaker raised his voice:

"You, who think you have encountered Joy; you who mock and scold her because you believe she has made you even more miserable, you all do not know Joy; for know that she is no bout of intoxication followed by the disgust of the morning after, she is not a fraud that makes sport of you. Joy is eternal light like the sun above you. She is present only where she is life itself, where she reigns supreme. You are servants of Labor, not for the sake of Labor, no: for the sake of Joy; and wherever it is not thus, there you are not true servants. Therefore lift your eyes and listen to me. Go forth into the world and preach to all men and women the new doctrine: Labor is our salvation. We want to serve her in liberty. We want to stir our hands and fortify our minds, through their power we want to master the forces of nature. But we do not want to be slaves to a slave. For everything we do in her service we do for the sake of a higher goal. Through her we want to be the rulers of the earth. Inexhaustible sources—the blessed floods of Joy—shall open up for us through her. Joy shall enter our minds and hearts; Labor shall prepare the way for her. Joy shall be the deep melody of our life; Labor is but the accompaniment. Joy shall rule over us, and in her name we want to wreak miracles. I say unto you: if you stand together in this force, victory will not be far. And the day will come when you go up to the mountains in large numbers, decked in white garments, laughter in your eyes, hand in hand. Your life will be a song of triumph. The love in your hearts, which now is buried under the ruins of the temple of Joy, will rise again in its heavenly glory. Your tears will turn into laughter, and paradise, which your forefathers sought above the stars, will descend upon you.

The last words faded away as if they came from far, far away. Muffled sounds struck my ear. I woke up. A gloomy morning was rising on the horizon. Factory smoke stacks loomed like ghosts out of the fog. The call to work sounded shrilly. And from all directions they came—men, women, and children; gray their clothes; clouded their glance; tired their limbs. Poor slaves, who did not yet know anything about what had been preached to them.

TWO FESTIVITIES

Our heathen ancestors greeted the beginning of summer with merry song, with games and dance; they shouted at the golden lady sun and celebrated the long yellow tresses of the harvest goddess Sif. And the beauty conscious nation of the Greeks proffered redolent flowers to the shining god Apollo; in honor of summer, his youths and maidens wound their curly heads with red roses. Have we lost the ability to rejoice as they did? It almost seems so. No laughter can entirely wipe away the ascetic mien that Christianity has imprinted on the faces of humankind. The word for our festive period, Carnival, is derived from *carrus navalis,* the ship "Skidbladnier" of the sun god Freyr. But Carnival does not remind us of the sun god. Artificial roses are supposed to deceive us about the winter during which it takes place; not glowing sun rays in free nature greet us but electric light in a confined ballroom, the sound of violins rather than jubilant bird song sounds in our ears.

But, just as longing pervades the world, not for the bliss of a heaven above the earth, but for a happy future here on earth, so also a longing for joy pervades it, and today as long ago human beings thirsting for beauty and joy choose the sun to be their goddess.

Over two festivities the sun recently shed its radiant golden brilliance. The one had been prepared by the German Writers' Association in the Berlin Exhibition Park, the other was organized by the Social-Democratic party in the little Müggelsee Castle on the lovely shores of Lake Müggel near Friedrichshagen. A ticket for the former cost twenty marks (half that if bought in advance), one for the latter twenty-five pfennigs. Four thousand persons assembled between suburban railroad arches and streets for the "Festival of Roses"; forty thousand, according to newspaper estimates (I would have guessed three times as many), populated the woods and meadows at the lake, which glittered in the sun. Numerous

"Zwei Feste," *Ethische Kultur,* 2 (no. 20, 1894).

supervisors, identified by badges, with untiring endurance from early morning to late in the night maintained order and saw to it that those attending the people's festival would have fun. The organizing committee of the Festival of Roses practically did not show any concern for the public; indeed, it went so far as to delay the opening ceremony at the exhibition, for which the guests and the artists had all assembled, because no committee member was present. In the end, the singer, Mr. Rothmühl, ran out of patience, and he asked those present whether the festivities should get started. The supervisors at the people's festival faced a difficult task. At the landing of the ferry, which took people across to the little Müggelsee Castle, they stood tightly pressed together waiting in long lines and often pushing forward impetuously; but the supervisors were able, mostly with kindness but when necessary with all their energy, to keep things calm. The superpatriotic committee of the Festival of Roses had personally invited government ministers but had not found it necessary to trouble with them any further; the supervisors at the mass festival greeted every single participant as if he were a guest of honor.

The amusements offered at both festivities were copious. In the hall of honor of the Exhibition Park, the Festival of Roses was opened by a concert of famous artists and by a prologue that could be enjoyed, however, only by those who were ready to sacrifice an additional donation (one mark) on the "Altar of Charity"—the whole thing had been staged, of course, "for the benefit of communal service institutions". Indignation over this additional expense was great, but curiosity was greater and won out in most people. The priestess of the Festival of Roses greeted the guests in fiery verses. The author of the prologue obviously had great difficulty weaving into his joyful paean a reminder of the poor who were to benefit from the proceeds of the festival. His public does not like to hear about need and misery. And so he inserted only a few lines about this:

> The money for the poor—for us alone
> The blooming roses and the sunshine!

That was supposed to sound frugal and unpretentious, but in reality sounds so crude and in all its crudeness is so horridly true. The clinking coins remaining to all these happy people after they have paid for their festivities are tossed into the laps of the poor as alms, but the sunshine and the blooming roses that ought to give their light and their scent to all of humankind, they want for themselves alone.

The next day, in the woods out by Lake Müggel, the people saw a
performance of *King Mammon's Funeral.* His giant body lay on a bier
between cannons and money sacks; a museum and a panopticon contained memorabilia from the era of his rule: Justice as understood by
Brausewetter; big agricultural interests suffering economic hardship with
"wine and women" in the dance palace; civilization brought to Africa
under the banner of Christianity, which lets the bull whip dance on the
backs of hapless native women the same way in which at home it wields
the rubber truncheon.

The priestess at the Festival of Roses called on her listeners to enjoy
life:

> Hence ere your leaves dry up in sorrow
> Enjoy the youthful time of roses!
> Roam through them, earthly guests of this day of gods
> Welcome, welcome to the Festival of Roses.

At the mass festival, the priestess called the people to struggle and work:

> Poverty and need and squalor
> Mammon's pallbearers will be!
> When you lower him into the earth
> Throw the bearers in with him!
> Act to put an end to need
> And to vanquish servitude.
> Sisters, work and stir your hands
> That our holy cause may win!

At the Festival of Roses the high point was the "Inkville" fair, which
seemed just the right thing for innocently merry visitors. There were
booths with the strangest, often very witty curiosities: a roving troup of
circus riders who ably performed out in the open, a shooting gallery, a
speed painter who was kept busy all the time, a charming fruit vendor
with a horrid old huckster woman sitting next to her, a menagerie; in
short, nothing was missing except—the public. Not that I want to say
that it was empty there; not at all. They all came: the fat banker and the
brewery owner, now visibly pained by the beer boycott, the guards
lieutenant and the aristocratic estate owner who looked bored; the artist,
the writer, and the elegant female stars of the theater; they passed each
other stiff and distant or greeted each other with courteous phrases; they
criticized and flirted as in the ballroom or the theater lobby. But a public
for a fair they were not. Tirelessly the vendors extolled their wares, with

restless energy the cheerful shills invited the public to visit their shows. They themselves were gazed at as part of the show. The modernized version of Schiller's *Die Räuber* in the "Inkville National Theater"—a magnificent achievement on the part of the author as well as the actors— did not unleash the storm of merriment one should have expected; those who really laughed heartily were almost ashamed! And the graceful ballet *Sleeping Beauty,* performed outdoors with clever lighting effects, evoking a veritable fairytale mood, did not elicit much applause.

At Lake Müggel there was also a fair. Neither slide nor the merry-go-round was missing; here, too, there were shooting galleries and speed painters, concert and choral singing, dance and games. Vendors of roses and cherriers were there also, but they plied their trade not for fun, for "charity." They were painfully waging the struggle for their daily bread, as attested by their pale cheeks and bent backs. Today a reflection of the general merriment lay on their faces as well; they belonged to the large family that *one* distress, *one* struggle, *one* hope, *one* goal have welded together far more tightly than ties of blood could do. Here nobody walked past another as if past a stranger; in "good" society it goes without saying that one should speak to one who has not been introduced only in an emergency, and then only after a "beg your pardon"; among the "uneducated" masses it is equally understood that one should exchange a few words with whoever happens to stand nearby. Every joke evoked a merry response from the participants in the mass festival; if in the crush anyone got violent, there surely were ten who would calm him down. A young lad who wantonly was breaking green shrubs out of a hedge was admonished with the argument that he should not give the innkeeper an opportunity to say that workers were destroying his property. Loud applause rewarded the popular singers on the small stage; when the men's glee clubs were singing, the crowd of many thousands joined in with enthusiasm. And, what is the main thing, the most grateful public of fairs was not missing; the children. Among the old people, particularly among the women, one saw enough tired and careworn faces, who had forgotten how to laugh. But the children took care that there was plenty of laughter. The youngest ones were being pushed in wicker prams by their fathers—the "proletarian's coach" one of them called it—; once in a while a father might load other people's children into the buggy who were too heavy for their mothers to carry; the older ones played all the countless old children's games under the green trees or they watched the Punch-and-Judy Show with shining eyes. On the slide and the merry-go-round, old and young sat together; in the ballroom of the restaurant, couples turned in dance. In lieu of the breakneck feats of circus clowns and tightrope dancers at the Rose Festival fair, you could see here 150 gymnasts of the workers' athletic clubs in a gymnastics show that had to get them highest marks for their strength and skill, and the light boats of the "Vorwärts" rowing club cut through the water with arrow speed.

At both festivals, I observed those who came and went. On most of the faces of those who strode down the wide stairs to the Exhibition Park in costly gowns, glittering uniforms or in an elegant dandy coat in the newest fashion, one could read plainly: "I have come in order to be seen"; whereas the expressions of those who in their simple Sunday best impatiently waited by the lakeshore until the ferry took them expressed the idea: "I have come to see." And when the guests were leaving the Festival of Roses, most of their faces wore that tired, bored, blasé mien that leads to the conclusion that the orgy of enjoyment in which they spend their lives has destroyed their ability to enjoy. Slowly, and tired, the participants at the mass festival also went home. The closer the train brought them back to the factory smokestacks of the city, the more the merriment disappeared from their faces. For once they had breathed fresh forest air and seen the sun; but now they had to go back into the dust and steam of the factory, into the unlit tenement dwelling. Worry, heavy, pressing everyday worry I read in the eyes of the men and women and even on the pale brows of the children. The roses lay fading in the dust—here as well as there.

No, we no longer know how to celebrate the sun god's festivals, and I would believe that we will never learn if I had asked none but the priestess of the Rose Festival. She had nothing to offer except the fleeting present; the future was as a fading flower to her. But the spirit that animated and joined the thousands outside by the lake pointed beyond the present. Whoever could evade its influence had to be blind or deaf or evil, because it is the spirit of indestructible hope, the spirit of self-sacrificing brotherly love.

It seemed to me as if I were hearing the voice of the Germanic seeress who prophesied the fall of the gods in these words: "The sun begins to darken, the earth sinks into the sea, from the sky the merry stars vanish," but then continued, "and then I see emerging once again from the sea the earth, fresh and green. . . . Of all evil improvement will come." Then the bright gods will return, and a rejuvenated race of men will offer red and redolent roses to the sun as sacrifice!

HOW WE NONBELIEVERS
CELEBRATE CHRISTMAS

Come ye children, come ye all to the manger in Bethlehem's stable and
see the great joy which in this most holy night the heavenly father has
brought you.

Thus the bright children's voices are singing today in all schools, and
wherever there is a musical instrument in the house, one can hear in all
keys the melody, "O sanctissima." Be they devout churchgoers or modern
heathens, a joyous mood of expectation and hope, spread by the mysterious power of suggestion, fills them all. Among some, of course, its light
is as bright as the Christmas tree in the home of the rich; among others it
is as dim and feebly flickering as the flames of the thin candles on the
spruce branch in the hovel of poverty.

Among the high priests of the nonbelievers there are strict moral
clerics who count these little flames in their hearts and on the Christmas
tree as sins—who zealously condemn all hypocrisy and want to rob the
kids of all enjoyment in the beautiful old Christmas carols. Similarly
there are people who do not tell them fairy tales just because they are not
true. It would be better to cast such false prophets into the deepest depth
of the ocean than that they should cheat humanity out of its festivals and
youth out of its festive season.

We nonbelievers also celebrate Christmas, and we celebrate it as
believers. We do not believe in the Virgin Mary who as a pure hand-
maiden gave birth to the son of God; but we do believe in the deeply
afflicted mother of the son of man, who has merited sainthood not by her
virginity but by her love and devotion. Nor do we believe in the loving
kindness of a heavenly father who gave his son to redeem the sinners, but
in the divine powers inside the human being that is destined and capable

"Wie wir Ungläubigen Weihnachten feiern," *Neue Gesellschaft,* 3 (no. 12, 1907).

of liberating itself. Further, we do not believe in Jesus Christ who took on the sins of the world and atoned for them by his martyr's death, but we do believe in him and people like him whose great heart and widely shining mind comprehend the unlimited fullness of life and suffering and who, therefore, become the prophets and poets, the discoverers and thinkers and the crossbearers of humanity. They have forever been choked and stoned to death, burnt at the stake and crucified, and yet they alone remain immortal! Nor do we believe in eternal heavenly bliss, but we do believe in the bliss of life, of which all those will partake who know how to drain the well of suffering and ecstacy to its very bottom. Hence, we do not exhort our believers to defeat Satan's powers through mortification of the flesh, fasting and prayer, thereby to gain the eternal bliss of paradise; instead, we preach to them that in untiring struggle they must overcome the forces of darkness on earth—physical and spiritual poverty, hunger and thirst for bodily, emotional, and intellectual nourishment—in order to conquer the promised land for the coming generations.

Faith in God, in its clerical narrowness, has turned out to be a will-o'-the-wisp, deceiving the eyes, paralyzing our energy, luring us deeper and deeper into the dark depths of misery. We proclaim the sunlight of our faith in human beings! For that reason we, and we alone, are entitled to celebrate Christmas. For after all, it blends the winter solstice feast of our heathen ancestors, which in the midst of snow and storm gently heralded the coming of spring, with the birthday celebration of the son of man, when Christendom bows down before the poor little child in the stable at Bethlehem, that marvelous symbol of all those born to take the woe of the world upon them. Go ahead and light your Christmas candles! Let the star of the Magi shine on top of the tree! What paralyzes our will and our readiness to fight are not festivals in which devout tradition is irradiated with the light of energetic hopes for the future. Instead, what robs our soul of its élan is the gray emptiness of uninterrupted everyday life, with its senile reasonableness, and the icy coldness of its purist lack of faith, which freezes the blood in our veins!

There is abroad today a mighty yearning that aims for far more than the mere satisfaction of bodily needs, indeed more than the slaking of the thirst for knowledge; emotion and the heart, long misunderstood and maltreated, claim their birthright. They have had to sacrifice their childhood belief in fairy tales to harsh reality—now they are impoverished and desolate. Unless we give them a new content, they will be in danger of falling into the clutches of false prophets of superstition, of returning into the chiaroscuro of the church, and thus being lost to the demands of life. The grand task of socialism is to give the masses more than shorter work hours and higher wages, more than the prospect of ruling and always having their bellies full; the task is to open the eyes of their soul for the sun of belief in humanity, the only true faith that can move mountains. Every baby's cradle is the altar of this faith, for each and every one of the very poorest carries in him or her the redeemer's destiny.

And now deck your chambers with spruce branches and kindle lights around ye. But wherever the windows are dark, there ye should enter and bring the Christmas taper of your new faith with ye. And do not tire of lighting the candle of faith, love, and hope, so that ye may triumph even over the darkest night of winter!

AGITATING

When the ancient Germans sat at a festive meal or were throwing dice, when they were sleeping soundly or were chasing the wild boar across rocks and ravines, when they were sacrificing to their gods in the sacred grove, and suddenly their tribal war call sounded in their ears—then they threw cup and dice down, jumped from their cots, forgot about the boar and interrupted the sacrifical ritual. With shouts of elation they grabbed sword and spear, flaming enthusiasm shining in their eyes, for fighting—fighting against enemies—was the part of their lives that contributed most to their happiness.

We do not arm ourselves with murder weapons but have not therefore lost the feeling of exultation that swelled their breasts. Many a person gets tired intellectually and physically on the rails of everyday existence; all sorts of petty rubbish paralyzes his political enthusiasm so that often it seems to have withered. And then a call to war sounds—and everything bad and depressing is forgotten; one sentiment only, one idea still rules head and heart: Forward to battle against the enemies!

There probably is not one among us Social-Democrats who picked up the gauntlet thrown us by the Reich Chancellor on 13 December with anything else than jubilation. There are no complaints here about Christmas vacation disturbed, about holidays lost; everyone is filled with the same desire to be able to go to work as soon as possible. The first task, as with the general staff officer after a declaration of war, was to orient oneself concerning the general situation, to find out the enemies' forces, their equipment, their position, to reconnoiter their weakness and plan one's own strategy accordingly. The next task is to inspect and replenish one's own armament of knowledge in order to be fully prepared. And now out into city and countryside! First into the glistening white winter days. How rare they have become of late here in Prussia is evident from the fact

"Auf Agitation," *Neue Gesellschaft*, 3 (no. 17, 1907).

that in the small country towns it is difficult to obtain a sleigh; the poor overworked plowhorse—if he had any sense he would run away like the agricultural workers—pants while trying to pull the ramshackle rack wagon through the deep snow, which soon turns into a deep morass or an endless expanse of water; the *Spreewald* region now looks like a lake from which trees and willow shrubs and haystacks erected on some sort of pile scaffolding stick out. In the Oder marshes the foot sinks deeply into the black-brown soil. A soft, floating fog, as in March, gives nature a dreamy mood: Spring is in the air!

When I arrived in Frankfurt-on-Oder, heaven had just opened its sluice gates. In quiet, old-fashioned gentility the city stretched along the river; fortress moats have long ago been converted into idyllic green spaces; little is felt here of the feverish industrial growth in other cities that are found in more favorable locations, on a big river and an important rail line. I expect few visitors. But there is busy activity already in the trade union house. The old building, one of Frankfurt's oldest, may be greatly astonished at its new guests who took possession of it barely a year ago, no less astonished probably than the Frankfurt bourgeois who will never get over the fact that the reds found such a beautiful home in the very heart of their city! Today they were typical men of labor who flocked together here: Miners from Bossen who, undaunted by long distances and bad weather, had come to Frankfurt as good fighters to report for duty, since at home they have no meeting place at their disposal. How excitedly these usually taciturn sons of Brandenburg soil talk with each other, then listen without talking, and then give joyful expression to their agreement! The next meeting took place the same day in a large hall on the outskirts of town; hours before it began everything was filled to the bursting point; hundreds had to be turned back. Even in 1903 the waves of enthusiasm had not risen so high; the bourgeois visitors who are never entirely lacking here went home even quieter and more depressed than usual. Perhaps they felt the pulsating life of spring, despite the raw weather outside.

Shortly afterwards I came to Pomerania, into the Randow-Greifenhagen district. There I heard how the conservatives are now trying to deceive the peasants with the same means that Potemkin once used to deceive an empress, except that the clever Russian's stage sets of villages were replaced here by photos of fabulous fairy-tale landscapes. They were to represent our colonies; I guess they came from New Guinea or New Zealand. As for political speeches, the gentlemen didn't strain themselves with any real effort. Neither was there any discussion. Why should there be? Mice are caught with bacon, stupid peasants with pictures. But suppose they are badly mistaken in this? In Bredow, outside Stettin, the masses were crowded together in a giant ballroom: mostly the brawny figures of the workers from the Vulkan shipyards, but in between many others who had wandered in from far away. They were aware of the seriousness of the fight that had to be waged, and when I, myself deeply moved by the tempestuous eruption of their feelings, strode through the hall, I sensed that every hand stretched out toward me was raised as if for a solemn oath.

Further west I traveled. But as far as the opponents were concerned, on the other side of the Elbe I had the same impression as in East-Elbia. What the photos were to accomplish there, here it was the task of a parade-African who was supposed to arouse enthusiasm for the colonies. Except that this old former sergeant was basically an honest Joe: He faithfully described the waterless sand deserts, the meagerness of the soil, the ugliness of the landscape. Perhaps he meant to create the right background for the trump card he could play at the end, to wit: Diamonds, which he claimed to have found himself. Of course, he did not show them, so that one could not determine whether they might be equivalent compensation for the millions that the German people have tossed into all this sand. Besides, a primary school teacher had entered into a promising competition with him. He told these Hannover peasants about the fertile lands that would be at their disposal without any ado in this African fool's paradise; and about the Social-Democrats he told on the basis of his very intimate knowledge that on the 26th they would expropriate the German peasant if on the 25th he got the bright idea of voting for them! In the Harburg-Wilhelmsburg district, which can boast of such a socialist-killer, the comrades developed a feverish activity in order to pry the district out of the hands of the united opponents. This is shown by the impressive meeting they had organized in Harburg. Nothing but genuine proletarians were there, but more careworn, pale faces, more bent backs than elsewhere, and so many women whose tired eyes told of the entire misery of their lives. All one needs to do in order to know the whole truth is to look at them: Poor wages, lousy treatment, long work hours. Lots of foreigners among them. Nonetheless they all understood me: Destitution speaks an international language. And when at the end they rose the wide wooden hall seemed to tremble under their roaring shout, long live Social Democracy! At that moment I sensed stronger than ever before the world-conquering might of the proletariat, that might that helps the poorest and the weakest to lift themselves up to heroism.

Soon afterwards another image: I was riding into the "Brandenburg Alps" (*Märkische Schweiz*), where handsome little homes rise on the slopes and hills of Buckow on wintry dark Lake Scharmützel. Old Buckow, the people say, has been swallowed by the ravenous lake. It is said to have been a rich town. Now Buckow's sole wealth is the beauty of the forests, ravines, and lakes, for even the summer guests it welcomes each year do not belong to the capitalists. Our meeting place lies outside the dumpy lanes of the town, leaning close to a wooded hill. A mixed bunch of visitors inside: Bricklayers from Berlin who chose the Brandenburg poet's corner, far from the noise of the big city, to be their and their families' home: Perhaps they also built themselves a little house here; local craftsmen, agricultural laborers and peasants; also a few town big shots and a fat, portly constable in front at the police table. Here too as everywhere many women, including some who up to now have not dared to go to a meeting. Here also as everywhere, burning enthusiasm! Every mention of Basserman, who had been the delegate from their district, evokes anger and indignation.

I rode back home through the night, and I thought of the history of this Brandenburg soil, of the ancient families that used to own it and still do very often; of the young generation that wants to conquer it. It is sad for anyone to see the old die off, but only he can despair of this who does not, who will not see the sprouting new life. And yet nothing in the world is as certain as the eternal return of spring. Therefore happy he who knows how to ally himself with spring!

The train rushes through the Spreewald. Here the degenerate children of Berlin capitalists purchase that bit of good health that their parents' neurasthenia leaves attainable for them: They suck it out of the breasts of this region's daughters, who for this business have to sacrifice their children. *

Beyond Kottbus the charm of the landscape stops, and in Forst factory smokestacks once again tower against the sky; beside them the elegant manufacturers' villas mushroom out of the ground. The hall in which I spoke was still shining with the white of newness. Against its walls the

---

* Wet nurses for well-to-do mothers in and around Berlin generally were hired from the Slavic peasant women of the Spreewald.

tightly packed crowd was a black and heavy contrast. It was one-third women, all of them textile workers. No doubt: if on 25 January Germany's women were allowed to go to the polls, the Social-Democrats would win an unprecedented victory, for the government's policies have accomplished what our agitation never succeeded in doing: they have shaken up the most inaccessible and the dullest among them and have made thinking human beings out of them. I saw the poor people, prematurely aged in the struggle for existence, cry bitter tears when I reminded them of their children, and many a glance that met my eyes was more eloquent than words: Should the men be negligent we will drive them to the polls! But such a roundup will hardly be necessary. The unscrupulous campaign methods of the opponents, who do not hesitate to wage their campaign with the weapons of slander and lies, has spurred the party comrades to muster all their energies, and even if in one or another district their confidence in victory should be disappointed, we cannot overestimate the success of this campaign. It has spread enlightenment like none before it and has cast so glaring a light on the opponents that the repulsive picture they present cannot be forgotten so easily.

And now into the Oder marshes that I love so dearly, perhaps because they symbolize our endeavor: "I have conquered a province peacefully," said Old Fritz (Frederick II) after he had tamed the waters of the Oder. We too are conquering the world peacefully.

In the midst of this fertile plain, self-sacrificing party comrades, bricklayers and builders employed in Berlin, have built their trade union headquarters that makes this inhospitable area, in which no pub was obtainable, accessible to us. This did not make the ghost of old Derfflinger,* who once owned Gusow Palace close by, rise out of his grave in horror any more than it enabled the rich marsh peasants to prevent it with their anger. Here they now assemble in droves and come from all the surrounding villages: building workers and agriculturalists. They listen with greater devotion and attention than the big city comrades, and the work they have to do in the election campaign demands more sacrifice and energy. Only too often do they pay for their conviction with ostracism and isolation, because within the narrow confines of the village everyone knows the "red" to whom in the big city no one pays attention any longer. On the long roads of their agitational work they have to take,

*Georg von Derfflinger, 1606-1675, Field Marshal General in Brandenburg.

on many a farm, insults of the worst kind if indeed people don't unleash their dogs on them. But the conflict has steeled these sons of Branden- burg's soil as well: They will conquer this province peacefully.

Back to the station in the old familiar rattletrap. I am once again in the train that the likes of us now greet as a welcome resting place: One gradually learns to sleep anywhere. I still face Saxony, red Saxony, which let us hope will get even redder than before, and then in the end Brandenburg once more, on the eve of the battle the confidently prosper- ing manufacturing town, Fürstenwalde.

I have spent many a night hour chatting with old party comrades after the meetings. And it was always like a banquet of old war buddies telling each other of their adventures, their battles, their victories, and their wounds. They all were agreed on one thing: This must be the decisive battle. And when afterwards we bade each other farewell as good friends, another conviction was in us firm as rock: Come what may, victory or defeat, we will go on fighting until death defeats us!

MAY

It was a year in which spring simply did not want to come. At Easter, snow whirled about in thick flakes, and, during the height of the day, the sun's eye looked down brightly yet coldly and severely. Weeks passed, and still the icy wind whistled over the roofs, swept across bare fields, rustled in leafless branches. Men and women were gripped by a nagging disquiet, and all worried about their bread, their roses, about bird's song and sunshine. A thousand letters arrived in editorial offices every day asking for the cause of those disquieting phenomena and demanding consolation and hope. Astronomers and meteorologists published learned treatises about the position of the earth's axis, about sun spots and barometer minima. But the thermometer stayed below the freezing point. No one cared any longer to hear about the standardization of weights and measures with which a wise parliament was just then dealing, nor about the customs war between Brazil and Ecuador, nor even about the seven-times rape-murderer Schulze, whom the Dresden District Court had just declared capable of standing trial. They all only cried for the sun and for spring.

Miserable business of news writers, who had to write about spring every day, and it would not come! Their fingers got calluses, their brains became empty, their hearts numb, their hair gray at the temples. One of them died; the grave digger, with stiff hands, dug up the soil, which was frozen hard as stone, and a friend, whose heart trembled in his body under a warm clock, spoke at the grave: "He died of impatience, but nonetheless happy, because he believed."

Those, however, who died waiting for the springtime of nations, did not die in vain; and those who fought did not fight for a lost cause. Let us remember in hours of impatience that the progress of humankind is not dependent on the phases of the moon, but that human beings are the weathermakers of world history.

"Das ist der Mai," *Neue Gesellschaft,* 4 (no. 5, 1907).

Of course, man is man's eternal disappointment. What has seduced many a Socialist to make false predictions was not miscalculation of societal forces working mechanically but the overestimation of human powers of understanding and will; and such errors of prediction are not any less honorable for these Socialists, merely because thoughtless philistines can make them the butt of their stupid jokes. Hence, we need not be ashamed at all for confessing that, seventeen years ago, when for the first time we celebrated the first of May, the time we would celebrate it for the seventeenth time appeared much more beautiful to our hopes than it is in reality.

To look this truth in the eye is something everyone who wants to celebrate the holidays of the proletariat in the proper spirit will have to learn. This truth confronts us with the merciless reality of life but forever has been hardened in the right kind of fire; it contains not a germ of fatigue and renunciation. It is the destiny of our generation to consume itself in struggles, the great successes of which beckon only from afar— and yet, there may one day in the future be a quieter, richer generation, who will, with a bit of awe, but also with a secret feeling of envy, make a pilgrimage to the graves of a generation that fought the greatest battle of world history.

If we really wanted to, we could also talk about *successes*. Much has changed; much has improved. If today the Berlin construction workers fight for the eight-hour day, one might remind the reader that in 1848, the attainment of the ten-hour day and a standard wage of five thalers a week at public construction works was hailed as a tremendous victory. Thanks to the political and trade union movements of the workers, the material and intellectual condition of the proletariat has been raised, and far greater successes might accrue within months or a few years.

So, we can indeed talk about successes, those we have won and those we may soon be winning. But the real and most profound significance of the proletarian movement is reflected not in these successes, but rather— as paradoxical as this may sound—in its disappointments and failures. The enormous tension between reality and the desired state of affairs has generated the mighty current of moving energy that courses through the proletariat of our time. And thus, the May festival symbolizes that great longing for spring that gives oppressed but upward-striving human beings the strength to persevere in harsh storms throughout the long winter and to struggle on while looking forward to the day when awakened humanity will give itself the gift of its spring.

V.

Children's Liberation

All her life Lily Braun resented the upbringing she had received and most children still were receiving. Child rearing, she argued, should have as its purpose the bringing out of all the talents and potentials slumbering in the individual. Hence it ought to be individualized and sensitive to the young person's needs and interests. The standardized education children now receive, she argued, breaks their will and destroys their potential; it robs them of their youth and often drives the best children to suicide.

Indeed, her earliest attempt at expressing her ideas in essay form, a fragment entitled "In Opposition to the Lie," argued that most education was miseducation. The socialization of children for their class roles is education for pretense, for the lie.

While the children of the rich were taught to lie, the children of the proletariat, she thought, were cheated out of all opportunities as well as of their childhood. By their schooling they were channeled into blue-collar jobs, so that proletarian status became hereditary; and by forcing their mothers to leave the home in search of wage work, capitalism was robbing them of their mothers. "Proletarian Mothers" addresses that problem.

Braun believed that German and Prussian schooling was especially alienating. She admired the American system of education, asserting that American schools educate, while German schools indoctrinate; American schools provide choice, while German schools impose uniformity. The reason for these differences, she thought, was that American schools are created and run by the people, whereas German schools are controlled by state bureaucrats.

All these ideas and more come together in the pamphlet *Children's Liberation*, in which she argues at length that children are being crushed by teachers as well as by parents. To the children of the world she cries, Assert yourselves; liberate yourselves! Ultimately, liberation from the misery they impose on you is up to you.

PROLETARIAN MOTHERS

I am aquainted with two proletarian mothers and know the relations they have with their children; and it seems to me that there is a profound lesson to be learned from the difference in their relations.

One of them is nothing else than a petty-bourgeois housewife and mother. She cooks, scrubs, washes, mends, and takes care of her proletarian dwelling and her small children. But with these she lives in a state of war from morning to night. They run away, get dirty, tear their clothes and then tear them again, lose their toys bought with money that the mother has carefully saved from her skimpy household allowance. They run into water, beat each other up, get into fights with other kids—in short, they are the inescapable and uninterrupted curse of her toilsome days. This mother therefore shouts, beats, says No, scolds, is constantly angry, and curses her children ten times a day. Of course, it is only the outside observer who sees this clearly. She herself is hardly aware that with all this scolding and ill feeling the kids don't hear one friendly word out of her for entire days. And she herself probably would never even suspect that the observer might consider her treatment of the children unloving and hardening—because most women in comparable situations treat their kids just the same way. And they all would tell you that their exhausting toil and worry about their children is, well, that great maternal love.

The other mother is herself working in a factory and must leave her children to chance, to good neighbors, and to the street. Basically these kids are not a hair's breadth less bratty, that is, less wild, less cheerful, less drunk with freedom, or less wilful, and if their mother had to be around them without interruption from morning to night she would probably also be vexed half to death over them every day. But the sad compulsion

"Proletarische Mütter," *Neue Gesellschaft*, 2 (no. 22, 1906).

of her absence from the children has one great good side: it does not give her time for this eternal faultfinding and scolding, it lets her come to the children with a heart full of love, and every day it lets these kids experience that great strong bliss: mother is coming!

Hardly one proletarian mother these days can be a real mother, and all proletarian children are stunted not only physically but also in their psychological life. Nonetheless, I call those children happier who, notwithstanding all the lack of mothering, have a relationship to their mother that still knows joyous excitements; happier than those whose mother fills every one of their days with petty worries about little things and with futile scolding.

CHILDREN'S LIBERATION

To all those of you, I address myself, from whom the load of books in your backpack ever pressed groans, or whose straight spines were bent crooked by the briefcase under your arm. To those of you whose right to an individual existence is denied by family, school, and government in that they sacrifice your childhood on the altar of adulthood—not suspecting that the fire gradually consumes much that could still nourish many flames later.

To those of you who are altogether mute—well-bred children at the table of the grown-ups. And yet you have found a language that makes a frightful noise in our ears—the language of death. The number of the accusers is growing. But they complain in vain if your ears do not open up to them. Already the blood of your martyrs reddens the soil. But they will have died for nothing if your lips remain sealed.

Come. Into a dark house I will lead you. Garlands of straw flowers are wound around the high columns of the hall; red roses, broken in their bloom, are fading on the threshold. A deeply folded curtain, black and heavy, divides the room.

One boy is leading, in a frayed little jacket, wooden clogs on his bare feet red with frostbite. He is only seven, but already he has an old man's disconsolate expression of being tired of life around his bloodless lips. Instead of sitting in the dreary classroom with its grim teacher who brandished his cane over all the boys and girls, he preferred running into the woods to the birds and the flowers and the red berries. And from the miserable shack with six noisy siblings, the mother who was always tired, and the father who always smelled of booze, the sun had lured him into

Die Emanzipation der Kinder: eine Rede an die Schuljugend (München: Albert Langen Verlag, 1911).

its warmth and brightness. And then everybody had been against him. He saw no way out and threw himself in front of the locomotive.

There is one, tall, pale, his high boyish brow deeply lined from brooding, who is wearing good clothes. He had an insatiable hunger for knowledge, for understanding of what is and was; what he did not have was a memory for words and numbers; they bored him. He was the son of a poor widow, of a good little house mother who would shed tears over bad grades. Until he could not take it any longer. In the attic, between boxes and crates containing the ancestors' household things in scrupulous order, he placed his neck into the noose.

Two walk behind him, a girl and a boy. They loved each other with all the romantic ardor of tender feelings when they first awaken. With cynical, derisive laughter the father had confronted his sixteen-year-old son when he learned about it. His words dropped like muck on the pure spring flower of his feelings. The girl, however, now labeled as "corrupted," was to be sent to the country under the severe discipline of an old parson in order to protect her siblings from her influence. Their love was not strong enough to make them tolerate all this. They jumped into the lake together—it rippled a little over the light bodies, but then it once again lay blue and still in the embrace of green forests.

And now look at that slim lad with dark eyes. How full of hopes and youthful strength he may have rushed to meet life head on! How was it that he too mingled with this roundelay of death? In front of the class, an angry teacher tossed him a nasty word that burnt his cheek as if it had been a lash with the whip. He was only fifteen, but his sense of honor was that of a man. Thus marked, he could no longer show his face to his school mates. He knew no other way than by a bullet in his temple.

Whole troops crowd across the stage—boys and girls, poor and rich, big and little. Despite all the differences they resemble each other: the expression of fear and anxiety in the eyes big with horror erases all individuality in their faces. It was fear that drove them to hang and drown themselves, to jump out of windows, to point the pistol at themselves. Fear—not of life, which beckoned magically from an unfathomable distance, but of the horrid abyss that separated them from it. Fear of the torture of eternal admonitions, of continually repeated punishments. Fear of those who called themselves their educators.

There are hundreds of them. But now that they have passed—the sound of their irregular steps still echoes through the room as the only sound—others come whose feet touch the floor slowly, with calm consciousness of where the road is leading. They are not afraid. Instead, the senile expression of life denial is engraved in their soft features.

A girl is the first to enter. She is beautiful, has white hands and soft curls, her eyes are deep as if they were exhausting the world. A sad weeping envelops her as if from a great distance. Alas, father and mother, whose pride and hope she was, do not know why she departed of her own free will!

Now come pairs of friends—young lads. You recognize them, don't you, those from whose wounds the red blood drops are still seeping? Some of them shot themselves, each one alone in his room, at one and the same hour. In incomprehension their mothers stared at the lifeless bodies—good mothers who had cared for and protected them from earliest age. And yet, their children had to die in order to make them conscious of the fact that they had never lived for them.

Others sneaked up into the forest together through the autumn fog. They pinned little ribbons red as blood into each other's white shirts at the place where the heart beats. And the friend aimed at the friend and hit the target. Had one of them been too many in the world in a conflict over a girl? Had they decided to throw away their lives together because its burden seemed unbearable to them, because, like Negro slaves, they were dragging iron balls on their feet even while their longing drove them onward with the speed of the wing?

The dead file past and are silent.

Daylight once again receives us, and the noises of life. In front of the gates through which we have passed, the crowd is waiting, and it whispers and claps and screams. They stand in groups, gathered around those who speak for them.

"Those are the consequences of godlessness," preaches a man in a black gown with a white dog collar under his wide Luther chin. The devout around him nod their heads ostentatiously, while a few old crones, carried away by emotion, dab their eyes.

"They lacked all moral foundation," a man standing close by cries out with gestures of pathos; "It is Nietzsche and Oscar Wilde whom these green boys were reading; no wonder they lost all moral certainty!" His audience murmurs approval, a few elegant ladies throw amorous glances in his direction.

"It is women's liberation that turned these girls' heads," a skinny woman standing in a group of excited people nags in a toneless falsetto voice; "instead of standing behind the cooking pot they flirt with every rascal at the *Gymnasium* and the university."

A man with a deep beery bass voice is seeking to outsmart her: "The party of revolution is to be blamed for everything. It undermines the god-given authorities of school, family, government. . . ."

"Children's suicides are only a symptom of the decadence of bourgeois society." A hostile voice counters his.

"The capitalists greed for profit drives our children to their death," adds a woman whose angry eyes flash from under her black head kerchief.

New groups crowd into the scene. A black banner waves above them on which in white letters is written "down with the school."

"Here is the enemy who bears the guilt for what happens to our children," their leader begins. "Hour after hour they are locked into overfilled classrooms with fossilized teachers; under the garbage of dead rules and numbers, their natural thirst for knowledge is smothered, their tender souls hardened by cruel treatment."

"The school is to be blamed, the school," a thousand voices answer him.

By and by the people disperse. Some return to their desks, their workshops, their evening drink; they have relieved their souls of its excitement; their conscience has been quieted. Others, however, hurry to their class, to their political meetings, eager to use the latest student suicide for the purpose of making gains for their own ideology.

And now they begin to fight over reforms designed to lock the gates of death with an unbreakable safety catch to all would-be suicides.

More religion! we hear from one side. And people who remember the church only at the time of baptisms, weddings, and deaths, who have long forgotten all the commands of Christian neighborly love when they are within their own four walls, among their wives, their subordinates, their colleagues—these people suddenly demand even more Bible verses and hymn stanzas for their children. They do not know or do not want to know that religion is not something one can acquire through rote learning, and that the contemporary kind of religious instruction cruelly kills that childish religiosity with which the six-year-old enters school and makes hypocrites out of those who believe in miracles.

A great movement that has its protagonists in all civilized states recognizes these facts and consequently strives to ban religious instruction from the school altogether; many of its adherents desire to replace it with a doctrine of moral virtues. They expect it to provide that strengthening of character that enables young people to cope with the dark sides of life. But, even if we assume these desires could expect fulfillment in Prussia-Germany in the foreseeable future, would this change the spirit of the school? The religious form would disappear, but the teachers would continue in authoritarian fashion to drum in the moral doctrines, as before they drummed in the catechism; and that student would continue to be called the best who knows how to recite them by heart without omissions. Whether they turn into a living force inside the student is something even the best teacher cannot know as long as he is facing half a hundred pupils.

Others expect salvation for our imperiled youth from an educational reform comprising a thorough change in curriculum. They have recognized that a high percentage of secondary school students are not up to the demands made of them and that the burden of intellectual work leaves them far too little time for the necessary bodily training, and they explain their lack of willpower, their weaknesss of nerve, by these causes. The growing number of reform *Gymnasiums* have come into being because of these agitations. These schools enable the student to postpone the choice between a classical and a scientific education until a period of greater maturity, which provides a little bit more space to individual aptitude. The same considerations have brought about a shortening of school hours and the abolition of the surprise quiz, that frightful bogeyman for countless children.

But the most radical voices in this movement go much further in their demands:

They want to push scientific instruction into the background in favor of technical subjects and practical crafts. They demand the abolition of all compulsory instruction in classical languages. They declare war against the very institution of the humanistic *Gymnasium*.

Does that not mean throwing the baby out with the bath water? Just because many students have neither an aptitude for nor an interest in classical languages, should all be denied access to an intellectual universe from which the greatest writers and thinkers of all times received inspiration and still receive it ever anew?

Just because in our pragmatic and pedestrian era many boys would rather build a railroad or an airplane than immerse themselves in historical or literary works, for that reason all of them should be compelled to do the same?

That is a method of leveling that, if it is pursued consistently, will end up by making the least talented children into measuring sticks for the intellectual education of all.

We have seen that the majority of young suicides take their own lives because of nervousness from overwork out of fear of punishment, of poor grades, or of having to repeat a school year. Their number might go down if the demands made by the school were reduced to a minimum.

But we have seen also that in recent times those cases have increased in which highly gifted students resort to poison or the pistol. Not out of fear, but because already life (and therefore also the school, which fills such a large space in their lives) no longer offers them anything, no longer satiates their minds, and, instead of ever blowing new winds into the sails of their hope, lets them hang limp in motionless air.

Their number will grow as long as educational reform is limited to a merely mechanical limitation of the material to be taught and the homework to be accomplished. The strong will be sacrificed to the weak.

Grave internal ailments will not be cured with a few pills and lotions.

But here we are not just dealing with an ailment that is occasionally lethal. Behind the unfortunate children, whose desperation is so much stronger than their life-affirming youth that they choose death by their own free will, there stand thousands who do not die but whose lives are poisoned.

We are dealing with an epidemic that endangers the very future of our nation. And its cause goes much deeper than it has been comfortable, so far, to assume.

Are we permitted to believe that children kill themselves because they have to work too much?! Children, with their hunger for knowledge, with all that energy demanding an outlet! They become tired of life because they are given stones instead of bread. One does not lock lions and tigers in the same stable together with lambs and horses and before the same feeding trough. One does not ask sparrows and eagles to soar to identical heights. Only human beings are all measured by the same yardstick. The only distinction we make in their education—by sending some into secondary schools and others through primary education—depends, not on their aptitudes, but on the class prejudices and very much on the pocketbooks of their parents. The son of the official, the businessman, and the officer is sent to the *Gymnasium*, however unsuitable his brain is to absorb Latin and mathematics. Most recently it is getting to be fashionable to send daughters also to the *Gymansium* indiscriminately; and the women's movement, which aims for the liberation of women from all legal, social, and economic restrictions, boasts about this as if it were progress. But the children of workers are stuck in primary schools, regardless whether their intellectual ambition seeks to move far beyond this level. And while the talentless *Gymnasium* student tortures himself trying to make it from one class to the next, coming closer and closer to the last dreadful ordeal—the graduation exams—the primary school student has already left school and is toiling in the shop or the factory, embittered at his fate.

None of the proposed educational reforms would remedy this situation.

But with this we have only barely touched the deepest cause of the epidemic that victimizes our youth.

The most gifted children, those destined to be the leaders of the future, suffer far more from school than those without talent. They are offered almost nothing once they have gone through the lowest classes. They sit aside in boredom while, for the sake of all the mediocrity filling the classroom, the material to be studied is gone through again and ever again. They have long grown beyond it and yet are treated as dependent and unself-reliant. To have an opinion of their own, to voice and to defend it in the face of the teacher, is regarded as a punishable offense. And, what is worse, only the smallest minority of these children are compensated in their families for what the school fails to give them. The teacher's authority position corresponds to the authoritative stance of the parents. For children, the prime token of good breeding still is thought to be their silence. Not to join the conversation when the grown-ups speak, not to have their own opinion and, if they are so arrogant as to claim to have one, to keep it to themselves—that is the alpha and omega of pedagogical wisdom in "good" families. And so, naturally, the young person is alienated from parents and teachers; none of those who could assist him or her in these intellectual and spiritual struggles knows anything about the young person. With all the adolescent soul's need to communicate they go their own way. And there they find comrades in misery who, to be sure, are not able to help them but only intensify their torments by their own.

And should the oh-so-reasonable adults notice anything about the anxieties of the young person's soul, they smile with condescension from the high platform of their self-possession. They declare the pains of young love to be "juvenile infatuation" and seek to suppress their children's intellectual conflicts as "deplorable manifestations of unhealthy pre-cocity."

They do not wish to know that the pains and struggles of young people can wound and scar them as badly as us adults, indeed, that for a person's whole life they are more meaningful and have greater determining power than the battles we have to fight later in life. For them, childhood is of value only to the extent that it is a preparation for maturity.

Whereas in fact every phase of life, like every season of the year, has a validity of its own.

It is taken for granted nowadays that the intrinsic aim of teaching is to make sure that whatever is learned be of practical usefulness for later life.

Whereas in fact learning should also enrich the child's present life, warm his or her young heart, expand his or her intellect.

Therefore we demand. . . *We?!* No: *You. . .*

Never in the course of human history has one class or one generation liberated another. Not because of ill will, nor from ignorance. It often is the physician, after all, who tells the patient what is ailing him. But the patient must have the will to become healthy again. Once the oppressed recognized their oppression, it was they who had to fight for their own liberation: the slaves of antiquity, the peasants in the Middle Ages, the bourgeois in the age of the French Revolution, the workers and the women of the present time. It is not only the fate of the individual that is in his or her own hands but also that of the class and the generation.

"But," I hear indignant cries, "it has always been adult, mature human beings."

Surely! But also, in the eyes of those against whom they rebelled, legally incompetent like the children today!

"Those who struggled for their liberation," I hear another respond, "are always those who in the course of their development had become intrinsically mature."

Surely! But who would want to assert that the children in the era of Charlemagne are the same as those today?!

Those who praise the "good old days"—all of them people who walk on crutches and therefore cannot keep in step with historical develop-ment—in moving tones complain "that there no longer are any chil-dren." When they were young, they say, girls at fifteen still played only with their dolls, and boys at the same age had no higher interest than playing cowboys and Indians. They are right. Except they consider those things unnatural and unhealthy that are nothing else than consequences of changes in conditions. Such consequences may be deplorable the way much is deplorable that the past has taken with it to its grave. But we cannot change it. History cannot be slowed down; instead, it demands that we keep in step with it.

The noise of the world in Grandfather's time sounded only from afar; today it penetrates into almost every home. The child of the big city especially need only look around with bright eyes and listen with alert ears, and in no time at all he or she will know more than an adult could have known a hundred years ago. But at every step he or she will also be challenged to criticize things and judge others, because from early on the child will be able to hear the parents' authority contradicted. The child learns about world events from the flood of the newspapers that even under the strictest educational regime can no longer be withheld from her or him; and, particularly when it is the case of proletarian children, he or she will be introduced to the horrors of the struggle for existence from tender youth. Children, as long as they are not morons, are forced to think and feel independently.

The child has changed: But the spirit of education in school and home has remained the same. It still wants to function solely through the force of authority; it still sees in the child nothing but soft wax to which it must give form and shape. And for most parents the child is their creation in the same sense in which the artist's work is his creation: an expression, a mute witness of his own personality. Whereas, in fact, respect for the child's individuality ought to be the basic principle underlying their behavior toward the child—a task all the more difficult to carry out, since parents would like to see nothing but their own qualities reflected in their children, the good ones enlarged tenfold, as in a magic mirror.

As in school and home, the position of the child in the state has remained the same. Beginning with the fourteenth year, children support themselves by their labor or contribute to the support of their families. They must suffer like adults under poor working conditions and high food prices. It would not only be their right but in fact their duty to enlighten themselves about the causes of all these conditions through exchange of ideas with their comrades in fate or with their older colleagues at work. But they are not permitted to do this. In school they had to study pages of grammar and Bible quotations *ad nauseam* but learned practically nothing about the constitution and the laws. So also later the adolescent is forbidden to deal with them altogether, as if they were mysteries accessible only to the initiated.

Gymnasium students, to be sure, are standing amidst the mechanism of modern life; over backstairs and through back doors it sneaks up to them in the form of its meanest phenomena; the dirt of the back alleys shamelessly presents itself to their searching eyes. But woe to them, thrice woe, if they descend down the front stairs freely and openly and get together with their comrades to discuss the serious questions of their lives, or if they openly voice their ideas on those things that distress or insult them in the classroom or in the family drawing room. Student associations are forbidden.

Surely, the authority of state and school must be standing on a rotten foundation when it must protect itself against the assault of the young by the barbed wire fencing of laws and decrees! And neither of them will learn to understand that today's youth shares only its age in years with the youth of long ago. If only it would gather courage by itself instead of just going mutely to its death!

I hear the philistines rage and the good bourgeois weep and wail. I see the scoffers shrug their shoulders.

"Children's liberation!!!"—derisive laughter accompanies that word, the same laughter with which the pioneers of the women's movement were received one hundred years ago. Today, when hundreds of thousands are following, when they have gained entry to the universities and to the parliaments, nobody is laughing any longer.

"Children's liberation!"—and menacing fists are raised, the same fists brandished against the first workers when they demanded equal political rights. Fists are still being made today, but since millions are already confronting them victoriously, they no longer frighten.

But I also see questioning, expectant glances turned toward me from shiny young eyes; and I feel wildly beating hearts, as if they were waiting for a brisk, merry fight. Instead, what beckons them is only a rough and rocky trail. The first steps on it do not give even an echo. Yet it is they that demand the greatest courage, the greatest endurance.

There are few parents who do not love their children. What makes their love barren most of the time is only the fact that they do not know them.

Begin by having the courage to make your parent acquainted with you! Express your desires, your views, your hopes and fears, even if for the time being you encounter nothing but astonishment, reproofs, prohibitions, and commands. Obedience is no virtue except when it is joyful affirmation of the command.

Listen to one of our greatest contemporary writers, Richard Dehmel, who sang to his own son: "And if one day of filial duty,/my son, your aged father speaks to you./ Obey him not, obey him not—"

Speak frankly about all things the school takes from you and denies you. Your parents' class prejudices have not yet eaten so deeply into your hearts as to repress your inclinations. Demand the right to choose a profession corresponding to your aptitudes. Protest if mathematics or Greek or Latin poison the most beautiful years of your youth while the artist or the engineer in you demands altogether different intellectual nourishment. Resist your father who forces you into the *realschule* only because he has decided that you will become a businessman like himself, whereas your own dreams lead you toward writing and philosophy. And before you ruin yourselves with intellectual work for which your brains are not fit, have the moral courage, which is rarer these days than intelligence, to want to become a good craftsman rather than swell the huge ranks of the intellectual mediocrities who are a burden to themselves and to others.

You lower your heads?! Oh, I see: you will still have to sit out the six years of secondary school to gain the privilege of one year of military service! So, then, you young people who secretly mock the philistines want to prostitute yourselves to show that it is class arrogance, not love of knowledge, that guides your steps? Are you really suffering already from the same conceptual confusion as the adults, who think it a disaster if their sons have to serve for two years, whereas to sacrifice their genuine calling to the idol of class prejudice is a far greater disaster?

You must learn to speak frankly not only about the what and how of school. Inside the school, too, you shall not deny your own selves. As soon as the time begins when not only do you learn rules, numbers, and facts, but also your teachers begin to give you their opinions about these facts—a right that all human beings prossess—and try with that same high-hat assuredness to teach them to you as unchallengeable truths like the rules and the numbers earlier—from that moment on, give up your ambition to be a model student, i.e., one who is nothing else than a phonograph record that faithfully reproduces the teacher's voice. Here, too, have the guts to have your own opinion. You will be placed on the dunce's bench, because in the school as well as in the state those who keep their mouths shut and those who voice approval are the most convenient citizens. But that will prove nothing against you, only against the method of education. Perhaps—in fact, probably—your opinions will be false; but who will prove to you that those of your teachers will be correct?

"I prefer a young person going astray on his or her own path to one who walks on someone's else's right path." Let this word of Goethe be your guide.

I am tossing a flaming torch in your midst. With it, light a bonfire. Into that fire, toss all the things that are constricting your hearts, smothering your free breathing, and forcing your feet to walk in other people's footsteps. After a while, when the flames rise high into the sky, strong auxiliary troops will link up with your small contingent: your parents.

Not all of them. Certainly not. Many of them have had their eyes blinded, their feet paralyzed forever by the desolateness of everyday life, by the wear and tear of the struggle for existence. Pass them by, notwithstanding all your compassionate love. But there are others who would be your allies if only they got to know you. Through your pains your mothers would grow strong, through your struggles, the long forgotten youth of your fathers would be reawakened.

In the final analysis, you have only one enemy: yourselves. Your own careerism, your hypocrisy, your cowardice. Overcome those, and the road will be free.

Where does it lead? "To utopia!" your antagonists will sneer. Even if that were so, many a new world has been discovered on the road toward utopia! Anyone whose fantasy grows strong wings need not hesitate to place his aims above the clouds.

All the aims toward which I want to direct you are no more than way stations on the road to the one single goal: the young people's right to self-determination. That is no more utopian than the self-determination of women and of workers.

There are schools in Germany that are called free school communes, rural school homes, or schools for education. There members—teachers and students of both sexes—constitute a citizenry in miniature. Their form of government is democratic. Questions concerning internal and external school relations are discussed and resolved in general meetings in which teachers and students have an equal voice. Classroom instruction is essentially guidance to independent work, not rote learning or indoctrination. The teachers are no authorities by virtue of their titles, but only in so far as they can give themselves authority through their personality. They relate to the students as if to younger friends, not as if to subordinates.

The essence of these schools is to be found not in what they teach but in how they teach. The most diverse curricula can be taught in one and the same manner, which is characterized chiefly by the fact that it respects the autonomous human being already in the child.

In the United States, colonies for the education of neglected or delinquent children have been created in which the principle of administrative autonomy is carried out scrupulously. The young colonists give themselves their own laws, punish every offense according to their own judgment, and elect their own leaders. The teachers only conduct classes and are at times consulted for advice. And the system works so well that again and again new such colonies come into being.

What is revealed here is that only the possession of freedom can educate people for responsibility and for the ability to make use of it. A child who has always run about in a safety harness held by the mother will more easily stumble, once it becomes necessary to let it go free, than a child who has relied on his or her own feet from early on.

While in our country student associations are banned, they play a major role in the associational life of North America. Almost every school has several of them. During summer vacations, youth congresses meet, to which the various associations send their delegates and where the problems of these adolescents' schooling and living are discussed in front of adult audiences paying serious attention. Many an educational reform has been suggested first in such congresses.

The children's position at home naturally corresponds to that in school. The young American learns very early to defend his own opinion; his female age-mate is granted a degree of freedom of movement that a German schoolgirl could obtain for herself only through lies and secrecy.

Now I do not wish to praise foreign achievements as exemplary, nor suggest that all children should be educated in boarding schools like those I discussed earlier.

My only aim is to show that the new spirit of education, which alone corresponds to the recent development of our youth, has already established itself in many places and that, the warnings of the sceptics notwithstanding, this has neither destroyed family life nor violated discipline or morals. Subordinate problems of the curriculum can be resolved properly only where this spirit reigns. Once this point of view is adopted, it will become apparent also that the subjects to be taught should not be adjusted to fit the intellectual level of the masses but that the individual minds of the children demand very different treatment. Thus, no unity school, but a rich variety of schools, so that every aptitude, every talent can find the right source to nourish it. The aim is to transform the work of the children into what it ought to be: an exercise of their own energies, rather than painful toil. One way station on the road in this direction is necessarily the liberation of the children's future from the parents' pocketbook. Fulfillment of this demand is so obviously necessary that coming eras will consider us barbarians for still having to make it: energy and talent alone must be the deciding factors in the choice of school and profession.

You see the dead pass in review—they are your martyrs. And your hearts stopped beating, and your eyes filled with tears.

See now what I will show you while the magic mantle of recognition carries you high above the round earth.

Down there, wheels are rattling and machines are thundering; the fires of iron works glow like brightly flaming torches; black chimneys belch clouds of gray smoke. Small cottages stand in narrow valleys. Inside them there is hammering and knocking; and, activated by hurrying feet, the sewing machine is whirring. Great cities appear, a dark, conglomerated ocean of stones. Weak light escapes into the night from cellars, garret windows, and tenement houses. Wherever the eye may turn: tired children stand among all the grim men and pallid women, whom misery and need kicked in the back so that they might learn to bend over the work. A last gleam of longing for the sun still glows in the children's young eyes. It will go out in the eternal night of suffering. Dreams stir their heart; how long before they flee before the noise of the workshop? Many a brow shines in the light of great ideas; the pestilential breath of the factory will gradually cause it to die. Red lips only recently sounded a sweet song—it will be silenced forever by the shrill cry for bread.

How much promise has misery killed in these children even while wealth coerced others to sit at the full banquet tables of intellectual lives, and they did not have energy enough to help themselves?

The dead called you with loud voices. If you were still hesitant to listen, the mute languages of the living will pursue you until there is no escape left for you.

History tells about a children's crusade. Today the task is to liberate more than Christ's grave from the hands of the infidel.

The century of the child, only a pious wish so far, must be the work of the children themselves.

INDEX